GENERAL UNION
A STUDY OF THE NATIONAL UNION OF GENERAL AND MUNICIPAL WORKERS

GENERAL UNION

A Study of the National Union of
General and Municipal Workers

by

H. A. CLEGG

Fellow of Nuffield College, Oxford

BASIL BLACKWELL
OXFORD
1954

PRINTED IN GREAT BRITAIN IN THE CITY OF OXFORD
AT THE ALDEN PRESS

To G. D. H. COLE

to whom all Students of the British Labour Movement
owe so much

CONTENTS

ix

CONTENTS

PART III

THE N.U.G.M.W. IN INDUSTRY

CONTENTS

CONTENTS

PART IV

THE N.U.G.M.W. IN THE LABOUR MOVEMENT

PART V

AN APPRAISAL OF THE GENERAL UNION

PREFACE

THIS study is based on the records of the union at head office and at some of the district offices, on attendances at union meetings, from branch meetings to Congress, on visits to each of the union's districts, and on interviews and conversations with officers and members of the union, from branch members and shop stewards to the General Secretary.

The work was carried out in 1949 and 1950. The first draft of the book was completed in the summer of 1951, but progress was thereafter delayed. The book remains substantially as it was then written, although there has been opportunity in the meantime to correct many errors, and it has now been brought up to date by including reference to the most important events in the union up to the end of 1952.

The book was thus written before the publication of Dr. Goldstein's study of the Transport and General Workers' Union.[1] It will be clear to the reader of both works that I am not entirely in sympathy either with Dr. Goldstein's methods or with his conclusions. It is, however, of perhaps greater importance that the two studies are in many ways complementary. Dr. Goldstein gave his attention mainly to an attempt to derive information about trade union government from the statistical records of the Transport and General Workers' Union, and to a detailed inquiry into the working of a single branch. The present study makes little use of figures, and contains no close study of a union branch. Its main aim is to describe the working of the governing bodies of the union, both nationally and in the districts, in internal union affairs, in collective bargaining, and in relation to the other elements of the labour movement.

It is objective in the sense that its author is an outsider with no strong reason for grinding any particular axe. My objectivity is, however, limited by my keen sympathy with trade unionists and the purposes of trade unionism, which would

[1] Joseph Goldstein, *The Government of British Trade Unions*, Allen and Unwin, 1952.

xiii

PREFACE

make me reluctant to write anything likely to bring into disrepute either the trade union movement in general or this union in particular.

I take this opportunity of recording my gratitude to all those who have helped me in making this study — to Jack Cooper, Southern district secretary and Chairman of the union, who encouraged me to undertake the work and first introduced me to the union; to Tom Williamson, the General Secretary, who gave me permission to proceed and placed every facility at my disposal; to the district secretaries, national officers, district organizers and members of the head office and district office staffs, who gave unstintingly of their time and energy to show me the union and to discuss its work with me, and who provided valued companionship in my travels about the union; and to the many branch officers, shop stewards and 'rank-and-file' members who willingly helped a stranger in his strange task. Finally, and above all, I must express my deep thanks to Bob Roberts, the union's Research Officer, and to the staff of his department. Without his constant and unfailing help, and his friendship, the work could never have been completed.

I should also like to thank Professor G. D. H. Cole, Mr. Kenneth Knowles and Mr. B. C. Roberts for suggestions and advice; and Mr. D. W. Kelly and my father for help with proofs. Responsibility, of course, rests with me.

H. A. CLEGG

PART I

THE AMALGAMATION

THE AMALGAMATION

THE N.U.G.M.W. was formed in 1924 by an amalgamation of the National Union of General Workers (founded in 1889 as the National Union of Gasworkers and General Labourers of Great Britain and Ireland), the National Amalgamated Union of Labour (founded in 1889 as the Tyneside and General Labourers' Union) and the Municipal Employees' Association (founded in 1894). The form of general unionism which has been such a distinctive feature of modern British trade unionism was thus finally established, for the Transport and General Workers' Union had been set up, also through amalgamation, three years before. Subsequently, the two unions continued to absorb small bodies, expanded and reorganized, but the pattern then laid down has not been seriously altered. We are mainly concerned with the development and work of the N.U.G.M.W. since that time, but some account of the growth of its constituent unions and of the rise of general unionism is a necessary preface to this. A full history is beyond the scope of this study. We must content ourselves with an attempt to mention some of the most important features.

The Origin of the Labourers' Unions

Both great general unions look back to 1889 as the year of their foundation. What happened in this year was not that labourers were organized into trade unions for the first time; but that unusual success enabled several of the unions which were continually being set up for labourers to attract a large enough membership to cut a figure in the trade union world and to build an organization which could survive. The Gasworkers' Union was founded in March, 1889. By July it had over sixty branches. In August it won the eight-hour day in London without a strike. This victory, followed by similar concessions elsewhere (not always gained so peacefully) gave the union a good start. The famous London dock strike, which began in August, established the Dock, Wharf and Riverside Labourers' Union on the Thames. The Tyneside Labourers were granted recognition by a number of local employers. Success encouraged imitation and in that and subsequent years dozens of labourers' unions were set up, some soon to die, others to struggle on until they were absorbed.

Every student of trade unions knows the difficulties of classification. There are unions which approximate to craft, occupational, industrial and employmental unions, but so many defy classification. The Amalgamated Engineering Union is no longer a craft or occupational union; the engineering industry is a unit only for the purposes of collective bargaining, and many of its members do not come within the scope of those bargains; but if we called it a general union we should be forced to find other names for our general unions, for almost all its members are to be found in the engineering and shipbuilding industries, or in engineering maintenance in other industries, and apprenticed craftsmen still dominate its counsels. So it is only in deference to the thought of the time, which clung to the categories of apprenticed craftsmen and labourers, that we call these new unions labourers' unions. There were labourers' unions for instance, many county or even more localized associations for builders' labourers; but the larger unions cast their net wider than that.[1]

The traditional categories applied pretty well in the building and engineering industries and in the shipyards. The new unions organized both craftsmen's mates and general labourers. Already, however, the number of machinists in engineering establishments was growing rapidly, and these too were taken in. The gas industry was like so many modern service and productive industries in employing no apprenticed craftsmen apart from maintenance workers at the gasworks (although outside the works the gasfitters are an important group, and

---

[1] In 1895 the Delegate Assembly of the N.A.U.L. changed its rules to allow recruitment of 'such classes of labour as the E.C. shall from time to time decide', instead of 'all classes of labour other than those employed as artisans, mechanics and as members of professions' to allow all South Yorkshire colliery surfacemen to come in.

the Gasworkers always claimed to organize them). The yard labourer could hope for promotion to any job apart from these, including jobs requiring considerable skill or carrying responsibility. The regular docker did not think of himself as entirely unskilled, although the 'aristocracy' of stevedores and lightermen generally kept apart. The labourers' unions entered the rubber, chemicals, boxmaking and similar industries on much the same terms as the gas industry, and for this reason new 'all-grades' unions such as the Municipal Employees' Association or the Amalgamated Tram and Vehicle Workers had closer affinities to them than to the older unions. Finally, the new unions took in groups of recognized skilled workers, who for any reason were not or did not wish to be included in the older unions. The Gasworkers organized the doubling mill operatives of Derbyshire since they were outside the normal area of the Lancashire cotton unions, and the cotton unions refused to recognize the shift system which many doubling employers had adopted. Engine drivers in docks or at collieries and Yorkshire dyers also came in. Sometimes the new unions were conscious that in thus expanding they were moving away from their original purpose.

The spread of the new unions was, in part, haphazard. There was no obvious logic in the inclusion of South Wales' tinplate workers with London dockers. We can understand that Tyneside labourers should bring in Grimsby dockers, and shipyard labourers in Liverpool, Belfast and Glasgow, but not so easily that South Yorkshire colliery surfacemen, Sheffield metal workers and Thames cement workers should be in the same union. Affinities between London gasworkers and gasworkers elsewhere are clear, but there were half a dozen other unions which included gasworkers, and Will Thorne's union, even in its early years, spread to scores of other industries. In 1894 the Bristol district had branches for cotton operatives, pipemakers, boxmakers, sanitary workers and quarrymen besides gas workers and general labourers; and the Birmingham district for builders' labourers, polishers and grinders, steel toy makers, glass bottle makers and brickmakers. Their willingness to organize in this way was due to the class theories which their socialist patrons provided for them, and to the ease with which a labourer might move from gasworks to roadmaking, from roadmaking to building, from building to brickmaking and so on, but success was due to the abilities of organizers and branch secretaries, to chance visits, to grievances opportunely taken up. It was largely due to J. R. Clynes that Derbyshire doubling mill workers and quarrymen brought their associations within the Lancashire district of the Gasworkers. In 1891, W. H. Blow, the first official delegate of the N.A.U.L. outside the Tyne area, brought the Grimsby dockers into the union, and from there made contact with a labourers' association in Sheffield. Two years later T. Hough, of Sheffield, was made official delegate for a new Lincolnshire and Sheffield district and began to organize builders' labourers, metal workers and colliery surface workers around Sheffield to form one of the strongest centres of the union.

The new unions were thus, in a sense, general unions almost from the outset. Certainly no other classification suited them. Each had its base in a particular industry — gas, docking, or shipyards — and worked outwards from it, the London dockers more cautiously, the gasworkers over most of England and Wales and in almost any industry. They went far afield, but only rarely did they dig deep in other industries. For the first twenty years their numbers remained very small compared with the field open to them. The Gasworkers' membership in 1910 was about 30,000, no higher than in 1890, and the total of the ten larger labourers' and all-grades' unions fluctuated between something under 100,000 and 150,000 over the same period. If we picture the vast tracts of British industry left unorganized by the older unions as dotted by widely scattered groups of organized workers, with a fantastic pattern of repeatedly crossing lines joining many of the groups together into a few dozen larger bodies, some by area alone, some by industry alone, and a few by both, we have some idea of the character (up to 1910) of the unions in which we are interested.

Other interesting features were their low contributions and their close connection with political parties. The low contributions were essential for recruiting labourers, and precluded the

4

payment of friendly benefits, except perhaps a funeral benefit of a few pounds. Although at times, again under the influence of class warfare theories, they made a virtue of necessity, and attributed their low contributions to a desire to prevent the corruption of a fighting spirit by considerations of security, and although some of them, particularly the London dockers, took part in famous strikes, they were not markedly more aggressive than other unions. Where opportunity offered, as it did to the N.A.U.L. on the north-east coast, they were perfectly ready to cultivate good relationships with employers. Indeed their stability has been attributed to their success in achieving recognition from a relatively small number of employers,[1] so that they maintained a solid base on which to retreat in bad years, and from which to expand in good years. Certainly a very large proportion of the membership of the Gasworkers came from a small number of large works in various industries.[2] They early learned the lesson that, amongst general workers at least, unions can rarely build a satisfactory organization without winning the goodwill of the employer, and J. R. Clynes understood the nature of general unionism far better than Tom Mann.

The founder of the London dockers' union, Ben Tillett, was a member of the Social Democratic Federation, and had the assistance of Tom Mann and John Burns. Will Thorne's Gasworkers were even more closely connected with the socialist sects, for not only was he an S.D.F. member, but Eleanor Marx-Aveling served on the executive of the union for a number of years, and the union's expansion over the country was considerably helped by local socialist groups.[3] The practice of the unions rapidly diverged from their Marxist tenets, but the connections lingered for some time. The two most notable amongst the second generation of general workers' leaders, Ernest Bevin and Charles Dukes, were active members of the S.D.F.'s successor, the British Socialist Party, before the 1914-18 war. The new unions had, however, other reasons, besides the affiliations

[1] E. J. Hobsbawm, General Labour Unions in Britain, 1889-1914, *Economic History Review*, Second Series, Vol. I, Nos. 2 and 3, pp. 129-33.
[2] Ibid.
[3] Ibid, p. 126, note 4.

of their leaders, for close interest in politics. They could provide no serious friendly benefits, so that if their members were to have other provision than higher wages and better conditions to assist them in sickness, unemployment and old age, it must come from the state. Because they had no monopoly of labour supply in any market they were far more ready to rely on political action as well as industrial strength. They took a large part in the foundation of the Labour Representation Committee and provided their share of funds and M.P.s for the young Labour Party. The Gasworkers were notable in this respect. J. R. Clynes and Will Thorne were elected to Parliament in 1906 and they were joined by Pete Curran in the following year when he won a by-election at Jarrow.

General Unionism

Although the goodwill of an employer may be of assistance to the general union in its organizing work, the government can do an even bigger job, and the vast growth of the new unions from 1911 to 1920 must be attributed mainly to government action. First, the workers were attracted into the union by the 1911 National Insurance Act. Having to enter Approved Societies large numbers of them chose trade unions, and the general unions which covered vast areas of industry, but covered them very sketchily, naturally gained greatly from this influx.[1] Before the effect of this factor was spent the war came, and from 1915 compulsory arbitration under the Munitions Acts forced trade unions upon the employers. Although all the general unions, and indeed all unions, benefited greatly, the Gasworkers, being more widespread, gained more than most, and increased from 30,000 in 1910 to 80,000 in 1913, 300,000 in 1918 and nearly 450,000 in 1920. Even more rapid was the expansion of a relatively new union, the Workers' Union, which was founded in 1898 by Tom Mann. It was intended by him to cater mainly for the growing class of machinists in the engineering industry, but showed itself prepared to be as omnivorous as the Gasworkers when its chance came. From 5000 in 1910 it had risen to about 100,000 by the

[1] See S. & B. Webb, *History of Trade Unionism* 1660-1920, Longmans and Green, 1920, p. 498.

6

outbreak of war and by 1920 claimed 50,000 more members than the Gasworkers' Union.

These are not the only factors explaining growth. Between 1911 and 1914 there was a storm of angry trade union activity, connected with the theories of syndicalism and industrial unionism, and the industrial upheavals of war made the protection of the unions even more necessary than in normal times. The first is often attributed to the failure of real wages to continue their nineteenth-century majestic sweep upwards after 1900, even in these years of high industrial activity; and the rapid rise of prices during the war taught workers a lesson which was easily learned. Apart from the dockers and the Irish Transport and General Workers' Union, the new unions did not take a leading part in the famous pre-war strikes or in the shop stewards' movement. The 'industrial unionists' amongst the engineers, railwaymen and miners were to the fore. But they, the new unions, were not unaffected.

The influx of membership changed the character of the general unions. From associations of scattered groups of workers in a variety of industries they grew to have, between them, real control over a number of industries. They had benefited greatly from dilution, and had made great strides in munitions factories and in the war-inflated engineering, metals' and chemicals' industries. Elsewhere scattered groups had become solid blocks of membership. At any time before 1911 the general unions might have been considered exceptions. If they had collapsed, or been absorbed by unions of a more regular type, or forced back on their bases to become all-grades' unions in one or two industries, no one would have been greatly surprised. By the end of the war they had clearly come to stay. Individually, several of them were very powerful unions; together they would be impregnable.

Joint Action and Amalgamation Projects

From the first the labourers' unions had had some recognition of their common interests, and on occasion looked forward, perhaps remotely, to a common organization for all labourers. The first practical step to joint action was a meeting of repre-

sentatives of eleven labourers' unions in December 1906, convened by the General Federation of Trade Unions (which had
been set up in 1899 to provide a more powerful organization
of joint action than the T.U.C. and an insurance system for
strike funds). A General Labourers' National Council was set
up, but it did not become a very strong organization. There
was little for it to do. The Gasworkers drifted out but returned
just before the war when a more serious project of amalgamation was being considered. During those years of ferment, the
National Union of Railwaymen had been formed by amalgamation, the Miners' Federation had emerged as the most powerful
union in the country, and there was widespread propaganda in
favour of amalgamations to form industrial unions amongst
engineering, building and transport workers. The labourers'
unions saw that such amalgamations would be the end of them,
and argued that organization by industry would reduce the
labourer to the subservient position from which they had sought
to raise him. It was in the interests of labourers that they should
all stand together. So the National Council set up a committee,
with J. R. Clynes (now President of the Gasworkers) as chairman, to draft their own scheme. The project, like the schemes
of other groups, was left in abeyance at the outbreak of war.

The war gave a powerful impulse to 'amalgamationism'.
Before that time unions had normally bargained with individual
employers or with associations of employers covering relatively
small districts. War-time national advances and the intervention of the Committee on Production forced industry after
industry into a system of national bargaining, so that joint
action between unions became a necessity instead of a luxury;
this was especially true of the general unions with their haphazard collection of members over a wide range of industry.
In 1917 the National Council was succeeded by a more work-
manlike body, the National Federation of General Workers,
which took over national negotiations in industries such as
Aluminium, Chemicals, Candles and Soap, the Explosives
Trades, Flour Milling and Quarrying, and acted with the
Federation of Engineering and Shipbuilding Trades (of which
several of its constituents, including the Gasworkers and the

8

N.A.U.L., were members independently). In addition many of the general unions which catered for building workers (and most of them did) were forced into the National Federation of Building Trade Operatives in order to maintain their hold in that industry.

Amalgamation did not come through the new federation, although when pre-war schemes were taken up with fervour in 1919 it mooted projects and tightened its organization by setting up districts. There were far too many jealousies and other difficulties to be overcome, and arrangements were made more easily between groups of constituent unions. The first important attempt at complete amalgamation was between the Gas-workers (now the N.U.G.W.) and the London dockers. A ballot was held late in 1919. Both unions voted heavily in favour, but the proportion of dockers voting was insufficient to comply with the law (which requires at least 50 per cent to vote) and the project was abandoned. Perhaps the dockers' leaders were not enthusiastic. They had already a different scheme in mind for a grouping in which their 100,000 members would not be dwarfed by the N.U.G.W.'s 400,000.

Early the following year they began discussions with the other important dockers' union, James Sexton's union, based on Liverpool. Nearly all the other unions catering for dockers, stevedores, watermen and the like were then brought in (except the N.A.U.L.) and next the unions of road transport workers were approached. Ernest Bevin attracted support for his plan of trade groups to give the industrial groupings wide autonomy, and late in 1921, fourteen unions voted in a sufficiently large ballot to ratify the scheme. The Transport and General Workers' Union began its work on January 1st, 1922, with something like 300,000 members. At the time it was not yet a general union in the sense that the N.U.G.W., the N.A.U.L. and the Workers' Union were. It was an amalgamation of dockers' and road transport workers' unions, many of whom had brought in odd groups of workers in a variety of other industries. But it was a union with energy and ideas, and made progress during the difficult years of the twenties.

As early as 1917 discussions had been opened between the

Workers' Union and the N.A.U.L. They did not favour a full amalgamation, but ratified a project for a joint executive committee, with control of a common fund out of which salaries, strike pay, and legal and propaganda expenses were to be met. In August, 1918, the Municipal Employees' Association decided to come in on the same terms. The joint executive met for the first time in November of that year, and gradually took over its functions as governing body of the federal National Amalgamated Workers' Union during 1919. Schemes for full amalgamation were further considered and in January 1920, the N.U.G.W., rebuffed by the dockers, was interested in the project. A joint sub-committee was set up, but soon matters began to drag very slowly.

From the first the N.A.U.L., perhaps the most democratic of the general unions, had suspected the appointed and powerful officials of the W.U. The N.A.U.L. soon became convinced that they were using the superior numbers of their union to establish a complete domination of the federal body. Disaffection was inflamed by local disputes between two unions. In 1921, with industrial depression, there began a decline in trade union membership which soon became catastrophic. The general unions suffered most heavily, for their membership was the most vulnerable, although the new T.&G.W.U., with its strong grip on the docks and the expanding road transport industry, managed to hold on well. Schemes for amalgamation had to be radically revised as funds declined and salaries and staffs had to be cut and cut again. In 1922 the engineering lock-out, which deeply concerned the N.U.G.W., the N.A.U.L. and the W.U., occupied all their attention.

Meanwhile, the W.U. was clearly losing its interest in the project. Its membership was slipping away faster than that of the N.U.G.W. and it would clearly no longer dominate any joint organization. It fell behind in its contributions to the joint fund and in March 1922, when the three other unions rejected rules which it wished to include in the scheme for amalgamation, and refused an individual ballot of all the members on each rule (an impossible procedure), it withdrew, and the partial amalgamation was wound up.

For a time it seemed that was the end of the affair, but the three remaining unions arranged a ballot which gave them the necessary majority, and the scheme was taken up seriously once more. Throughout 1923 difficulties were ironed out. Rules were drafted, salaries, contributions and benefits were agreed, and the allocation of posts nationally and in the districts (the most invidious task of all) was settled. By the end of the year they were almost ready for a conference of delegates to consummate the project.

Before the constitution of the new union is described it would be useful to give a brief description of the three unions, since we have so far been concentrating on their common characteristics.

The National Union of General Workers

The N.U.G.W. was certainly the greatest of the general unions up to this time. In numbers the T.&G.W.U. just surpassed it, but it was a new union with a relatively new general secretary. Will Thorne was already the 'father' of the T.U.C. General Council, and J. R. Clynes had been a minister of the Crown.

The most powerful centres of the union were in London (which was the centre of a vast district covering the whole of the south of England and East Anglia) and Lancashire. The London district had been built up by Will Thorne himself, and by such men as Harry Picard, Pete Curran, Arthur Hayday and Jack Jones. In Lancashire the work of Clynes and Fleming Eccles and of a group of young men led by Charles Dukes and Arthur Seabury had built the Lancashire district up into the strongest union in that area outside the cotton industry, with a branch of several thousands in each of the important South Lancashire manufacturing towns. Hugh Lynas had built up a strong district in the north-east although that was the centre of the N.A.U.L. and from there John McKenzie had gone to Scotland to succeed, where an earlier attempt had failed, to recruit a considerable membership into a district based on Glasgow. Amalgamation with the Amalgamated Society of Gasworkers, Brickmakers and General Labourers — a real general

union, but localized, with its core amongst Birmingham municipal workers — had added greatly to the strength of its Birmingham district. There were centres of membership in Nottingham
and Leeds, and more scattered groups over the rest of Yorkshire,
on the east coast and in South Wales.

Probably the largest section of the N.U.G.W.'s members was
in the group of industries generally referred to as 'Engineering',
so called because wages fluctuate in accordance with the agreements made by what is now the Engineering and Allied Employers' National Federation. The union was by far the most
important in the gas industry (a heavy decline in its London gas
membership was partly offset by the adhesion of the Birmingham gas-workers) and probably the largest single union in the
electricity supply and cablemaking industries. In the gas and
electricity industries its members worked both for local authorities and for private companies. In other branches of local
government services it had a much smaller hold. The union
had a fair membership in shipyards in the south of England and
Dundee. In the north of England and on the Clyde the claims
of the N.A.U.L. were generally respected. Small unions of
government workers, mainly Admiralty Dockyard workers, had
been absorbed in 1920.

In Scotland and on the north-east coast there was a considerable membership in the iron and steel industry. Many
metal trade workers were organized in Sheffield and Birmingham, and aluminium and asbestos workers had been brought in.

In the building materials' industries quarryworkers, brickmakers and cement workers were organized, and there were
some groups of woodworkers, particularly boxmakers. Amongst
the food and drink trades, flour-mill workers, brewery workers,
distillery workers and sugar workers probably provided the
largest number.

Apart from these the chemicals and rubber industries contributed a fair membership. Besides doubling mill workers and
dyers there were groups of members in the textile industries
outside the main centres. Leather workers were organized,
especially in South Lancashire. There was, in addition, a
scattered membership in fifty or a hundred further industries.

The union had always made a virtue of organizing women, although it was not until the war that women had come in in large numbers. In 1921 the main separate women's trade union, the National Federation of Women Workers, had come in to form a special women's section of the union, bringing something like an additional 30,000 women members.

It must be remembered that the union had suffered a drastic decline in membership between 1921 and 1923, and that this decline was not uniform. Some industries held fairly well; others collapsed. So that in many industries all that remained was a few shrunken branches, scattered members attached to general branches, and a claim to representation. Claims of this sort might not mean much at the time, but they would become important once again when the trend in trade union membership changed. This was equally true of most other general unions, and even more true of the Workers' Union, whose recruiting had been almost entirely amongst the war-expanded industries, and which had little solid industrial basis outside.

The members of the union were organized into branches, some general, some catering only for a particular class of worker and some for workers in a particular factory or other place of employment. A commission was paid to branch secretaries and to collecting stewards, and this made possible the growth of very large branches. Contact could be maintained through the stewards, and if a branch grew very large the branch secretary could devote his whole time to its affairs, relying for income on his commission, which, in exceptional cases, would even allow him to employ an assistant. Not unnaturally, the full-time branch secretary might become a powerful figure in the union.

The branches were grouped into districts with elected committees to govern them, a district secretary, and full-time organizers to assist him, in number roughly proportionate to the size of the membership. In the pre-war days of local collective bargaining and less-developed transport and communications, growth depended on the energy and ability of the district secretary more than anything else. District secretaries, like Hugh Lynas in Newcastle or John McKenzie in

Glasgow, had built their districts and would carry their districts with them. Their power was recognized by an unusual provision in the constitution of the union. In the nineteenth century most national unions, to avoid expense, had entrusted the government of the union between delegate conferences to an executive committee of working members from the district in which Head Office was situated; the general unions had followed suit. As funds grew a change was made to national executives. When the Gasworkers made the change in 1908 they chose to elect a governing body composed partly of working members from the districts and partly of district secretaries, in place of the entirely 'lay' committee of other unions.

A biennial delegate congress was the union's final authority. Its meetings were too infrequent to give it much say in industrial policy; the union's rules could be altered by it alone. At Head Office there was only a small staff. Will Thorne had, at the time of the amalgamation, been general secretary for thirty-five years. Clynes, the President, was the union's most famous figure, and probably had greater influence than anyone else in its policies. He had long championed moderation, avoidance of strikes where possible, the use of all possible means of conciliation, the establishment of good relations with employers, and the virtues of political action, and, by and large, the union had come to accept his philosophy. There were one or two other officers at Head Office — Jack Jones had been there for many years, and Will Sherwood came from the Northern district in 1920 to deal nationally with engineering, shipbuilding and iron and steel — and a small clerical staff.

Within this framework there were a number of enclaves of semi-autonomy, due to amalgamations. The Women's Federation had originally come in as a separate district, but this proved too much for the secretaries of the geographical districts, and a scheme was arranged between the Women's Committee and district secretaries under which this national district lapsed at the end of 1922. But special women's branches were to be kept within the districts, where necessary; Miss Bondfield, previously the women's secretary, was to set up a Women's Department at Head Office, to which the women organizers were to be responsible; there was to be a Women's National Committee; and at the union's congress and on the General Council women were to be entitled to separate representation. A number of local amalgamations gave groups within individual districts certain rights. Sometimes they amounted to no more than the inclusion of representatives in any wage-negotiations affecting the group, as with the Hawick Hosiery Workers. Government dockyard workers in the South had their own contributions and looked after their own finances, paying over a *per capita* sum to cover only the union's services in collective bargaining. The cranemen had a separate section, and an organizer attached to Head Office.

The National Amalgamated Union of Labour

As we have said, the centres of the N.A.U.L. were on the Tyne, and at Liverpool, Belfast, Glasgow and South Yorkshire; its main strength was in the shipbuilding, ship-repairing and engineering industries. It had members in the iron and steel industry on the north-east coast and was the only union for dockers there. In South Yorkshire it had a large membership amongst colliery surface workers, and workers in the lighter metal trades. In the chemicals and cement industries its members probably outnumbered those of the N.U.G.W., for it organized chemical workers in the north-east, South Lancashire and Cheshire, and had a considerable hold in the cement works along the banks of the Thames. In London some engineering workers were in the N.A.U.L. and it had a few members in the south-west in cement and one or two other industries. It organized amongst builders' labourers and in a wide variety of food, drink and consumer industries similar to that already listed for the N.U.G.W., but it had considerable membership in these industries only in its own strongholds. In some of these centres it organized corporation workers, for instance, in Belfast and Sheffield and on the Tyne, and specialized in the 'black squad', the tramway maintenance workers. In Northern Ireland some textile workers had come in.

The government of the union was the nearest approach to simple democracy amongst the general unions. Having grown up in the shipyards and engineering shops it had imitated much of the terminology of the craft unions. Its organizers were called official delegates, and its constitution was intended to give the working members absolute power over them. This explains its executive committee's suspicions of the powerful officers of the Workers' Union during partial amalgamation. The numbers of the N.A.U.L. had declined even more rapidly than those of the N.U.G.W., probably because of its concentration in areas and industries most severely hit by the depression of the early twenties. Its figures for affiliation to the T.U.C. had fallen from 170,000 in 1920 to 53,000 in 1924. Although in its first years it had not included women, it claimed 25,000 in 1921, but this figure had fallen to a mere 2000 by 1924. The general secretary, J. N. Bell, died just before the negotiations for amalgamation were completed, and the correspondence secretary, R. Spence, acted in his place.

The Municipal Employees' Association

The Municipal Employees' Association was not a general union in the sense that the N.U.G.W. and the N.A.U.L. were. Almost all its members worked for one class of employer, the local authorities. It could not, however, be classed as an industrial union, for by no stretch of the meaning of the word can gasworkers, tramway workers, roadworkers, dustmen, pier attendants and gardeners be included in one industry. Even if an industrial union is defined as an 'organization which seeks to unite and co-ordinate the bargaining of all groups whose bargains affect each other substantially'[1] (a vague definition, at best) we can hardly include the M.E.A. in the class, for the bargains made for tramwaymen, for instance, were more affected by decisions affecting tramwaymen in private companies than by decisions affecting roadmen, especially after the setting up of Joint Industrial Councils to cover all gas undertakings, all electricity supply undertakings, and all tramway concerns, whether private or municipal, separate from the local authorities 'non-trading' council. The ugly word 'employmental' must be used to classify the union.

[1] E. J. Hobsbawm, op. cit., p. 123, note 3.

If the M.E.A. was not a general union, it recognized that its interests lay with the unions which organized general workers, if only because they competed with it. The M.E.A. could erect no craft barriers. Will Thorne's Gasworkers and the Birmingham Gasworkers had organized council employees before it existed. There was strong competition from the various vehicle workers' unions which amalgamated into the T.&G.W.U., and to a general workers' union roadmen and other corporation labourers naturally appeared to be within its province. So the M.E.A. joined the General Workers' Federation soon after it was founded, and, as we have seen, came into the negotiations for amalgamation as early as 1918.

In that year the union conducted a census of membership. Out of a total of roughly 50,000, over 13,000 were in the Scottish district, which included Ireland. The bulk of these were in Glasgow, and 2000 of the remainder were in the Belfast branch. The next district was London with just over 10,000, mostly in London itself. There were, however, large branches at Bournemouth and Brighton, and some members in other south coast towns. Liverpool provided a district on its own with one large branch at Southport attached. The Manchester district had branches scattered from Blackpool to Huddersfield, but does not appear to have had a very firm hold in any of the large centres included in that area. Of the 5000 odd members in the North-Eastern district half were on the Tyne and more than half the remainder in a large branch at Hull. In the Midlands, Leicester, Derby and Northampton were well organized, but there were very few members in Birmingham or neighbouring towns. There were branches in many towns in South Wales, the largest at Cardiff.

The M.E.A. had, like other unions, expanded greatly during the war, but, unlike others, it maintained its membership very well. At the peak in 1921 it claimed 65,000 members (5000 of them women), and it brought more than 40,000 into the amalgamation. The reasons for this are probably that unemployment was lower in local government service than in almost any other group of industries, and that joint industrial councils had been set up over the whole field in which the union organized, so that the war-time practice of collective bargaining was maintained. In many other industries, once compulsory arbitration procedure was dropped, trade union organizers were shown the door with drastic results on their membership figures.

Although the main strength of the union was amongst manual workers, and local government officers had already their own association, promotion naturally brought the M.E.A. into that field, and after the war it made a determined attempt to extend its influence. G. P. Dean, perhaps the most important official, other than the General Secretary (Peter Tevenan), was detailed to concentrate on work amongst local government officers.

In 1907 the first General Secretary of the union, Albin Taylor, had been dismissed by the Executive Council. This action led to two court cases and a considerable controversy within the union which ended with the secession of a number of branches to form the National Union of Corporation Workers under Taylor's leadership.[1] Compared with the M.E.A. it was a small organization, approaching any strength only in London, but with members scattered over the country. It was, however, in direct competition and a potential menace. The M.E.A. always regarded it as a break-away union, and this attitude was taken over by the amalgamation, for trade union memories on matters such as this are very long. In 1925 the N.U.C.W. changed its name to the National Union of Public Employees.

The Amalgamation Conference

From February 12th to 15th, 1924, 102 delegates from the N.U.G.W. and 52 each from the N.A.U.L. and the M.E.A. met at the Memorial Hall, Farringdon Street, to take the final decision on the proposals for amalgamation. The Standing Orders' Committee had received 2012 amendments (1536 when duplicates were omitted) to the proposed rules, but, in fact, there was little opposition to the arrangements which had been made for the allocation of offices, or to the proposed

---

[1] One account of these events may be found in Bryn Roberts, *At The T.U.C.*, published by the National Union of Public Employees, 1947, pp. 137-42.

clauses on union government, which did little more than carry over the N.U.G.W.'s constitution into the amalgamation; serious controversy was confined to the financial provisions.

The old address of the N.U.G.W. — an entirely Marxist document drawn up by Marx's son-in-law, Aveling — was adopted without division, and the title of National Union of General and Municipal Workers agreed (on the insistence of the M.E.A. who required that a municipal section be set up under the control of Tevenan and Dean). A. P. Borgia, of the London District of the N.U.G.W., moved a number of 'Communist-inspired' resolutions, demanding, for instance, affiliation to the Red International of Labour Unions, and measures for fuller control by working members. His only success was, however, to insert a clause allowing dismissed officials the right of appeal to the General Council. Then the conference turned to finance.

Although the three unions already had the same rate of contribution — 6d. — and fairly similar benefits, the stringency which falling membership and contributions demanded would not permit the most favourable terms to be maintained in each class of benefit. The M.E.A. was, naturally enough, far less liable to heavy demands for strike pay than unions which organized amongst engineering and shipbuilding workers and miners. Its rates for funeral benefit were, therefore, higher than those of the others, and these were adopted for the amalgamation. The N.A.U.L.'s accident benefit had, therefore, to be dropped, with a promise of reconsideration when funds improved. Annual income was estimated at £300,000 (for the 6d. contribution, with a fairly rapid turnover and lower rates for women yielded, on average, only 19s. 6d. per member per annum). Of this, expenditure on officers' salaries was estimated at 15.27 per cent. Office staffs, travelling expenses, rents, telephone and post, affiliation fees and the officers' pension fund would take 23.03 per cent. The commissions of branch secretaries and collectors at the rate proposed would, with other branch officers' honoraria, take 17.96 per cent. Political expenses and the proposed funeral benefit were estimated at 15.96 per cent. This left only £83,254 or

27.78 per cent to cover all trade benefits, and in 1922 the N.U.G.W. had spent over 50 per cent of its income on strike, lock-out and victimization benefit. These estimates were made on the assumption that cuts would be made in the pay of officials (a grading scheme had been arranged to bring the different practices of the three unions into line as easily as possible) and the proposed commissions for branch secretaries and collectors (10 per cent and 7½ per cent respectively) were each 2½ per cent below the old rates of the N.U.G.W. To preserve the old rates would have cost a further £14,125 or 4.71 per cent of the estimated income.

It was on this point that disagreement broke out. Delegate after delegate spoke against the proposed cut in commissions and claimed the solid support of the branches. Most of the officers and staff of the three unions had already been guaranteed a place in the new organization. It is true that their salaries had been reduced more than once, but their numbers had not been reduced to keep pace with the decline in membership. The branch officers' income, being by commission, had already been nearly halved, on average, by the decline in membership, and this cut in the rate of the commission, seemed to be a second reduction in order to maintain an inflated number of full-time officials (in the new union there would be one officer or clerk to 1700 members). After a long debate the chairman intervened to say that the reduction was a necessary precondition to amalgamation for the other two unions, and the whole financial proposals were then put to the vote and carried by fifteen votes. The chairman then gave a promise that the new General Council would be empowered to consider an increase for collecting stewards as soon as funds permitted, without awaiting a Congress.

Differences about the rate of strike benefit, the distribution of the political fund between the districts (mainly for municipal elections) and Head Office (for parliamentary elections), and the correct method to ensure special representation of women by women on the governing body, were settled with much less trouble. One or two matters, such as the status and remuneration of officers when elected to parliament, were deferred, and the re-arrangement of the officers' superannuation fund to cover the officers of the N.A.U.L. — previously not provided for — was entrusted to the new General Council, when elected.

Amalgamation was now fully accepted, and was finally accomplished on July 1st when the three separate unions ceased to exist.

The New Constitution

We have already noted that the arrangements for the government of the new union were taken over bodily from the N.U.G.W. The final authority was to be a Biennial Congress elected by the branches with one delegate for each 3000 members. No full-time officer could stand as a delegate, and although a proportion of them were to attend each Congress, and were to be allowed to speak, they were to have no voting rights there. Each district was to have a Council of working delegates, which would meet every six months, and elect from its number a Committee of not more than seven members and a Chairman to act between Councils. Each district was to send its secretary and a 'lay' member to the General Council of the union, and the four largest districts were to send an additional lay member, so that full-time officers would be in a minority. The General Council was to meet every quarter, and to elect five district secretaries and five of its lay members, from districts other than those of the five elected secretaries, to serve with the General Secretary and President as an executive committee. This executive, naturally enough, became the most important organ of government.

The branches of the three unions retained their identity but were re-allocated into twelve districts. These districts were roughly the old districts of the N.U.G.W. — London, Lancashire, Northern, Scotland, Birmingham, Leeds, Sheffield, Midland, East Coast and South Wales — with a new Liverpool district carved out of Lancashire, and a district in Northern Ireland. Since the N.U.G.W. had no members in Ireland, this district was composed entirely of the other two unions. In the London, Lancashire, Leeds, Birmingham, Northern, South Wales, East Coast, Midland and Scottish districts, the old

N.U.G.W. secretaries — respectively S. J. Wright, F. Eccles, W. Wood, T. Hurley, H. Lynas, W. E. Hopkin, R. H. Farrah, A. Hayday and J. McKenzie — took over. In Sheffield, Liverpool and Northern Ireland, A. J. Bailey, T. Williamson and S. Bradley, the old N.A.U.L. delegates, were appointed district secretaries. Other officers of the three unions became their district organizers.

At Head Office Thorne and Clynes naturally retained their positions. Tevenan, General Secretary of the M.E.A., and Spence, Correspondence Secretary of the N.A.U.L., were appointed to new posts as Assistant General Secretaries, and G. P. Dean, of the M.E.A., joined Jack Jones, Will Sherwood and Miss Bondfield. The new Municipal Section in fact amounted to little more than the institution of a department at Head Office for the supervision of collective bargaining with local authorities and on the joint industrial councils to which they belonged, very much as Sherwood had general responsibility for negotiations in engineering, shipbuilding and iron and steel. For all other purposes the old M.E.A. members were as much under the control of the district committees and district secretaries as the other members.

The five district secretaries to serve on the first Executive Committee were S. J. Wright, F. Eccles, A. J. Bailey, H. Lynas and J. McKenzie. Size of district was the determining factor, for the London, Lancashire, Northern and Scottish districts were the four largest districts, with an additional lay member of the General Council, and, therefore, an additional vote, and Sheffield came next to them in numbers.

Full-time officers might in the first instance be appointed, but they remained temporary until they were confirmed by an election in which they competed with any other members of the union whom a branch or branches might wish to nominate. Each district voted on its own officers, and the national officers came before the whole union. All posts came up for election every two years, but it was expected that these elections would confirm the holders, as they had almost invariably done in the past.

The subsequent history of the new union may be briefly outlined. It suffered from the gradual decline of membership which affected all unions during the twenties, and steepened during the depression of the early thirties. It played its full part in the General Strike, but repudiated it most emphatically afterwards. At the same time it became one of the most firmly anti-Communist of the trade unions. In the middle thirties numbers began to recover. Charles Dukes succeeded Will Thorne and carried through a reorganization of the union's structure following on the institution of compulsory retirement for full-time officers. Expansion continued during the war, and, after a pause, into the post-war years. During the war the union accepted its share of responsibility in the tripartite schemes of the government for advice and even for administration of industrial and social policy, and since the war, with Tom Williamson as General Secretary, it has been amongst the foremost supporters of the policies of the Labour Government and the T.U.C. for increasing productivity and for wage restraint.

From now on, however, we are not concerned with the strict chronological sequence of events. Our aim is to describe the union as an organization rather than to write its history.

PART II

THE ORGANIZATION OF THE N.U.G.M.W.

THE MEMBERSHIP

THE difference between total membership and financial membership in the table overleaf is due to the rule that only members whose contributions are less than six weeks in arrears are 'in benefit'. The membership of the union can thus never be exactly determined, for many of those 'out of benefit' may soon pay up and suffer no penalty unless they had reason to claim some benefit before they paid. The rest are members who will ultimately be crossed off the books. Naturally an effort is made to get in contributions before the books are made up, so that at the dates for which figures are given financial membership is likely to be at a peak. Branch secretaries 'may' strike off the books the names of those whose arrears exceed twenty-six weeks. In normal circumstances it is unlikely that a secretary would go to the trouble of carrying the names of such troublesome members over into a new book, but if he has any reason for inflating his total membership the rule allows him to carry a certain amount of dead wood. There is no 'political' incentive to do this, since for voting purposes financial membership alone is taken into account.

The figures of growth do not reveal the turnover, which is considerable. A certain turnover due to deaths and retirement is inevitable (although many retired members continue on a reduced contribution in order to retain their funeral benefit rights), but the figure has always exceeded any that could reasonably be attributed to this cause. Between 1932 and 1933 total membership fell by a little more than 500. As there were 38,000 entries during the year, the loss must have been over 38,500 or about 16 per cent of the total. Between 1940 and 1941 the union gained 273,000 new members, but increased its total by 118,500, so that it must have lost 154,500 members, or over 32 per cent of its total membership at the beginning of the year. A proportion of these, of course, went into the forces.

Year	Total Membership	Female Membership	Total Financial Membership
1924	359,697	32,638	298,197
1925	348,859	34,227	295,920
1926	322,345	30,378	262,956
1927	308,305	26,997	256,991
1928	283,906	25,512	239,120
1929	290,877	26,701	247,433
1930	282,903	24,876	239,979
1931	267,734	20,588	228,456
1932	241,998	19,394	207,701
1933	241,447	20,460	210,844
1934	269,357	23,427	235,639
1935	300,145	25,929	262,522
1936	366,467	35,691	313,297
1937	439,287	47,351	376,785
1938	452,367	47,023	387,640
1939	467,060	55,780	394,315
1940	479,318	70,624	403,742
1941	597,890	162,381	515,514
1942	720,666	257,138	631,017
1943	726,487	243,710	638,487
1944	660,604	193,830	582,566
1945	604,753	129,529	537,287
1946	795,173	149,058	715,171
1947	823,612	159,628	742,614
1948	816,261	155,962	736,471
1949	804,564	152,041	732,071
1950	785,040	146,147	715,460
1951	808,533	161,142	738,258
1952	808,238	162,691	737,802

Between 1948 and 1949 entries were 160,000, the total fell by 11,500, and losses were, therefore, 172,000 or 21 per cent.
Caution is always required in interpreting turnover figures. It may be true that the average length of membership is about four or five years. It is certainly most unlikely to be true that most members stay in the union for only four or five years. Claims for death benefit show that a considerable proportion of memberships is of far longer duration, and this probably holds for most memberships, so that the majority of the losses in each year (except perhaps depression years) are of members who have not long been in the union. If this is accepted it is still possible either that this year's gains are last year's losses, or that the bulk of new members, even in years in which total membership is not expanding, have not been members of the union before. The answer could only be determined by an exhaustive study of branch books. An ex-member may well join a different branch from the one to which he previously belonged, and even if he comes back to the same branch the secretary is likely to accept him as a new member, unless a very short period off the books, or repetition, suggests that his only concern is to avoid payment of arrears. Although there is no proof, it is probably best to assume that a large number of new entrants in any year, especially in years when the total changes little, have been members before. This is widely believed to be true by union officers, who grumble that there are many who join the union when they have an industrial grievance and leave as soon as the matter is settled.

Turnover varies between industries, and is likely to be affected both by labour turnover within the industry concerned, and by the strength of the union's hold. When low industrial turnover coincides with something approaching a closed shop, the union's membership must be fairly stable: for instance amongst the employees of many boroughs, especially before the war, when municipal employment had the attraction of a sheltered industry. Building labourers are notoriously difficult to keep. They may be organized on one site, but they soon move off on to a new job, and are lost until a new effort is made elsewhere. Turnover amongst laundry workers, whose industry

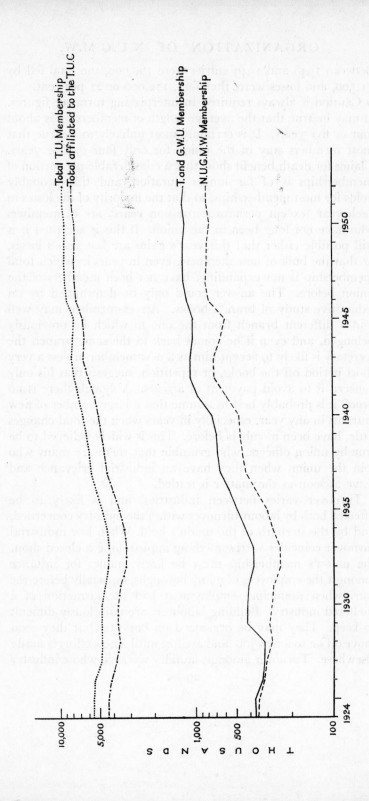

Total T.U. Membership
Total affiliated to the T.U.C
T. and G.W.U Membership
N.U.G.M.W. Membership

10,000
5,000
1,000
500
100

1924   1930   1935   1940   1945   1950

THOUSANDS

has itself a high turnover and over whom the hold of the union is at best insecure, may be even higher.

The growth of women membership needs little explanation. The war of 1939-45 brought an even greater number of women into the union, and into other unions, than did the first world war, partly because they started with a larger proportion of women in 1939, so that union membership came more naturally to women, and the unions were more acquainted with their special problems, and partly because women were brought into industry to an even greater extent. The very different economic developments after the second war have left the union with a considerably larger proportion of women than it had when there was a separate women's district and staff of organizers.

The graph opposite shows that the membership of the union has roughly kept pace with total trade union membership since the amalgamation. During the twenties the T. & G.W.U. took the lead over the N.U.G.M.W. This was at least in part due to the amalgamation of a number of unions, especially of the Workers' Union, with the T. & G.W.U. Since 1933 the N.U.G.M.W. has grown at about the same rate as its sister general union. The numbers of the N.U.G.M.W. today only exceed the aggregate of the N.U.G.W., the N.A.U.L., the M.E.A., the Birmingham Gasworkers' and the Women's Federation in the peak year of 1920 by about 50,000 (or roughly 6 per cent). In that year, however, total trade union membership[1] touched a figure which it was not to reach again until 1946, and even in 1949 total trade union membership exceeded the 1920 figure by no more than 10 per cent.

It is not possible to give exact figures for the industrial distribution of the union's members. In recent years the union has begun to take censuses of industrial distribution, but the results are regarded as confidential. We are, however, not wholly without guidance. For the 1926 Congress of the union an estimate was made that, out of a total of almost 350,000,

'The membership in the various groups of industry is approximately as follows:

---

[1] Chief Registrar of Friendly Societies' figures, quoted in the *Ministry of Labour Gazette*.

Public Services, i.e. Gas, Waterworks, Non-
Trading   110,000
Engineering, Shipbuilding and Metal   80,000
Building Trades   25,000
General Transport   10,000

The remainder are mainly general workers employed in
various trades, whose wages and conditions are governed by
the various Joint Industrial Councils and Trade Boards.'
For the Congress of 1938 far more thorough figures were
prepared in order to estimate the cost of a proposed accident
benefit scheme (which was not in fact introduced).

Textiles	18,000
Building and Constructional	43,500
Heavy Engineering	40,500
Shipbuilding	9,000
Docks	9,000
Claystone, Brick, etc.	7,500
Chemicals (Paint, etc.)	13,500
Quarrying	12,000
Iron Ore Mining	8,000
Coal Surface Workers	8,000
Gas	40,000
Electricity	14,000
Municipal Service	146,000
Food, Drink, Tobacco	24,000
Factories, General and Miscellaneous	27,000
	420,000

Since that time membership amongst municipal workers,
textile workers, building workers, dockers, iron ore miners and
coal surface workers has probably expanded but little. All the
other groups have greatly expanded. Nearly all of them
have at least doubled, and the engineering and factories'
groups have grown even more rapidly. Some of the divisions
in the table are not easy to interpret. Membership amongst
workers whose wages are determined by, or follow, agreements

between the Engineering Employers and the Engineering Unions is now probably at least four times as great as the figure given for heavy engineering at that time. But the majority of these members are in works which would be classified as 'light' rather than 'heavy' engineering. Probably the term was chosen to cover all members whose wages were determined in this way, as opposed to the 'Light Metal Trades' who have their own machinery for collective bargaining, but do not cover most of what would normally be considered 'light' engineering trades.

Today the union has three groups of members of roughly equivalent size: the public services, including mainly local government employees, gasworkers, hospital workers, electricity supply workers and waterworks employees; engineering, ship-building, metal and allied trades (including, for instance, aluminium workers, and Ministry of Supply and Admiralty Dockyard employees); and workers in other industries. The form for the union's census lists nearly 250 industries or sub-divisions of industries, and even then there are groups of workers in every district who cannot be classified under any of those heads. Despite this the majority of those outside the first two groups are in a few industries — building, civil engineering and building materials (mainly bricks of all kinds, and cement), quarries and mines other than coal, chemicals (heavy and light, explosives, drugs, paint and varnish, soap and candles), rubber (tyres, general rubber goods, rubber floors and rubber reclamation) and catering. Membership in a few other industries, such as sugar refineries, breweries, distilleries, flour-milling, rayon, doubling, dyeing and wool-combing, docks and laundries, may be numbered in thousands, but under many headings on the census list the total will be given in hundreds.

Since 1924 amalgamations have not greatly affected either growth or distribution between industries. The Cumberland Iron Ore Miners came in in 1929, the Cleveland Miners in 1931, the Quarryworkers and Settmakers in 1934, the Welsh Artisans in 1935, the Woolcombers in 1936 and the Air-craft Inspectors in 1944. Besides this a number of very small associations have arranged to transfer their members to the

N.U.G.M.W. None of these unions brought in either large numbers (the most important accession was the Quarryworkers and Settmakers' union, and that had no more than 6000 at the time when it was merged) or a claim to organize a wide field of industry.

An analysis of distribution between industries is not always a good guide to distribution between occupations. How far, for instance, is the union still a labourers' union?

In shipbuilding and in building the traditional division between craftsmen and labourers who service the craftsmen has been maintained more than in any other important industry, except perhaps the printing trades. Here the N.U.G.M.W. organizes in the main the same groups of workers as did the early labourers' unions, although many of the jobs its members perform may require skill.

In the engineering and metals group of industries the division has largely disappeared. There are still many craftsmen, in toolrooms, on maintenance, and operating machines especially reserved for them, and these are almost invariably organized by the A.E.U., the E.T.U. or the craft unions. There are still labourers, who are catered for almost exclusively by the two big general unions. But a large proportion of the workers are now semi-skilled — machinists, assembly workers and the like — for whom the general unions compete with the A.E.U. For a long time the two general unions alone represented women, but since 1943 the A.E.U. has also opened its doors to them, and has been followed by the E.T.U. and the Foundryworkers.

In civil engineering, as in docks, there have never been many craftsmen and the general unions are almost alone in the field. Amongst local government manual employees they meet severe competition from the N.U.P.E. but the competition is for all classes of workers.

In the gas industry the union organizes all production and distribution workers and, in addition, most of the largest group of craftsmen — the gas fitters — and some maintenance craftsmen. In the electricity supply industry the union has, due to upgrading, members amongst all classes of workers, including craftsmen. It draws its membership, however, mainly from other grades and meets severe competition, especially from the E.T.U., even there.

Elsewhere, in a wide range of productive industries, the craft unions are normally confined to maintenance workers. The general unions organize the labourers and the whole range of productive workers. This holds good, for instance, in the chemicals group, in rubber, in most food and drink industries and in laundries.

Some of the small groups of skilled workers in various industries who have come into the union, such as engine drivers or woolcombers, have already been mentioned. A more recent addition are the typewriter mechanics in London who joined after they had failed to set up a union of their own. Besides this the union has small numbers of members from a wide variety of crafts, even so exclusive as the boilermaking and pattern-making trades. This is most likely to occur among maintenance workers in an isolated rural factory where the union already covers production workers, but it may be the result of successful retaliation against 'poaching' by a craft union. In South London the union has a large proportion of the gas maintenance craftsmen.

The union is not confined to manual workers. In each of the public service industries which it covers it has some clerical and administrative workers, although the majority are in their own associations such as the National and Local Government Officers Association or the British Gas Staffs Association. Elsewhere it has tried to organize the staff of many works where it already has a hold, with varying success. Over the whole country it must number its clerical and administrative members in thousands, if not tens of thousands. Perhaps the largest single group is amongst North London gas staffs.

'Flat-rate' wage increases during two world wars have reduced the difference between the wages of craftsmen and of labourers. In many industries semi-skilled production workers under systems of payment by results earn more, as apprenticed craftsmen bitterly complain, than craftsmen earning time rates. For both these reasons the general workers' unions cannot be so accurately described as 'lower-paid workers'' organizations as they could before 1914. There is, however, still some basis for their championship of the cause of the lower paid. In building and shipbuilding their position is clear. In the building industry earnings are about the same as the national average, but the earnings of members of the general unions must be below the average for the industry. In the engineering and metals group of industries earnings are above the national average, but since the general workers organize nearly all the labourers and very few of the craftsmen, and compete for the semi-skilled workers, and since they between them have most of the women trade union members, the average earnings of their members are probably below the average for the industry. Earnings in all the public services are below the national average, in municipal service very much below the average as far as male workers are concerned, and the very large membership of the union in this group must outweigh the high earnings of its members in some of the other industries, such as heavy chemicals and rubber. Finally, the general unions represent a large number of workers whose wages are governed by Wages Councils, and earnings here are almost invariably well below the national average.

The N.U.G.M.W. certainly speaks for the lower paid in some industries, and, although no statistical demonstration is possible, it is probable that it has a stronger interest in speaking for the lower paid workers in general than have most other trade unions.

CHAPTER II

THE BRANCH

THERE are about 2250 branches in the N.U.G.M.W. so
that the average size of branch is between 350 and 360.
The minimum number of members for setting up a new
branch is twenty, but smaller branches exist, mostly in rural
areas. A branch of twenty may lose members, and in exceptional circumstances permission may be granted for a smaller
branch to be set up if there seems a likelihood of attracting
recruits by such a move. There is no upper limit to the size
of a branch. The system of paying branch secretaries a commission, as we have already explained, encourages branch
secretaries to build up their branches until they can afford to
devote their whole time to the work. At the end of 1947 there
were 64 branches with over 2000 members. Between them
they held 216,000 members, or over a quarter of the total.
The number of whole-time secretaries of all sorts has since
increased, and is now over eighty, so that it is probable that
the proportion of members in branches of this size has also
increased.

From the earliest days of the Gasworkers, there have been
general branches and specialized branches. The general
branch is perhaps most fitted for rural areas and the specialized
branch for industrial areas, but, although by and large that
may be the general practice, it is a practice to which many
exceptions are made. In one industrial town several thousands
of workers from a wide variety of trades may be brought into
one large branch. In another town of comparable size, a
similar number of workers may be split up into gasworkers,
electrical workers, municipal workers, waterworks employees'
branches, with perhaps half-a-dozen other branches attached
to the various large works, and one or two general branches
besides to cover the rest. In Lancashire, where large branches
are strongly encouraged, nearly all the towns of the industrial
belt have large general branches. Only in Manchester itself,
where some method of division has to be found, is there special-

ization by industry and occupation. And, in fact, the large branch is more likely to be found in an industrial town of middling size — Dundee, York, Warrington, Reading — than in the largest cities, where there may be one or two large branches, but accompanied by a considerable number of small branches. Large branches are not necessarily general branches. The York branch is mainly a cocoa and chocolate workers' branch, and most of its members are employees of Rowntrees. The Banbury branch is entitled the Northern Aluminium Company Branch. Both have naturally attached to themselves other groups of workers in the same town (gasworkers, engineering workers and so on), but this is likely to happen to any specialized branch, to suit the convenience or the taste of members.

The main functions of the branch are to act as the local financial agent of the union, to serve as the local centre of administration — as the means of contact between Head Office, the district and the members, and as the electoral unit — and to conduct its own business so far as it is competent to do so.

All contributions are collected through the branches, and, after deductions have been made for branch commissions, honoraria, and approved expenditure, transmitted to the district. All benefits are transmitted from the district to the branch secretary to be disbursed by him. Most branch secretaries handle the income of a district accident, or sick, accident and burial fund as well as the income of the union. In all but the smallest branches collecting stewards are appointed, nominally by the branch, normally by the secretary himself, to collect contributions from the members and hand them over to the secretary. The collecting steward is provided with his own book for keeping his accounts. Collections are normally conducted at the place of work, although in Lancashire, following the practice of the cotton unions, house-to-house collections are common. Rule requires that the branch secretary 'shall hand over all moneys taken on behalf of the Branch to the District Secretary each week less a sum not to exceed 5s. retained in hand when required for authorized Branch expenses', although towards the end of the quarter he may retain enough to pay commissions. In fact, branches pay in weekly, fortnightly, monthly or even over longer periods, according to the size of the branch, and the 5s. limit is often exceeded even when money is paid in. By rule and in practice books are balanced, audited by elected branch auditors and the balance sheet sent in to the district each quarter.

The branch provides the regular means of contact between the members and the higher administration of the union. The district keeps all branches posted on union business, sending the minutes of district meetings, instructions for carrying out union decisions, and to each branch a mass of circulars containing information about changes in wages and conditions in any industry in which the branch has an interest. The branch secretary sends to the district office resolutions from the branch, any information which he thinks may be useful, and letters on all individual cases — claims for benefit, injuries at work, and the like — together with requests for assistance in matters he cannot deal with himself.

Elections are conducted within each branch for branch officers — chairman, secretary, auditors and a committee of not less than five in addition to the first two — and through the branch for full-time officers, for district council and for the union Congress. Rule provides for voting either by ballot or show of hands; the latter is the customary practice. When the election is for a position outside the branch the majority by show of hands casts the voting strength of the whole financial membership of the branch. Only occasionally are elections keenly fought. Branch officers are normally re-elected at the end of each two years of office, and even when the secretaryship and chairmanship are contested there is not usually any difficulty in obtaining a place on the branch committee. Sometimes the difficulty is to find members who are willing to serve.

In one district, between 1947 and 1949, the number of branches varied from 267 to 283. In elections to the union Congress, the number of branches making valid returns varied from 67 to 108. In elections to the district council the numbers of valid papers were from 82 and 109. In elections for district officers the figures varied from 76 to 85.[1] Although it is impossible to obtain accurate information on the size of attendances at branch meetings for the N.U.G.M.W. or for other unions, P.E.P.[2] has made calculations based on attendances in meetings at which voting takes place, in unions which vote by ballot at branch meetings. Its conclusion is that 'percentages vary from 2 to more than 30 per cent, but are mainly between 15 and 25 per cent.' There is no evidence to show that the N.U.G.M.W. differs markedly from other unions in this respect. P.E.P. also points out 'large branches show a lower percentage poll than the small branches'. In the N.U.G.M.W. a regular attendance of a hundred in a branch of 3000 would be considered good. It can be seen, then, that elections are determined by a small minority. The district quoted may be somewhat exceptional, for the elections of district officers, which are recorded in the union's annual report, frequently show that the votes of more than three-quarters of the total financial membership of the district have been cast by their branches. As it is less likely that the large branches will forget to record their votes, it cannot be assumed that this shows that the large majority of *branches* voted, and we can only guess what number of members were present at the meetings which determined the way in which the block vote should be cast. In the autumn of 1946 when Tom Williamson was elected General Secretary, the financial membership of the union was 623,261, and the total number of valid votes cast for him and for his opponents was 486,356, so that a considerable proportion of the branches must have failed to send in their ballot papers.

Before an official strike takes place, a ballot must be held. The rule is here far more strict than over elections. 'Two-thirds of the members of the Branch or body immediately concerned' must vote in favour. On this point practice also seems to be more strict.

The branch may get through a good deal of industrial business without calling in the district officers. The way in

[1] This proportion of branches making valid returns should not be taken as typical of all districts of the union. In elections held in the London district during 1951 the proportion varied from 48 per cent to 59 per cent.
[2] *British Trade Unionism*, P.E.P., 1948, pp. 25-8.

which this is conducted varies according to the composition of the branch. A specialist branch will discuss industrial matters, especially when trouble arises, in the branch and the branch committee, and decide what action shop stewards should take. In a general branch special meetings of the members or the shop stewards concerned may be held, either regularly or as occasion arises. If the matter is beyond their competence, especially if the terms of a collective agreement are in doubt, the district office is informed, and an officer takes up the matter. The amount of work conducted in this way will vary with the ability and temperament of the branch officers. A whole-time branch secretary, although he is not authorized to sign agreements, may do all but that, and may in fact take a great deal of work off the shoulders of district officers. On the other hand a branch may wish to keep matters in its own hands, and fail to bring in the district officer when it ought to do so.

Many branches run their own funds. These are normally financed by a 1d. levy on members above the union contribution, although some branches, particularly those of small groups of craftsmen, for instance, in the Sheffield cutlery and light metal trades, have far higher contributions, and elaborate benefits. The rules of these funds must have the approval of the District Council or Committee, but they are conducted at the discretion of the branch. They may be used for social events, or to remit the contributions of members who are sick or otherwise in trouble, and to provide small grants to them.

Social activities may rank high amongst the branches' activities. Outings, dinners and children's entertainments may be arranged. The branch will be connected with other local groupings in the Labour Movement. Except in the large cities, where Trades Council activities rank as district business, the branch sends its delegates to the local Trades Council, and gives them instructions. It is normally affiliated to the local Labour Party, and makes nominations for seats on local authorities. It may also be called upon to make nominations in the choice of Labour candidates for Parliamentary seats, but since this raises the question of official union recognition and aid for the nominee, the decision here must be left to the district and to the National Executive; the branch acts on instructions, and is reprimanded if it fails to carry them out.

We have already said that attendance at branch meetings is poor. This is not confined to the N.U.G.M.W., nor is it a new thing in union experience. The business of the meeting is normally to hear correspondence, which may be mostly circulars concerning rates or conditions, each of which is of interest to a few members, and letters on individual complaints. Members then raise any problems which they may have, and a common problem may lead to a general discussion. At the appropriate intervals auditors and Labour Party and Trades Council delegates report, and elections are held. From time to time a district officer addresses the branch, and occasionally an outsider may be brought in to speak.

Usually the business, by its nature, is not exciting. If meetings as a result are dull this is not for lack of trying to improve them. Every conscientious branch secretary and official of the union must have given his attention to making branch meetings more attractive and better attended. When a dispute concerning a large proportion of the members is in a critical stage, a large attendance can be relied on. Otherwise the matters which arise hold little interest for most, and since the members are rarely good speakers, they are unlikely to become more interesting in debate. The union might turn its attention to education through the branches. At one time Charles Dukes prepared a national scheme. But probably those members who are so inclined already attend adult classes. There seems little reason for the union to compete, and it could not afford to compete for tutors with state-subsidized bodies. The union's officers are already busy men, and not usually trained for that job. The only certain attraction is a dance, dinner or entertainment financed or subsidized out of the branch fund.

The branch committee is often a much more lively body. The interest and to a much greater extent, the knowledge, is likely to be there. In fact, most of the work of a branch, financial affairs, individual problems, methods of increasing membership in various works and so on, is the kind of business which a committee is much more fitted to carry on than a general meeting. The members tend to leave it to the committee. Although quarterly meetings are enjoined by the rule book, and branches may meet as often as they please (monthly meetings are common), meetings cannot be held without members, and it does happen that an attendance cannot be found. There have been occasions when branches, at least for a time, have given up the attempt and the work has been carried on entirely by the committee.

Interest, measured in terms of branch attendance, is generally reckoned to decline with increasing size of branch, and to be least in the largest branches, with whole-time secretaries. In these branches, however, attendance may not be a very accurate index of interest, as a brief description of the organization of a whole-time secretary's branch may show.

There are, in fact, three classes of whole-time secretaries. There is nothing to prevent any branch secretary giving up his job and living on his commission if he thinks it sufficient to keep him. The district committees, with the approval of the National Executive, may appoint a whole-time secretary for 'a large branch or number of branches amalgamated for that purpose'.[1] The secretary so appointed 'shall be at all times under the control and work under the direction of the District Secretary' and 'shall not be subject to periodical election by the members of the branch'. If the commission from all sources — union dues and district sick, etc., funds — does not come to a certain minimum figure, the secretary is subsidized. Finally, where the prospects of the branch seem good, and the secretary qualifies on age and medical grounds, he may be admitted to the union's superannuation fund. In fact, whole-time secretaries are almost invariably elected by their branches. If a branch has an official whole-time secretary for the first time, the secretary in office is, with rare exceptions, appointed. If an official whole-time secretary dies, retires or gives up his office, his successor is elected by the branch. The district reserves the

[1] There is no rule that this shall be done for branches above a given size. At least one branch of over 3000 members is run by its secretary as a spare-time activity, although he employs secretarial assistance.

right to reject an unsuitable candidate, and would only confirm the successful candidate and recommend him for superannuation after a trial period of a year or two.

The whole-time secretary may require clerical help, and the National Executive may allow him up to 40s. towards employing a typist. In the largest branches the commission will permit him to employ two typists, or perhaps a typist and an assistant secretary. The union may rent premises for him, or allow him to use part of a union building.

It may seem anomalous that a whole-time secretary should be considered a 'lay member', and not a 'full-time' official, by the union rules. He is thus eligible for election to the district council and committee, to the union's congress with full voting rights, and to the General Council and National Executive as a lay member. It is easy to see how the anomaly arose. There was no reason to alter the status of a branch secretary just because he gave up or lost his industrial job. Later there seemed little reason to change it when the district committee confirmed him in office.[1]

The whole-time secretary is likely to have a good deal of work outside his branch. He is usually interested in local politics and may well be a councillor or alderman. He is almost certain to be on a number of local advisory bodies — such as those serving the Ministry of Labour — and tribunals — Unemployment Insurance, Health Insurance, etc. — though he may try to spread a good deal of this kind of work amongst the more interested members of his branch. He may be a J.P. He will be a delegate to the local organizations of some of the great trade union federations. And he may well have union duties on higher bodies, such as the district council or committee. But if he has the details of finance and book-keeping taken off his shoulders, he still has time for branch work.

If his branch is specialized, his committee may in fact be the shopstewards' committee of the works concerned. If he

---

[1] At the 1950 Congress, a resolution asked that 'all full-time Branch Secretaries shall be classified as full-time Officials'. It was, by consent, referred to the National Executive, who reported to the 1951 Congress that 'after giving the question careful and detailed consideration, it has been decided that, in all the circumstances, the principle cannot be entertained'.

chooses the same group as his collecting stewards (where shop and collecting stewards are distinguished and, as we shall see, the two offices are frequently confused) he has a tight system of contacts with the members (provided that the stewards do their work well) and most business is likely to be taken up and settled before the machinery of the branch meeting could have begun to operate. In a general branch his main contact may be with the conveners of stewards at the various factories and through meetings with their stewards arranged from time to time. Even when shop-stewards, collecting stewards and committee members are different persons (and there is likely to be a good deal of overlapping even when arrangements are not made for the offices to be held by the same people) his system of contacts should be manageable. Industrial business in the general branch is then taken out of the branch and handled separately in each industry. Information on negotiations is duplicated and passed on to the stewards concerned for dissemination, instead of read out at an ill-attended meeting.

Besides this the branch secretary normally arranges to be available in his office for some period each day, and members can, and do, bring their troubles straight to him. In this way he is likely to have to deal with all manner of subjects besides industrial matters, which are most likely to come through the stewards. He acts as a medium between district office and members concerned in compensation cases, industrial injuries, common law claims for damages arising out of injuries at work, and perhaps conducts cases before local tribunals. He will have to advise and help members in all their difficulties — and they are many — with the forms and claims of the welfare state. He will have to deal with many cases of hardship and distress. He may be brought in family problems — divorce, choice of schools, choice of careers. He may be asked to help with income tax, or intervene with the local tax office. He will be a frequent visitor at the Local Employment Exchange with his members' problems. To spend a Saturday morning in a branch secretary's office, and see and hear the constant stream of members — or members' wives — who call in, is a useful experience for anyone who would define the functions of a trade union, and a corrective for anyone who would judge interest in trade unions by branch attendance alone.

Very different views are held within the union on the value of the large branch and the whole-time secretary. Some officers argue that interest diminishes in the large branch. Lancashire, with twenty-three whole-time secretaries, holds that they are far superior for administrative purposes, and provide a full-time, experienced officer on the spot. Certainly an energetic whole-time secretary is a valuable recruiting agent. In 1944 Lancashire methods were introduced into the Southern district with considerable success by Jack Cooper, an ex-Lancashire official who was then appointed Southern district secretary. Although all districts grew rapidly in the following few years, Southern outpaced the others. Secretaries of some other districts argue that whole-time secretaries are difficult to control and liable to get out of hand. Whatever the rule may say they are far less subject to day-to-day supervision than the district officers, and they control a considerable block of votes. A few large branches might try between them to rule the affairs of the district.

In 1939 and 1940 there was some debate on the subject in the National Executive. It was pointed out that the decline in membership in the twenties had left one district with seventeen whole-time secretaries to subsidize, and the 'recruitment officer'[1] was suggested as a superior means of achieving the same ends. When the Bristol branch was broken into a number of small branches in 1941 there was some feeling that the district secretaries had decided to avoid whole-time appointments where possible. But it was stated that they had never discussed the matter. A year or so later the Aberdeen branch was similarly broken up when it was thought to be under the control of a small group of Communists. The new branches soon doubled membership in the town. With the growth of members, however, new whole-time appointments have been made every year since then, and the successes of the Southern district affected opinion within the union. The matter is still open.

[1] A new junior grade of district officer created in the reorganization of 1935-36. See p. 75.

The rule book gives the district committee almost absolute power over the branch. The former may close a branch 'for any reason which it deems good and sufficient, or when, in its judgment, it is considered advisable to do so', and may remove or suspend from office any branch officer on similarly widely defined grounds, although the officer so treated may appeal to the General Council. Another clause of the same rule allows the district to authorize a new election in the branch or to 'take such other action as may be deemed expedient in the interests of the Union'.

The wording of the rules owes much to Charles Dukes, who took legal advice, mainly from Sir Stafford Cripps, on redrafting this and other rules to keep disputes within the union out of the courts, which meant, of course, phrasing the rule so that a branch should have no legal redress against an action of the district. It must not be thought, however, that the rule is constantly in use. Districts step in from time to time to deal with misappropriation of union money, to settle an unofficial dispute, to quash an election in which a small group have established undesired control of a branch, or to discipline an officer who has exceeded his powers or failed in his duties. But the district depends on its branches, and they are normally allowed wide latitude to get on with their own business, so long as no trouble comes to its notice.

One of the worst offences a branch or its officers can commit is to form an 'unofficial' movement within the union and undermine government through the district. Consequently, branches are prohibited from intercommunication, except through the district secretary, and from divulging business or information to unauthorized bodies or to the press. Members are not allowed to attend meetings of other branches without the district secretary's approval, and must not associate themselves with any attack on the union or its officials, nor act 'singly or in conjunction with any other member or persons' in opposition to the declared policy of the union. We shall see later some of the ways in which these rules have been used.

CHAPTER III

THE DISTRICT

SINCE the reorganization of 1936 the union has had ten districts. Apart from minor boundary adjustments, the vast area of the London district was split into a London and a Southern district divided by the Thames; the Irish district was amalgamated with the Liverpool district; the Midland district was united with the East Coast district; and one Yorkshire district was formed out of the Leeds and Sheffield districts. In this way extreme inequalities in size were reduced. At the time the largest district was London, with 70,000 members, and the smallest Northern Ireland, with 6000. The extremes were reduced to 43,000 (Lancashire) and 19,000 (South Wales — renamed South Western). Today the same two districts come first and last in numbers, with some 120,000 and 50,000 members respectively.

The District Council and Committee

The final authority within the district is the district council, which is elected by the branches for a period of two years. It can consist of between 16 and 120 delegates and within those limits there should not be more than one delegate for each 1000 financial members. Small branches are grouped for electoral purposes. No branch, however large, may send more than one delegate. The council meets every six months. Extraordinary meetings are very rare.

Despite its powers on paper the council is not a very important body in union government. Most of its decisions give formal approval to what has been done elsewhere. The district secretary presents a report mainly concerned with the state of membership and of district income, which is frequently followed by a discussion on recruitment in which delegates air their views on where and how new members can be gained, and attack the practices of competing unions. In some districts a formal report on the results of collective bargaining within the district, or which affects the district, is presented to the council. This may be followed by a discussion in which delegates seek information on a number of points and perhaps explain how new agreements, or delays in arriving at new agreements, are being received in the branches. A number of the district officers are present to answer on these points. The minutes of the district committee meetings are presented. Queries are again raised and answered, and then the minutes are almost invariably approved *en bloc*. Rarely a particular decision is referred back to the committee — for instance, a decision on the appointment of a whole-time secretary — but normally a motion to refer back is moved formally to express displeasure at some action, and, if pressed, is heavily defeated. Occasionally a national officer or an outsider may be present to give an address (the Northern district makes a practice of this), and sometimes a general resolution on union policy may be put and debated at length. Debates of this kind can lead to no action, for the council is not empowered to take decisions which affect the union as a whole, and the most that can result is an expression of opinion for the consideration of the General Council or National Executive. The main functions of the council are to bring together from time to time the leading members of the union within the district, to provide a convenient occasion for the explanation of union policy and the work of the district, and to elect the district committee and representatives to other bodies — the General Council of the union, the T.U.C. and the Labour Party Conference.

The district council elects 'from its own number a Chairman ... and a District Committee consisting of not more than seven members'. In fact, each district has a committee of seven or eight members except the Northern district, which has ten. The Northern district had a committee larger than seven before amalgamation, and on amalgamation, the district secretary, Hugh Lynas, a man accustomed to have his way, decided to interpret the rule—'At its first meeting the District Council shall elect from its own number a Chairman, the appropriate number of Lay Delegates to represent the District on the General Council, and a District Committee of not more than seven members'— as requiring the election of ten persons (since the Northern district has always been entitled to two lay members on the General Council) all of whom are to serve on the district committee. Nominations are grouped into geographical divisions each of which is allowed one or more of the ten places according to the size of the branches therein. When the ten have been chosen (the whole council voting for each place), the council proceeds to choose the chairman and General Council delegates from their number. Elsewhere the three elections are entirely separate. The same man may be elected chairman and General Council representative, or General Council representative and committee member, although some districts vote for six committee members in addition to the chairman, and others choose seven and regard the chairman as an *ex officio* member.[1] In other districts there is not the same careful regard for geographical representation as in the Northern district, but in the London and Southern districts places on the committee are divided between the London and country branches.

The district committee, which meets monthly, has to deal with a good deal of routine business. It has to take decisions on the appeals which come in from the branches for help from its contingent fund in cases of hardship; it has to decide whether applications for disablement benefit are worth sending in to Head Office; and it has to consider financial appeals from outside bodies (which are not rare) and allocate the district's political resources during local elections.

Reports of negotiations in the various industries in the district come before it — mainly for approval, although it may at times give guidance to the officers concerned, or decide what action should be taken on a resolution from the branches seeking a local application for improved wages and conditions in one industry or another. It may sanction an official strike of up to 300 members, or (more usual in recent years) may allow a grant equivalent to strike pay where it feels that in an unofficial strike its members are in no way at fault and the blame rests on the employer. Larger disputes have to be submitted to London.

[1] The latter interpretation of the rule is regarded as correct by the National Executive.

In any case the committee will hear reports on disputes. Since unofficial strikes are normally brief the committee usually discusses them after the event, and has to decide only whether a grant is appropriate, or whether unofficial strikers need to be disciplined.

The committee is the disciplinary authority of the district, and in this capacity it does take the decisions. Only rarely, and when urgency provides an excuse, does the district secretary act first and seek approval afterwards. The committee acts as a selection committee for choosing new officers, and normally[1] for selecting a new district secretary from amongst the district officers.

The district secretary wields very great power within his district. He is in sole charge of the day-to-day running of business and of the district officers and district office. He is usually far more experienced than the members of his committee, although the presence of whole-time secretaries — perhaps even a majority of them — on the committee may give him less advantage in this respect than district secretaries in other unions frequently possess. It is through him that the committee receives most of the information on which to base its decisions. If he is a powerful personality, or a clever handler of men, he should clearly not find it difficult to carry his committee, and almost always, therefore, his district, with him.

Besides this he is a member of the General Council and may be on the National Executive. Even in the five districts represented on the Executive by laymen, the district secretaries are the leading figures. Collectively the district secretaries wield great power within the union. Only in exceptional circumstances will the district secretary lack the support of his district. The district committee or council are unlikely to succeed in a dispute with their secretary.

It must not be thought, however, that the district secretaries are absolute masters within their districts. In 1940 one of the district secretaries, against whom complaints had been made, was suspended by his district committee. Their action was approved by a meeting of the district council held for the pur-

[1] See below, p. 77.

pose. The matter was reported to the National Executive by the General Secretary, who gave his opinion that the district committee and council had acted strictly within their rights. The National Executive thereupon retired the district secretary, with subsequent confirmation from the General Council, and the district committee was empowered to proceed with the selection of a new secretary. This was an exceptional case, but in more normal times there must be give and take between the district secretary and his committee. For although they are unlikely to succeed in a dispute with him, his power in the union will be sadly reduced if he has not their support.

The District Officers and the District Office

The district secretary is primarily an administrator. Although he serves on a number of national and local collective bargaining bodies, he does little of the preparatory work of taking up the complaints of members and interviewing employers. His work is mainly within his office. There he is in control of a group of district officers, in numbers roughly proportionate to the size of the district, and a clerical staff. He is the employer of the clerical staff, which has no official status within the union. Its members must join the union, but are not eligible for election to any representative bodies within the union, outside the branches to which they belong. The district officers, once confirmed in their posts, have a much higher status, but the district committee has the power to suspend them and to recommend their dismissal to the National Executive. In 1944 several officers in one of the districts who felt they had grounds for complaint against their district secretary, tendered their resignations in order to call attention to their case. They had failed, however, to present their complaints through the proper channels. The district committee, therefore, stood by the secretary and the resignations were accepted by it and, on its recommendation, by the National Executive.[1] But these are

[1] Subsequently, the National Executive brought the secretary to Head Office as a national officer, and sent another national officer to the district as secretary. This was almost the only occasion on which the National Executive has used its powers to take the choice of district secretary out of the district committee. The appointment was, however, subsequently confirmed by an election throughout the district.

the bare bones of power. The successful work of the districts depends on the secretary handling his staff wisely and sympathetically. Normally Christian names are used, as throughout the trade union movement, and although the secretary may reprimand his officers severely for any failures or mistakes, he looks after them and stands by them, and they stand by him.

The main work of the district officers is industrial. There are distractions: no district officers are now M.P.s, but many are local councillors or aldermen, they may hold office in local or regional labour parties, and they serve on various tribunals and advisory committees. Their main work, however, is to keep the branches informed of developments in collective bargaining, and to learn of the industrial complaints of the members of the branches; to correspond with and interview employers and their representatives; to conduct cases before conciliation and arbitration committees and courts, and to sit on a number of regional and national industrial councils and other negotiating bodies. Along with branch officers they have the task of organizing, of recruiting members in new works or new areas, and of trying to hold existing members when difficulties arise.

Most districts have sub-offices which are run by one or more district officers. The number of sub-offices has, however, declined in recent years. Lancashire has none, Scotland, despite its size, has only one — in Edinburgh. The Southern district had eight sub-offices before 1944, but these were reduced to one — in Exeter — during the reorganization of the district's administration in subsequent years. District secretaries tend to dislike sub-offices as outside their immediate control, and they do not fit in easily with industrial specialization of officers, which has become more and more the general practice of the union.

There is clearly advantage in specialization. No officer can carry the details of a hundred different industries at his finger-tips. On the other hand, it is argued that an officer will be able to present a better case if he knows what is going on in a wide variety of industries. Accordingly, some districts have followed Lancashire (which has long preferred this method) into specialization, and others, which profess no high regard for the principle, allocate duties geographically. The difference between the two is not as great as it might appear. An officer is forced to specialize to some extent according to the negotiating committees on which he serves. If he is a member of the regional and national joint industrial councils of the gas industry or of the various sections of the quarrying industry, other officers will naturally turn to him for guidance when dealing with that industry's problems. On the other side no district has enough officers to allocate one industry each. Normally each officer must deal with at least half-a-dozen. And geographical and industrial boundaries may coincide, as, for instance, in shipbuilding. The two Lancashire officers who deal with quarries and textiles naturally find the great bulk of their work in Derbyshire.

Responsibility for branches is allocated between officers. Where specialization is applied a number of officers share responsibility for a general branch. An officer cannot be expected to attend each meeting of twenty or thirty branches, but he will attend from time to time especially when trouble arises, and in the meantime, deal with the industrial matters which they refer to the district.

Most of the clerical staff of each district office are shorthand-typists, who deal with the large correspondence of officers with branches, with employers, with negotiating bodies and with national officers. Besides this there is a financial department under a senior member of the staff to handle the money sent in by branches, keep the books, remit what is due to Head Office, disburse benefits and salaries, and to manage the district accident, or sick, accident and burial fund, where there is one. Here similarity ends. All districts but one have a legal department (there all legal business is handled by the secretary himself) to handle compensation cases (now industrial injuries appeals) and common law claims, but in some an officer is responsible for the work and in others a member of the staff, and the duties of the department vary widely between districts. One or two districts give a member of the staff charge of research, which means in practice little more than filing industrial information. There remains a good deal of administrative work (arranging district meetings and delegations to Congress, conducting elections) which may be handled by the district secretary's secretary or by some other member of the staff.

The district offices are normally large private houses converted into offices. Most of them are at a distance, even at a considerable distance, from the centre of the main town within the district, and therefore at a distance from the homes and workplaces of most of the members in that town. This is not necessarily a drawback. In the centre of an industrial district of a large town it would be too easy for those members who live or work nearby to call in to pursue their cases and queries in person, disrupt the orderly routine of the office, and hinder the dispatch of the business of branches further away.

The District and Head Office

The powers of the General Council (normally exercised by the National Executive) over the district are much the same as those of a district over its branches. The General Council may 'grant permission to start new Districts, and to disband any District or District Council' and has final authority over district officers. This does not mean that the relationship is the same. When the London district defied the authority of the union in 1947 the General Council's powers were used,[1] but where no such acute conflict arises the district secretary is an effective guardian of district autonomy, because the authority of the union over the districts is exercised, to a large extent, by the collective body of district secretaries. A district secretary does not meet such a formidable body in his district committee, even with several whole-time secretaries amongst its number, as the General Secretary meets in the General Council or National Executive. For this reason the union is considerably more decentralized than other unions and is in strong contrast to the T.&G.W.U., in which devolution of authority is by industry rather than area.

The district secretary is the channel of communication between Head Office and his district. All information goes to

[1] See below, pp. 128ff.

Head Office through him, and instructions from Head Office come to him. He is left to carry them out pretty much as he and his committee think fit. In particular, all information about collective agreements within his district should go to Head Office through him, and the National Industrial Officers at Head Office can communicate only through him with the district officers who deal with their industries locally, and with the members who work in those industries. Even if these rules are not always strictly observed they allow the district secretary to limit centralization fairly effectively.

CHAPTER IV

NATIONAL INSTITUTIONS

Congress

AT the Amalgamation Conference it was decided to allow districts to send one delegate to Congress for each 3000 financial members, elected by the branches from nominations by the branches. In 1930 in view of declining numbers this was altered to one delegate for each 2000. Since then membership has greatly increased, but the National Executive has failed to persuade Congress to increase the stipulated number. The General Secretary, all national officers, the General Auditors, all General Council members (including the district secretaries), and one-third of the officers of each district (by rota) attend Congress as *ex officio* delegates with the right to speak, but not to vote (except for the chairman, who has a casting vote). Since the number of national and district officers has increased considerably since amalgamation, the total number of delegates has increased about threefold. There are in addition a number of fraternal delegates from foreign unions or international organizations with which the union has affiliations, and some distinguished visitors. Many delegates bring their wives and families.

Up to the war Congress met biennially in even years. The war situation prevented Congress in 1940 and 1944 so that it was held in 1941 and 1942 and again in 1945 and 1946. In 1945 Congress accepted annual congresses in principle, and the rules were altered accordingly the following year. At the same time, it was agreed to leave the revision of rules (emergencies excepted) to every third Congress, starting in 1947. Head Office quickly discovered that this entailed devoting many of the members of its staff and much of the time of the National Executive for a considerable proportion of each year to preparing for Congress or carrying out its decisions, and proposals have been made from the platform to return to the old practice. But the delegates, not unnaturally, will not hear of it.

Congress normally meets at a seaside holiday resort. The exceptions are Keswick, 1928; Belfast, 1930; Swansea, 1936; and Aberdeen, 1947; and each of these was either an inland resort or by the sea. The reason is partly that it is far more easy to secure accommodation in a seaside resort out of the full season (Congress meets in May or June), but the knowledge that most delegates treat Congress as an occasion for a family holiday is not without its influence in the choice of venue. Seaside towns appreciate the value of a union conference, and often do their best to make their attractions known to the unions and offer special facilities to union delegates and visitors.

Congress assembles on Saturday, has a preliminary meeting on Sunday and gets down to business for the first three days, or, since 1950, the first four days, of the following week. After that many stay on to finish the week out. Even with debates on rules reserved for each third year, Congress has a full programme.

The General Secretary presents a full report to Congress, mainly concerned with the progress of negotiations and gains secured in the wide variety of industries with which the union deals, but including a few pages on the work of other Head Office departments — for instance, research — union political activities, and reports from the districts. In the first Congresses this was formally accepted, but from the early thirties the practice grew up of taking the report page by page. It is generally accepted, as a result of rulings from the chair, that Congress cannot decide that particular claims should be submitted in particular industries. That is a matter for the appropriate Joint Industrial Council or other negotiating body. But delegates have a number of queries to raise on agreements reached; they wish to explain the effect of various national agreements in their district; and they want to find out what is going to be done about current problems. So for some considerable time delegates alternate at the rostrum with National Industrial Officers who take responsibility for the appropriate parts of the report.

At the 1932 Congress the President, J. R. Clynes, announced that:

'the National Executive some time ago, looking over the

Agenda felt that there were omissions that were natural, and branches had scarcely touched any of those big national and international subjects on which we felt you would like to express an opinion.'

Accordingly five resolutions had been placed on the Agenda, and the practice has been followed since that time. Two or three resolutions on the current issues in the trade union movement or in Labour politics are put forward at each Congress. There is no serious difference of opinion unless the topic is one on which Labour and Communist views are divided. Then there will be a few opponents from the floor, but almost invariably such resolutions are carried unanimously or by an overwhelming majority. The resolutions are moved and seconded by senior officers or by lay members of the General Council. Delegates are given an opportunity to display their fervour in a good cause, and the policies of the union are confirmed. In 1951, however, a Special Resolution came near to causing the defeat of the platform. The Executive had failed to gauge the opinions of the delegates in framing a resolution which sought to persuade the government to combat rising prices both by stimulating production and by the 'use of every possible expedient to maintain prices at reasonable levels'. A London resolution which detailed steps to reduce prices, including the removal of purchase tax from 'necessities' and the increase of subsidies, was taken as an amendment. It won so much favour from the floor that the General Secretary sought the permission of Congress for the Standing Orders Committee to draft a composite resolution to cover the substance of both motions. Congress approved and unanimously accepted the new draft.

Each branch and district committee, and the National Executive and General Council, are entitled to submit resolutions, and any number of resolutions, to Congress. Nearly all the resolutions, apart from official 'policy' resolutions, come from the branches. The district committees usually confine themselves to endorsing or rejecting the proposals of the branches. Hundreds of resolutions come in, trivial or important and on a wide variety of topics. The Standing Orders Committee has to reduce them to a manageable compass by cutting out duplications and persuading movers to withdraw or agree to the wording of a composite resolution. Most branches, of course, rarely or never send in a resolution. The most persistent are those known for their Left-Wing views. Their resolutions lend themselves readily to composition, and are often conveniently taken as amendments to 'policy' resolutions.

Every third year there is a similar task to perform with amendments to rule. The National Executive submit a number of proposals arising out of their experience since rules were last considered, and another crop of suggestions comes from the branches, amongst them a good proportion of 'hardy annuals', seeking regular election of officers, more lay representation on the governing bodies, more working members on negotiating bodies, and a committee to hear appeals against decisions of the National Executive and General Council. Most of these do not gain much support.

In discussion of branch resolutions and amendments to rule, the brunt of the work falls on the General Secretary. His job is to steer National Executive proposals through and to guide Congress in dealing with branch proposals. It is a weary task, demanding a grip of detail, considerable endurance, and much good humour. But year after year it is done, with very few hitches. The performance is relieved when from time to time a district secretary speaks for the platform in his place, and even more when he announces that the General Council have agreed to accept a branch proposal, or that they feel that there is something in it and would like to have the matter remitted to them for further thought.

More often than not there is an item on the Agenda on which most of the delegates feel strongly, and on which opinions are divided. This rarely occurs on an industrial matter, but on some aspects of Labour Party policy (for instance, the war-time ban on the *Daily Worker*), on relations with the Labour Party (particularly the terms on which officers and members of the union on the official parliamentary panel shall be allowed to sit in Parliament), and most of all on matters of internal organization (contributions, benefits, compulsory retirement for officers). Then, often in private session, Congress debates seriously and with vigour. The platform, if it has already taken one side, has no easy passage, and may even be forced to give way with grace, or lose the vote.

Besides all this, time has to be allowed for the Chairman's official address and speeches from the fraternal delegates, perhaps some presentations and the like. And Congress has its social side. Entertainments must be arranged, there will be a Mayor's reception, and some districts arrange their own outings or dinners. To organize Congress is no easy job.

Except when the handful of Left-Wing delegates differs on a particular point, party divisions are absent from Congress. Voting is normally by district. The rule refers to 'delegates to represent the District at the Congress'. Delegates sit by districts and on most matters the district secretary or another agreed spokesman gives the district's view. Before Congress each district delegation will have gone through the Agenda and agreed a course of action on many points, and from time to time during Congress the district secretary will call his delegation together for emergency decisions. There is, of course, no compulsion by rule on a delegate to vote with his district, and a branch resolution which is opposed by a majority of the district delegates must be moved by one of them or it falls. The Agenda for Congress must be circulated at least six weeks before Congress meets, so that branches have time to discuss it. There is, however, no general practice of 'mandating' delegates. One district secretary has described the practice of the union thus:

'. . . The function of the Branch is to put down resolutions for Congress; in other words, for the Branch to initiate policy. It was, however, important to appreciate that all delegates attending the Congress were district representatives, and it was the pooled opinion of the District to be put forward at Congress, rather than the opinion of any particular Branch.

'. . . It was the practice, when holding a preliminary meeting of district delegates, to give consent to any delegate who may wish to put forward a point of view which was opposed to that held by the majority of the delegates. . . .'

The National Executive has been through the business beforehand in the same way, and determined the line that the

General Secretary is to take. It is, therefore, only in the most unusual circumstances that there will be serious controversy in Congress unless there is serious disagreement between the district secretaries, or between the delegations which they must lead.

The General Secretary, the district secretaries, and the National Industrial Officers, as we have seen, have important parts to play in the work of Congress. The district officers present, however, take a less active part in the proceedings. Occasionally one of them will enter the rostrum to give information on a particular point, or to put a question, but they are not normally called to put resolutions, to defend the platform or to speak for their districts. At the Blackpool Congress in 1942 a district officer moved a resolution in favour of the withdrawal of the ban on the *Daily Worker*. Charles Dukes himself, in his customary forthright manner, opposed the motion. A delegate then queried the district officer's right to move. The Chairman refused to rule on the point, but gave his opinion that officers would be in a most difficult position if they 'come here and by vote and voice try to affect the policy of the Union under which they have to work'. After the motion had been put (and lost) Dukes again intervened to explain that it was right for officers, as specialists in certain fields, to move general resolutions coming within those fields, but that controversial issues should be left to the branches. 'We always had an unwritten law that an officer could speak, but he never moved a resolution and he never moved an amendment.' Otherwise officers would monopolize Congress.

This settled the matter. The example has not been followed.

The General Council and the National Executive

The rulebook invests the General Council, as the final authority of the union between Congresses, with wide powers over property and finances, over Head Office and the districts, and over the officers. Moreover, 'any matter not provided for in these Rules shall be decided by the General Council'. In practice, however, decisions are taken by the National Executive, and on most matters the Council approves its decisions

unanimously. Occasionally decisions — for instance on matters
of discipline — are referred directly to the Council, and from
time to time there is a full debate, on just the same kind of issues
as seriously divide Congress, and in the same kind of circumstances; that is, when there is a real difference between the
districts and therefore, probably, the Executive itself is not
unanimous. The main function of the Council is to bring
together the union's leaders for discussion of current issues, to
hear the decisions of the Executive, and to get general agreement on their meaning and implications. From time to time
the General Secretary makes a statement of union policy to
the Council, or gives it an account of the latest developments at
the T.U.C. General Council, and occasionally statements are
issued to the press.

The General Council acts as the supreme judicial body of the
union, except in regard to the union's one considerable benefit
— Total Disablement Benefit — on which appeal to Congress is
allowed. The Council hears appeals from members and from
officers against disciplinary decisions by District Committees,
and appeals of members on any matter in which they feel they
have a complaint — for instance a ruling of a branch chairman
— if they wish to pursue the matter further than the district
committee. Appeals are rare — three or four a year is the
maximum — and the decisions of the district committees are
almost — but not quite — invariably upheld. It would indeed
be unnatural for a supreme court to be continually reversing
the decisions of inferior courts. All appeals must be made in
writing, but the member concerned is often called in for further
questioning and then allowed to state his case in person. The
Council takes its duties seriously in this respect. Hearings are
full, and on one occasion two members from Dundee had their
appeals considered at one quarterly meeting of the Council,
were heard in person at the next, and then the matter was
deferred pending circulation of documents to all members of
the Council before a final decision was reached at a third
meeting.

The Council meets quarterly, with rare emergency meetings.
It is a considerable meeting, for besides the Chairman, General

Secretary and twenty-four members, most of the national officers, several members of Head Office staff, and sometimes special visitors, are in attendance. Meetings are normally held in London.

General Council members serve for two years, as do branch officers and district councils and committees. The change from annual elections was made in 1934 to fit in with biennial Congresses. When annual Congresses were introduced, however, the rule was not revised. In 1927 Birmingham replaced Scotland as the fourth largest district, and, therefore, took over Scotland's second layman's seat on the Council. The seat returned to Scotland in 1935, and, after reorganization, went to the newly united Yorkshire district. There it stayed until 1948 when Yorkshire was overhauled by the Southern district. London, Lancashire and the Northern district have maintained their position. The composition of the Council is fairly stable. Apart from retirements the district secretaries are constant members. Some lay members, particularly those who are also district chairmen, National Executive members, or holders of both offices, have long runs of membership, of ten or twenty years or even longer. J. Wilkie has sat for Scotland since the amalgamation, and G. Dempsey for Ireland (and then for the Liverpool/Irish district) since 1931, but these are exceptions. At each election there has been at least one change amongst the lay members of the Council, and in 1948, nine of the fourteen lay members were changed.

In 1930 the number of places on the National Executive was increased to give each district one place. The equal division between district secretaries and lay members was maintained, and W. E. Hopkin, the Welsh secretary, came on. This was a break with precedent, for his was by no means the next largest district. The Welsh and Irish districts had previously been excluded from the Executive altogether on the grounds that they were the two smallest districts. Reorganization brought further changes. The number of seats, along with the number of districts, was reduced to ten, and the new London district, although the second largest in the union, did not retain a seat for its district secretary; it went instead to the secretary

64

of the new Southern district. Since then, despite moves and retirements, those same districts have continued to send their secretaries to the Executive.

This allocation of places has aroused some feeling. It is only natural that the other district secretaries should feel some regret at their permanent exclusion from what is in fact the union's governing body; and it is possible for their districts to argue that they have less pull in important decisions because their lay representatives on the National Executive have not the same weight and authority as their five official colleagues. So in 1934 when Charles Dukes, previously Lancashire district secretary, was elected General Secretary, there was some demand that the secretary of another district should take his place on the Executive at once, rather than that (as in fact happened) the place should be kept open until a new Lancashire secretary should be chosen, and then go automatically to him. At the 1938 Congress an amendment to rule was introduced proposing a rotation of office amongst district secretaries, the five lay members in any two years to come from the districts not represented by a district secretary. Two district secretaries supported the motion, and, fairly naturally, their motive was questioned. Charles Dukes opposed, saying that the proposal 'attacked the electoral system at its roots', and that when any important decision had to be taken he had called all the district secretaries together, had 'taken their mind on the particular matter, and placed it before the Executive. That is a better method than what you are proposing now'. The motion was lost, by 109 votes to 68.

The Executive has a good deal of routine work. It has to sanction all actions affecting the union's reserves and property — the investment of money, the purchase of property and amounts written off through depreciation. It has to consider appeals for grants to all manner of good causes. It has to sanction the pursuit of legal cases outside the competence of the County Courts (except in Scotland). It has to take decisions on political matters. Although most decisions about industrial negotiations will be taken by the members of the appropriate negotiating body (perhaps after the National Industrial Officer concerned has consulted the General Secretary), those involving questions of principle (as, for instance, a change from regional to national wage fixation), or those liable to arouse public controversy, will be referred to the Executive, which also has authority over all strikes outside the competence of the districts. The Executive sanctions appointment to all national offices other than the General Secretaryship, and may act as a selection committee for that purpose; more frequently it delegates the task. It carries through the arrangements for Congress and considers the Agenda. From time to time it is called upon to interpret the rules, and it has to consider all those matters which come up in every organization for which there is no satisfactory precedent, or which do not seem to come clearly within the field of responsibility of any officer or committee.

Like any other busy and responsible body the Executive appoints sub-committees, both standing and *ad hoc* committees. In 1952 its standing committees were entitled: Political, Organization, Property, Journal, Testimonials, Superannuation and Salaries. On the last of these only the lay members of the Executive are allowed to serve.

The powers and composition of the General Council and National Executive have not gone unchallenged, and amongst the 'hardy annuals' of Congress are motions to set up an Appeals Committee (on the lines of that of the A.E.U.) to hear objections to General Council decisions, to allow appeals to Congress against *all* decisions of the Council, and to increase the number of lay members of the General Council. Rule amendments of this kind usually come from branches known for their Left-Wing opinions. The platform's defence is as traditional as the proposals. It is easy to ridicule a proposal to add further and yet further stages to an appeals' procedure. And it has always been claimed that not only have the lay members already a working majority on the Council, but that division of opinion on both Council and Executive has never been a strict division between lay and official members. This appears to be true, and is perhaps not remarkable, for, as we have already seen, the government of the union is so constituted that any serious division of opinion is likely to be by district.

None of these proposals for reform has ever raised much support in Congress.

Head Office and the National Officers

The district offices have not radically changed since the amalgamation. The numbers of their staffs have increased, but not so fast as the growth of their membership. One or two new posts may have been added in some districts, but their organization, by and large, is unchanged. But it might fairly be said that Head Office has grown greatly both in size and in function. From the office of half a dozen national officers (most of them with parliamentary duties as well) with two or three rudimentary industrial departments, and a small staff to act as secretaries, take minutes of meetings, and manage the finances, it has developed into a considerable organization, with some thirteen industrial and administrative departments.

This growth was unavoidable. The main competitor of the union, the T.&G.W.U., which was organized into trade groups, had outstripped it, and the only way in which the T.&G.W.U.'s structure could be imitated without recasting the union was by adding national officers with responsibilities for particular industries. The advent of national collective bargaining in industry after industry, the growth of close relations between the unions and government departments, and the gradually extending power of the T.U.C. General Council, all inevitably added to the weight of work which had to be carried out in London. The transfer of the union's strong man, Charles Dukes, from a district secretaryship to the General Secretaryship, and the grant of power to him to reorganize the union in the mid-thirties, also led to an increase in the functions of Head Office.

The description of this tendency may seem in flat contradiction to what has been said of the power of the districts and their secretaries. It is, of course, true that the growth of Head Office functions has reduced the power of the districts, and that it represents, if one looks at the N.U.G.M.W. alone, a remarkable change. But it is equally true that the districts of the N.U.G.M.W. have limited Head Office expansion, and that their powers remain far greater than those of the territorial divisions of almost all other unions. Moreover, centralization has mainly concerned industrial negotiations; on internal administration its effect has been much less. If one reason for the willingness of the districts to countenance some expansion of Head Office is to be placed before the others, it should probably be their preference that new expenditure should be borne by the relatively far larger resources of Head Office.

By 1938 all industries which were not treated as the responsibility of a single district had been allocated to one of the five new National Officers who had come in as a result of the clean sweep caused by the recent retirement rule. H. N. Harrison had charge of engineering and metals' industries, H. L. Bullock of a group consisting mainly of building and building materials, Tom Williamson of gas, rubber and an assortment of factory trades, Mark Hewitson of the 'Non-Trading' employees of local authorities, electricity supply, waterworks and one or two others, and Miss Dorothy Elliott of 'women's' industries — mainly those covered by Trade Boards. Since that time there has been further subdivision of groups with the growth of numbers, and now nine National Officers share the responsibility for the various industries. Each of them has one major industry, and is or can become an expert on it. Perhaps he once worked in the industry, perhaps he dealt with it as a district officer, certainly he will not spend many days far from its problems so long as it is his responsibility. Each of them will also have to deal with a dozen, a score, or even more small industries in which they cannot usually claim expertise, and the files and responsibilities may more easily pass from room to room as convenience requires. The National Officer has normally only industrial functions, but in an emergency he may deputize for the General Secretary or take over the responsibility for a district whilst its secretary is ill.

There are four administrative departments at Head Office: Finance, Executive, Publicity and International, and Research. The functions of the first two are clear from their titles. The Finance department also covers some aspects of the Union's legal work, as well as all financial matters, which are discussed in greater detail in Chapter VII. The Executive department services the National Executive and the General Council. The Publicity and International department produces the union's monthly journal, deals with publicity and relations with the Press, and is responsible for some aspects of organizational work, including all arrangements for Congress and for international conferences. A Research department was first set up by Charles Dukes in the thirties, but it was not, in fact, much more than an office for collecting and filing information. Since Tom Williamson took over, however, it has become as large a research department as that of any other union in the country. It distributes information to the districts, briefs officers and M.P.s, and does a great deal of preparatory work for the National Executive and for Congress. It also acts as the political department, and deals with National Insurance and the union's scheme for training officers and shop stewards at technical colleges. The General Secretary has the same control over Head Office staff as the district secretaries over their staffs, and is directly responsible for all the administrative departments.

CHAPTER V

THE OFFICERS OF THE UNION

THE union's officers and staff have already been mentioned a number of times, and some aspects of their work have been discussed. Several points concerning them, however, including the changing rules on method of selection and their salaries and conditions of work, require systematic treatment, and to this we now turn our attention.

Election and Appointment

The amalgamation rules required that all officers' posts should come up for re-election every second year. The first elections under this rule were accordingly held in 1926 and the results reported to the Bournemouth Congress of that year. The places of all the general officers and of almost all the district officers in London and Leeds had been contested, and several elections in other districts had been fought. It was clear that most of the opposition candidates were associated with the National Minority Movement (the Communist-sponsored, and T.U.C.-condemned Left-Wing organization amongst trade unionists) and it was naturally assumed that their action had been inspired and arranged by the Minority Movement. In terms of votes the challenge was not serious. Against J. R. Clynes's 204,257 votes for the Presidency, C. J. Moody had 22,770, and few of the other unsuccessful candidates had done so well. The leaders of the union, however, took a very serious view of interference of this kind in the union's elections, and determined that the opportunity should not again occur.

In his opening address, Clynes strongly criticized the Minority Movement. Commenting on that movement's attacks on the established leaders of the unions, he asserted that 'officials can have no interest whatever apart from that of the members whom they serve . . . The men who fulminate against leaders are themselves always striving for leadership'. Later, when the election results were reported, he stated that 'it was the first time in more than thirty-five years' service that the General Secretary and President[1] and certain other officers had been opposed'. He went on:

'. . . Any person in the Union had the right to oppose an old established officer if there was any ground for complaint with regard to his fitness as an official, but he would deplore the tendency to organize opposition to existing officials on grounds other than those relative to their duties and the general discharge of them. He felt it would not be in the interests of the Union or its members if opposition were offered upon other grounds, or that any political motives should direct or influence hostility to officials who did their best for the members.'

The Leeds district introduced an amendment to rule requiring election to all posts in the first instance. Once elected officers were to retain their positions unless they failed to perform their duties properly. They were to have the right of appeal to district and national councils and committees, and, if necessary, to 'the branches throughout the Union'. (The last clause was subsequently cut out.)

A Scottish officer who seconded the proposal 'said that the recent election indicated that the provision of compelling officers to seek election was democracy run mad and a farce'. The proposal was agreed by sixty-two votes to twenty-three. The Communist press was heavily sarcastic at the union's expense.

The procedure which was followed for the next ten years was accordingly that districts should appoint temporary officers when permitted to do so by the Executive, that after a period these officers should stand for election against any other candidates the branches might choose to put up for the job, and that district secretaries and National Officers should be elected, by the district or by the union respectively, from amongst these permanent elected officers.

There were, however, very few elections under the rule until 1934. The reason for this was the decline in membership. Already at the time of amalgamation the ratio of officers to

---

[1] This was incorrect. The elections for both these positions in the old N.U.G.W. had been fought many times, including 1920 and 1922.

members had seemed high, and as district officers died or retired their places were left unfilled. The average age of the officers increased rapidly, and each year it became clearer that the union was being led by a group of men of advanced years.[1] The National Officers and district secretaries remained obstinately active and healthy, and there seemed very little hope of promotion for the district officers. Compulsory retirement was a fairly obvious remedy, and the demand for it increased from Congress to Congress.

Although compulsory retirement seemed an obvious solution it was not an easy solution. The solvency of the superannuation fund was already in doubt at the time of amalgamation. Since then there had been demands for the inclusion of officers' widows, whole-time secretaries and the office staffs within the scheme.[2] The compulsory retirement of a considerable number of hale and hearty officers in addition would have bankrupted it on the spot.

In 1930 a motion from the London district for compulsory retirement at sixty-five was 'heavily defeated'. Charles Dukes opposed on the grounds that 'you cannot dogmatize about age'. In 1932 a similar resolution was lost by fifty-eight votes to thirty-nine. Its opponents heavily stressed the extra cost which would be involved. In 1934 twenty-six resolutions concerned with compulsory retirement were before Congress. Its temper was demonstrated by its rejection of the proposals of the Standing Orders Committee to deal with them. After a long and heated debate an amendment to the composite resolution requiring compulsory retirement was carried instructing the General Council and National Executive 'to go fully into the question of the retirement of officials, whether from age or inefficiency, and its bearing upon the Superannuation Fund in all its ramifications and report to next Congress'.

[1] In 1932, for instance, of the 108 officers of the union, only 37 were under 50, and 24 were over 60. If there had then been a rule requiring compulsory retirement by 65, 14 would have had to go by the following year.

[2] Clerical staffs and whole-time secretaries were included in 1928. It was later decided to allow officers of the union's Approved Society to come in, but the scheme had to be abandoned, and contributions returned when, in 1936, the Ministry of Health required the union to set aside £50,000 to guarantee the pensions of the Approved Society's officers. In 1934 it was decided to allow officers to allocate a portion of their pension to their wives.

The volume of support for compulsory retirement made it clear that the report to the next Congress would have to include positive proposals, and Charles Dukes, who had been elected to the General Secretaryship in February of that year,[1] decided to use the turnover in personnel which the acceptance of compulsory retirement would involve to effect a reorganization of the structure of the union. Accordingly the report, which was approved, not only recommended that 'a retirement age of sixty-five be fixed and an assurance shall be given to Congress that in the two-year period up to the 1938 Congress everyone over that age shall definitely be retired' but concluded with a request that 'the National Executive be empowered to devise and put into effect such plans of reorganization as may be deemed expedient'. The resources of the Superannuation Fund as arranged at that time could not support the burden, but this was held not to matter, for, as Dukes pointed out in debate 'the Fund is merely a book-keeping arrangement and the real guarantee is the whole general fund of the Union'.[2] He stressed that reorganization was really a matter of men and that a similar opportunity would not recur. The districts withdrew the various alternative motions on the subject and approval was given to the whole scheme with only two dissentients.

All the National Officers except the new General Secretary himself, seven of the twelve district secretaries, ten district officers and seven whole-time branch secretaries were retired under the new rule, and there followed the redistribution of districts and the reorganization of Head Office which we have already mentioned.[3] In order to facilitate the change, new procedures for the selection of National Officers and district secretaries were introduced.

The reorganization of Head Office had already begun in 1936, and it was reported to the Congress of that year that in appointing new industrial officers the National Executive and General Council had agreed 'that if officials who had already

---

[1] Will Thorne had agreed to retire at the age of seventy-six.
[2] Subsequently it was decided to set aside in the accounts each year a sum to guarantee the fund.
[3] See p. 48.

passed through the process of election by the members were appointed to the Head Office departments, no further election would be necessary, but if any candidate was chosen who had not previously been elected, an election would be entailed'. Accordingly, Harry Harrison, an elected officer of the Lancashire district, had been directed to Head Office by the National Executive, whereas H. L. Bullock, their other selection, who had previously been a whole-time secretary at Bristol, went before the branches for election in order that his appointment might be confirmed. Later during the same Congress the rules were amended to cover this point.

At the following Congress, in 1938, the General Secretary reported that, since seven new district secretaries had to be appointed:

'. . . Without in any way being prejudicial to, or decrying the merits of, lay members, I do not think that anyone with a proper sense of responsibility can reasonably suggest that men totally inexperienced and without official service could have been permitted to become candidates for these major positions. In the exceptional circumstances we simply could not, in the interests of the Union, afford the risk of the haphazard chances of election whereby any unqualified candidate might have been elected.' District committees had, therefore, been asked to submit from amongst those of their officers who had still ten or fifteen years before reaching retirement age a panel from which the National Executive should make an appointment. Five districts submitted only one name, which was accepted; the two others affected submitted two names and the Executive made its choice. Three district secretaries were not affected, and the two others who were not retired were chosen by this process as secretaries for the new districts into which their old districts had been amalgamated.

At Head Office the two Assistant General Secretaries were not replaced and the office of President was allowed to lapse on the retirement of J. R. Clynes. In its place a new rule provided for the election of a Chairman by Congress from amongst its members. The Chairman was to hold office for two years and be eligible for re-election. His post was not a full-time office, and it has, in fact, been held either by a district officer or by a district secretary.[1]

When Congress approved reorganization it also approved a scheme for the appointment by districts of 'Recruitment Officers' with approval from the General Secretary. These new officers were to be chosen 'from amongst the younger element'. They were to be employed only on recruitment work, and not to conduct industrial negotiations. They might hope to become Temporary and subsequently Permanent Officers if they showed themselves fitted for that status.

Despite assurances to the contrary, this system rapidly became the regular method of recruitment for all officers, and if the recruitment officers served for a period of two years their promotion was a matter of course. During the war their salaries were not increased with those of the permanent officers, so that it became difficult to get suitable candidates to accept the position, and districts began to return to the device of the Temporary Officer. Accordingly in 1942 the General Council approved a new scheme under which the old titles were abolished. In future 'Appointed Officers' were to be appointed by the General Secretary on the recommendation of the district committees. At the end of twelve months the district committee might seek the permission of the National Executive for a second year's probation, and, when this was satisfactorily completed, for authority to proceed with an election. Once elected the officer should be termed an Elected Officer. He was to be allowed to contribute to the Superannuation Fund if he completed his first twelve months' service satisfactorily. During the six years it was in operation, seventy-seven officers were appointed under the Recruitment Officer scheme. Twenty were rejected as unsuitable or found the job not to their taste. By the time the scheme finished, forty had already become permanent officers.

[1] In 1952 W. E. Hopkin, the Welsh district secretary, who had held the office of Chairman for four years, retired from both offices on reaching the retirement age. Four candidates were nominated at Congress to replace him, and the voting was:

J. Cooper (Southern district secretary)	124
T. Eccles (Lancashire district secretary)	122
J. Yarwood (Northern district secretary)	60
G. Davison (Lay member of the General Council)	44

The amended scheme is still in practice. Consequently each Appointed Officer, should he survive two years' service, stands for election in his own district. In some instances there are no other nominations and he is returned unopposed. Occasionally the National Executive may support a district in rejecting the candidature of an opponent who does not come up to the standards required (a standard to be determined by the National Executive 'at its absolute discretion'). Usually, however, the branches submit several other nominations and voting papers are sent out. No temporary or appointed officer has ever lost his election, and normally he wins by an overwhelming majority. Once or twice, when the opponent has been a whole-time branch secretary, there has been something of a fight. Once elected the district officer may, should a vacancy arise, be selected by the district committee, subject to the approval of the National Executive, to the post of district secretary,[1] or by the National Executive to the post of National Officer. He only submits to another election if he is a candidate for the General Secretaryship. It is open, however, to the Executive to appoint a lay member to office as district secretary or National Industrial Officer. Such an appointment must be confirmed by a district or national election, as the case may be.

The procedure has its critics. Left-Wing opinion is in favour of regular elections to all posts. Proposals for a return to the old system have been made, without attracting much support in the union as a whole. On the other hand, the Yorkshire district has twice (in 1938 and 1941) moved that elections for district officers should be dropped on the grounds that it is wrong for a man to stand election when he has already given satisfaction; that 'members are not . . . able these days to judge of the negotiating ability of the organizer who has to meet in private the employer round the various Conference tables'; and that, since the elections are, in fact, never lost, they are rather point-less. On both occasions Charles Dukes opposed the suggestion. He stressed particularly that election gives an officer confidence

---

[1] In 1951 the Liverpool/Irish district, on the retirement of its district secretary, reduced the short-list of applicants for the vacancy to two, and asked the National Executive to make the final selection.

and the authority. The proposal gained some support, but was not carried.

Since reorganization there have been no elections to the post of National Industrial Officer, since all vacancies have been filled by district officers who have gone through the process of election. There have, however, been two elections for district secretaryships. In 1945 the National Executive instructed a National Officer, J. Cooper, to change places with the Southern district secretary, Tom Cochrane. At the subsequent Congress a promise was made to regularize Cooper's position (for he had not been selected by the district committee) by holding a ballot. It took place the following year, and he received the customary overwhelming majority. In 1951 the Yorkshire district secretary was due to retire, and the district committee recommended that a whole-time branch secretary should take his place. The National Executive decided that, as the district's nominee was not an elected officer as defined by rule, an election was required. Four other candidates stood, and when the result of the ballot was declared early in the following year one of these, an elected officer of the district, topped the poll, and was approved by the National Executive and the General Council. He received 39,219 votes against the branch secretary's 16,463. The other three candidates were well behind.

The Background of Officers

Officers are drawn from several sources. The majority have been lay members who have taken a prominent part in the union's work. Some have been whole-time branch secretaries, particularly in Lancashire. Some have come from the union's office staffs. And a few have come in as officers of amalgamating unions.

It is natural that the most active lay members of the union should be considered for vacancies for district officers, if they are willing to accept the position. Many officers have previously served on district councils and committees and perhaps as members of regional joint negotiating bodies. Others have attracted attention as convenors of shop stewards or holders of similar positions in industry. Sometimes recruits have made their names as strike-leaders, perhaps even as leaders of 'unofficial' movements, and may have been known for their Left-Wing opinions. The average age of recruitment to office is probably about forty, though from time to time much younger appointments are made of men who have shown early promise. During the war it was particularly difficult to recruit young men and a number of appointments were made from amongst those who might otherwise have been thought to be too old for the job.

In Lancashire the office of whole-time branch secretary is considered a regular training-ground for district officers. The Warrington branch (Charles Dukes' branch) has provided a number of district and national officers. Elsewhere this method of promotion is rare. Often such a secretary is content with his branch work and his part in local affairs and local politics. Transference to district office might in many instances entail a reduction in income.

Promotion from the office staff is also a fairly natural method of selection. The members of the staff must join the union and are, therefore, eligible. They acquire a wide knowledge of the union and its activities from their work, and the district secretary and committee have ample opportunity to form an estimate of their qualities. On their side, capable and ambitious members of the staff are likely to regard such promotion as the only means of 'getting on' in their job. Officers selected in this way are unlikely to have direct experience of industry, and their promotion is frequently criticized on these grounds. The reply is that today a considerable part of the work of a trade union officer is administrative, and for that they have been better trained than the lay member, and that many of those promoted in this way have quickly picked up sufficient knowledge about industrial conditions and industrial processes to become capable negotiators.

Relatives of officers of the union are frequently employed in union offices. This was particularly true in the early days when the staffing of a rather primitive office was regarded as essentially a domestic matter for the district secretary to arrange. Consequently, the method of promotion from the office staff has led to a number of family traditions in the union. The Lancashire district has had three generations of the Eccles family, the London district has known several Wrights, and so on. Several reasons for this deserve mention. First, the union was largely built in this way not only in the districts, but also in the branches. Families were known as union families; children would help their fathers with union work when union work might mean dismissal; the members would be only too keen that the son, who knew the ropes and had shown courage, should succeed his father as branch secretary. Secondly, to have 'grown up with the union', to be closely familiar with its work, and imbued with its traditions, is no mean qualification for office. Thirdly, some of the most able and successful leaders of the union have come up in this way — amongst National Officers, Tom Williamson, whose uncle was secretary of the Liverpool district, Fred Hayday, whose father was secretary of the Midlands district, and Jack Cooper, who was a nephew of Charles Dukes. In these instances district committees have made some of their most successful selections by promoting 'members of the family'.

The Salaries and Conditions of Officers

The determination of the right reward for a union officer's services has always been a matter of controversy. On the one hand, there are the 'militants' who argue that if a man's heart is to stay in the right place he should be paid no more than the men he represents. On the other side, the case is made out for paying the official a rate for the job, and for a job which entails long and awkward hours with no overtime, a great deal of travelling, and responsibilities far beyond those of the ordinary worker. In fact, most unions pay their officers a wage higher than that of most, though perhaps not all, of the workers they represent, but a wage far below that which any industrial or commercial concern would consider for equivalent hours and responsibilities.

Up to 1936 the salaries of the officers of the N.U.G.M.W. were determined by Congress and printed in the rulebook. At that time the General Secretary and President were paid £10 a week, district secretaries reached a maximum of £7 10s. after three years, and district officers a maximum of £6 10s., also after three years. National Officers were at that time paid as district secretaries. The National Executive proposed to the Congress of that year that all reference to rates should be taken out of the rulebook, and replaced by a new rule: 'The salaries of officials shall be determined by the General Council as and when necessary.' This arose, in the first instance, out of re-organization. The rates for the new appointments to Head Office had to be considered, and this had developed into a thorough review of salaries. The lay members of the Executive were asked to form a sub-committee with the Secretary and President as *ex officio* members.[1] Their inquiries led them to believe that the senior officers of the union were paid at rates considerably below those of much smaller unions, and that most unions did not publish their rates on the grounds that they might be used to their disadvantage. The proposal for the change in rule was, therefore, accompanied by recommenda-tions for all-round increases, and the effect of the new rule would be to empower the General Council to put the new rates into effect.

Questions were asked. 'The General Secretary made it clear, and gave a definite assurance, that there was no intention of seeking to deprive Congress of its power, but ours was probably the only Union whose Rules contained details relating to officials' wages[2] . . . It was necessary for someone to deal with questions between one Congress and another.'

So 'on the clear understanding that Congress would retain its right and power to confirm or reverse any decision which the General Council may reach, the amendment was agreed to'. Since that time the lay members of the Executive have con-tinued to act as the Salaries Sub-Committee and have recom-mended increases from time to time to the General Council.

Details of salaries today cannot be given, but it may be said

[1] Since then the office of Chairman has replaced that of President, and it no longer carries *ex officio* membership of the Salaries Sub-Committee which thus consists only of the lay members of the Executive.

[2] This is generally true. One or two unions, however (for instance, the E.T.U.) still publish their officers' rates of pay in their rulebook.

that increases since 1936 have roughly kept pace with the rise in the cost of living and increases in industrial wage rates. Most other unions have not granted increases to their officers on quite the same scale, so that today the officer of the N.U.G.M.W. is paid as much as any other trade union official and probably more than most of them. It is still true, however, that the salaries are not adequate compensation, when industrial equivalents are taken into account, for the long hours worked, the constant travelling and the responsibilities of the job. It is sensible administration to free the trade union officer from financial worries. If there are to be criticisms of trade union salaries, they should be levelled at the miserable rates paid by some of the craft unions, rather than at the salaries of the N.U.G.M.W.

Expenses are still regulated by the rulebook. Officers are paid their fares and an allowance for work away from home fixed according to the time away. Those who want to run cars — which are very valuable for the kind of work a trade union officer is required to do since they may save countless hours of his time, and of the union's time — are advanced loans to buy them, and given some assistance in running them. The rules also lay down rates of compensation for loss of working time and expenses for lay members attending committees or councils of the union, or otherwise engaged on union business. The planning of details of work, arrangements for time off and holidays, and similar matters are settled in the various offices and are at the discretion of the General Secretary and district secretaries respectively.

The staff are paid at least the rates which have been laid down by the T.U.C. in conjunction with the unions catering for clerical workers. Some of them in the more responsible positions are paid considerably more. After amalgamation it was discovered that some of those who were doing the work of officers at Head Office — amongst them G. P. Dean, who ran the Municipal Department and was in all but name a National Industrial Officer — had been appointed to their posts, and had not been through an election. Although they retained a status and salary commensurate with their job, the General Council determined that they could not be classed as officials. Time has removed these anomalies, but there is still some interchange of jobs between staff and officers in the district offices. In some districts, for instance, an elected officer is in charge of legal work, and in others a member of the staff.

In 1944 an officer of the Birmingham district set up a National Trade Union Organizers' Mutual Association. The National Executive determined that it could not be regarded as a district affair as he had recruited officers from other districts and from other unions, and that membership of the Association was 'inconsistent with the conditions of service of officers of the union and inimical to the best interests of the organization'. When he declined to appear before the General Council, it dismissed him. The whole affair was too involved with personal ambitions and personal antipathies for the Council not to regard it as a revolt, and an attempt to create a weapon for use against the union's leaders. If the General Council acted rightly, however, it does not necessarily follow that there was nothing of value in the scheme or that the other officers who joined the Association were entirely misguided in their action. Unions are often too ready to assume that the only employee who requires no protection is the union employee. Even where rates of pay and conditions are good, there is no *a priori* reason for the assumption that union general or district secretaries will not prove themselves as arbitrary as any other 'boss'. And, moreover, unions contend that they are required to represent even those who work for good employers, if the evils of paternalism are to be avoided. In at least one of the district offices a shop steward has been elected to meet the district secretary and to put to him the view of the officers and staff on all those points which may seem trivial, but are nevertheless so likely to cause friction in any organization.

CHAPTER VI

WOMEN IN THE UNION

The Women's Section

WE have seen how the original arrangement between the N.U.G.W. and the Women's Federation for a Women's District had been altered in 1923 to permit the inclusion of the women into the geographical districts, with provision for special branches and special representation.[1] This did not end the matter. One of the first problems to confront the new union was the means by which this special representation should be provided, and the whole question of determining the status and functions of the National Women's Committee and the Women's Department at Head Office, and the duties of the women officers in the districts, bristled with difficulties. The district secretaries wanted to be sure of their authority and towards the end of 1924 the Executive set up a sub-committee which reported in favour of giving complete control of women's affairs and women officers in the districts to the district secretaries and committees. The Women's Department at Head Office should be confined to:

(1) Propaganda and educational work amongst women.

(2) Representing women on public bodies, T.U.C., etc.

(3) Negotiating women's questions nationally.

(4) Collecting and distributing statistics on women.

(5) Administration of women's provident schemes.

A report from the Women's Department on the extension of its work was referred back, women organizers were forbidden to come up to London to attend the meetings of the Women's Committee, which was to be an advisory committee of lay members, and the scale of women's representation on several outside bodies was cut.

Miss Bondfield, the chief woman officer, felt that she was left with 'no field of action', and gave notice of resignation. This she was persuaded to withdraw and a new committee with four

[1] See p. 14f.

representatives from the Executive and four from the Women's Committee was set up to explore the possibilities of women's work within the limits of these decisions. The committee reported in July, 1925, and recommended that Miss Bondfield's status should be the same as that of Jack Jones and Will Sherwood, the two other National Officers, and that she should have 'complete control of all national women's questions'. This seemed to settle the question for some time.

In 1927 the Northern district reported that it was unable to find a suitable candidate to serve on the General Council as women's representative although its turn to nominate had come round. The district was informed that it could not substitute a male and the place was left unfilled. In May of that year another committee on the Women's Department reported in favour of abolishing the Women's Committee, and assimilating their department entirely to the status of those of the National Industrial Officers. In 1928 the Leeds district moved against special representation for women. The Congress of that year gave the proposal a large majority, and the last vestige of a special position for women within the organization was abolished.

This treatment may seem to have been harsh, and it is clear that the district secretaries were anxious to keep the reins of the union in their hands. At the same time a good case could be made out, on grounds of equality, for avoiding sex discrimination within the union. Before the Women's Federation had come in under this special arrangement, the union had organized women on the same terms as men, and organized them successfully. After 1928 it continued to do so. The figures for recruitment of women during and after the second world war give no ground for supposing that the union had become unattractive to women.

On equal terms with men, women have certainly not achieved an equal share of government, either in the districts or nationally. Both London and Lancashire have been represented by a woman on the General Council for a time, but no other district has sent a woman representative, and neither of these served on the Executive. District council meetings normally have one or two women delegates, if only from special women's branches, and during the war this figure rose as high as nine or ten. But it is very rarely indeed that any of these women delegates are elected to the district committees. Women hold office on occasion in mixed branches, and run their own branches seemingly to everyone's satisfaction. There are one or two whole-time women branch secretaries.

Women Officers and Equal Pay

Fusion with the Women's Federation had, in fact, created two classes of women officers — those elected in the old N.U.G.W. on equal terms with men, and those who came in with the Women's Federation. The rates of pay in the Federation were considerably below those of the N.U.G.W. and the amalgamation would have been jeopardized if the N.U.G.W. had been saddled with the cost of bringing the Federation's officers up to their own rates. With reductions in salaries during the depression of 1921 to 1924 the difference had been reduced from £5 (£10 for men and £5 for women) in 1921 to £2 (£6 10s. for men and £4 10s. for women) in 1936. But even this difference rankled in an organization which claimed to have amongst its objects 'to obtain legislation for . . . equal pay for the same work for women as for men'. Were women not elected to office under the old N.U.G.W. rules supposed to be doing a less satisfactory or less responsible job than their male colleagues or than women chosen under those rules?

Trouble was also caused over the position of Miss Dorothy Elliott. A woman officer of the Lancashire district (having come over with the Women's Federation), she had deputized for Miss Bondfield during her absence in the Labour Government in 1924, and had later been brought to Head Office to assist Miss Bondfield in her work. There was considerable trouble over her status, and the several committees on women's affairs gave it their attention. Eventually she was allowed to sit on Trade Boards and other negotiating bodies, and to attend national conferences for women, but her status was defined as that of a 'clerk'. In 1932, after she had once more carried on Miss Bondfield's work during the second Labour Government, the National Executive decided it was a waste of her talents to keep her as a clerk, and appointed her 'Temporary National Woman Organizer'. In 1935 her position was regularized by election and she took over the industrial work of the Department while Miss Bondfield confined herself to propaganda, and, on the latter's retirement, Miss Elliott was appointed Chief Woman Officer.

Meanwhile, the districts had in almost every instance of resignation or death of women officers, failed to appoint a successor, and the number of women officers dwindled. It is the firm belief of most of the district secretaries that men do not like to have women handling their affairs, whereas most women prefer to be looked after by men, who can handle them more easily.

At the Congress of 1938 a London branch moved for equal pay. There was some support from male delegates, but the big guns were turned on the proposal. Charles Dukes himself said that women officers had 'an entirely different job' and that they could not be put on to 'the rough and tumble work'.

'If you say here that a woman carrying full domestic responsibilities is as free to do her job as a man is to do it, I won't object, because you had better look the facts straight in the face; it is one thing in the Congress to exalt sentiment, and another thing on an Executive body. Face up to realities.'

Two district secretaries supported Dukes. Tempers were raised, and the discussion became acrimonious. Eventually the motion was put, and defeated, by 98 votes to 50.

Whatever the merits of the General Secretary's assertions, he was defending a very difficult position, and it is rather with relief that one reads that, in 1945, when the matter was again raised, the General Council decided to accept the resolution before Congress had debated it. It is much easier to square this with the stated objects of the union, and it seems more gracious that the women should be given the benefit of any doubt about the parity of the value of their services with the services of their colleagues.

Few women officers were left to benefit from the new rule. Miss Elliott was given leave of absence in 1946 to take over the

T.U.C.-sponsored National Institute of Houseworkers, and subsequently this has from time to time been renewed. Miss Horan of Lancashire was the only nominee for her place. Lancashire appointed a new woman officer, Miss Bates, to replace Miss Horan, and these two are now the only women officers in the union.

CHAPTER VII

FINANCE

IN the days when strikes were a frequent, but nevertheless irregular part of trade union life, careful budgeting was out of the question. The best that the union treasurer could do was to make sure that there was a large margin between income and regular expenditure and trust that it would be enough to meet commitments. A large-scale strike could destroy the most healthy reserve in a few weeks, and, at least in the bigger unions, levies on members still at work have at best proved stop-gaps for only very short periods.

Most unions accumulated large reserves during the first world war, when strikes were illegal, and lost them again during the years of conflict after the war. Strikes were not at that time the only drain on resources. The majority of the large trade unions were operating schemes under the Unemployment Insurance Acts which involved the payment of benefits over and above the minimum provided in the Acts. The heavy unemployment of 1921 and 1922 forced most of the unions which operated such schemes, including the N.U.G.W., to abandon them.

When the General Strike and the Miners' Lock-out brought the period of open conflict to an end, the unions were able to accumulate funds once more, slowly until 1934, and then, as trade union membership mounted, more rapidly. For nearly twenty-five years now the majority of unions have been able to budget fairly accurately. This has had its effect, although only slowly, on their customary estimate of the necessary margin. Consequently, trade union membership has become far cheaper. While trade union administrative costs have gone up with salaries, paper, printing, postage and fares, contributions have been increased since 1939 only by 10, 20 or 30 per cent — in a period in which the cost of living has at least doubled. And although trade union reserves are far higher than ever before, the increase in reserves per member has also failed to keep pace with the cost of living. In other words most unions are in a poorer position to finance a strike of a given proportion of their membership than before the war — or they would be if rates of strike pay had increased as fast as the cost of living. The fact that many unions' rates of strike benefit have not been increased, or have been increased only slightly, since 1926, is evidence that the official strike is now rarely used, and has been largely replaced by other trade union methods.

Income

We have already seen that the branches of the N.U.G.M.W. send the contributions which they collect in to the district offices, after deducting approved branch expenditure — which is almost entirely the commissions of the branch secretary and the collectors. A slight but steady increase in the proportion of branch expenditure to total income over the past few years is attributed to a growing tendency to rely on collectors. In other words fewer contributions are directly collected by the branch secretary, so that more contributions are subject to the full deduction for both commissions.[1] This should probably be related to the growth in the size of branch as membership has increased.

Between two-thirds and three-quarters of the total branch income is received by the district offices.[2] The districts are allowed to retain 50 per cent of what they receive for their own expenditure, but must send to Head Office 50 per cent of their bank balance at the end of each quarter as well as the other 50 per cent of their income. The effect of this is to concentrate all the reserves in the Central Fund. A district which attempts to save more of its share of the income it receives will only increase the amount it must send on to Head Office at the end of the quarter. Districts keep a small reserve, however, up to something like a quarter of their total income during the year.

[1] Between 1942 and 1948 the percentage of branch secretaries' commissions in total income stood at a fraction under 12.5 per cent. Branch collectors' share in the total rose from 11.7 per cent to 12.0 per cent. Since 1948 the percentages have remained almost constant.

[2] The system of branch commissions, and the rate at which they are paid by the N.U.G.M.W., probably make the proportion of income spent on branch management higher than that of any other union in the country.

So long as they do they are cushioned against the effect of declining income, for at such a time they are able to let their reserves run down and so pass on the reduction in income entirely to Head Office by reducing the amount it receives not only from income, but also from the balances. This occurred noticeably during the years of declining membership up to 1934. In addition each district is allowed to retain a small sum of up to £400, according to its size, which is called a Contingent Fund and may be used by the district committee 'to promote the objects of the Union or to support its members'. The National Executive is empowered to make additional calls on district funds at any time.

In addition to remittances from the districts, the Central Fund, since it accumulates the union's reserves, and since it is used to buy the union's property, receives a considerable income from interest and dividends (over £75,000 in 1952) and a small income from rents.

At amalgamation union contributions stood at 6d. for men and 3d. for women.[1] They remained unchanged until 1941, when the Executive, disturbed by the sharp rise in costs since the outbreak of war, raised them to 7d. and 4d. There has been no change since then.[2] Income from contributions has varied with financial membership, apart from the increase due to new contribution rates in 1941. In 1925 income from contributions was £339,559, in 1933 it had fallen to £217,440, and in 1949, the peak year, the figure was £926,539. Reserves reached their lowest at the end of 1926, after the General Strike. In 1935 they had risen to £636,487. In 1940 they stood at £1,130,649, and by the end of 1952 at £3,346,110.

Expenditure

Branch expenditure consists almost entirely of commissions and honoraria, although a total of a few thousand pounds is spent each year on rent of rooms and on postage. Districts have

[1] Women members may pay the full contribution and receive full benefits. Some do. In so far as they work in occupations in which 'equal pay for equal work' applies, it seems only right that they should.

[2] At the 1953 Congress an increase of 1d. a week for both men and women was agreed.

a more varied expenditure, but they do not have to meet any of the union benefits, nor the salaries of their officers. Both of these are borne by the Central Fund. Consequently their main expenses are the wages of their office staffs and the cost of running their offices, subsidies to whole-time branch secretaries, the payment of legal and medical expenses in cases which they fight for their members and become liable for costs, and the expenses of district meetings. Expenditure under all heads is duly accounted for to Head Office on a standard form.

The Central Fund bears the whole cost of Head Office, of national meetings (including Congress), of affiliations to the T.U.C., Joint Industrial Councils, union federations and international bodies, of all union benefits (including costs in legal actions sanctioned by the National Executive) and pays the wages and expenses of all officers. In addition it bears any extraordinary costs, such as those of the union's jubilee celebrations in 1949.

In 1934 the following break-down of expenditure for each 6d. contribution was put before Congress:

	1927	*1933*
Branch management	1⅜d.	1½d.
District management	⅝d.	¾d.
Affiliation fees, etc.	⅝d.	¾d.
Central Fund (managerial costs)	1⅜d.	1⅝d.
Benefits (despite no disputes)	⅞d.	1½d.
	4⅞d.	6⅛d.

The calculation was made to show that the fall in membership had proceeded so far that the union had ceased to accumulate any reserve. Fortunately for the union, membership began to pick up in the following year and the ratio of costs to income fell. A similar calculation today would show total expenditure per head just within the 7d. contribution, and would also show a different distribution of costs. All managerial costs have increased since that time faster than benefits, and branch costs most of all, due to an increase of 2½ per cent in commissions when the contributions were raised in 1941.

Besides strike, lock-out and victimization benefit (which invariably entails only a small expenditure — just over £1500 in 1952) the union pays a disablement benefit and a funeral benefit. The first, granted for total disablement, involves the payment of large individual sums (£30 after one year's membership, up to £100 after eight years), but the total expenditure in any one year is small (£1730 in 1952). Funeral benefit on the other hand involves smaller individual payments (the maximum is £10 to a member's next of kin on his death, and £5 to a member on the death of his wife) but the total expenditure is heavy (nearly £60,000 in 1952). Moreover, the cost of the benefit varies greatly according to the rate of growth of membership. When membership is falling, it seems that the young leave faster than the old, and that the prospect of funeral benefit keeps the oldest members loyal. At the same time, recruitment is low, and most of the claims for funeral benefit come from members of many years' standing, who can claim the maximum. In years of rapidly rising membership, the average age falls and with it the incidence of funeral benefit claims. At the same time more claims are in respect of members who have been in the union for only a few years. The following table gives the proportion of claims to total membership, and the cost per head of total funeral benefit at different periods.

	Funeral Benefit	
	Cost per head	*Claims per member*
1928	£.125	.017
1933	£.164	.021
1940	£.107	.015
1947	£.068	.010
1951	£.086	.012

It can be seen that the claims per head fell by 1947 to less than half those of 1933, the worst year for membership figures. The cost per head varied considerably more, but this is somewhat exaggerated by the change in the rule in 1938, which reduced benefit to those who joined the union over the age of forty-five. By 1951, with membership stabilizing, both figures were climbing up once more.

Even in 1933, when the average age of the members of the union was presumably at its highest point there was only one claim for each fifty members, and it must be remembered that two claims are allowed in respect of each member who is predeceased by his wife. We must, therefore, assume that the death-rate of members amongst the N.U.G.M.W. is preternaturally low, or that many retired members drop out and have no claim to benefit when they die, or that the turnover amongst members is such that many of them have not qualified for the minimum benefit at the time of their death (or that of their wife) by having at that time fifty-three full contributions without a lapse in membership. It seems reasonable to suppose that between them the second and third factors provide the explanation. Should the union's members stabilize at their present level funeral benefit costs are likely to increase. Should membership fall, they are likely to become a larger proportion of total costs. Should all union members contract the habit, which union officers tend to extol, of joining young and maintaining a constant membership to their death, the union would be forced to raise its contributions or lower its benefits, despite the growth of income resulting from more stable membership.

Administrative expenses are many, and since 1939 have tended to grow both with the growth of membership and with the increase of prices. By 1952 prices had more than doubled and union membership had nearly doubled, so that the cost of a Congress, for instance, has increased more than fourfold (and Congress is now held every year). The main single item in administrative costs, however, is expenditure on officers' salaries, and this item has not increased at the same rate. In 1939 total expenditure on officers' salaries was £47,427, in 1949 it had risen to £115,361 or about two-and-a-half times the 1939 figure. This slower rate of increase is not due to low salaries. Salaries in the N.U.G.M.W., unlike most other unions, have roughly kept pace with the cost of living. In 1939 the total number of officers was 130, and by December 1952 it had risen to 146. In other words, the number of officers has not kept pace with the increase in membership and income.

That the union contribution had, by 1952, only risen by 1d. in a period in which prices have doubled is to be explained, in the main, by the fall in claims per head for funeral benefit, and the fall in the proportion of officers (and office staffs) to members.

Financial Policy

The first Congress of the amalgamated union met at the end of May 1926. The General Strike, in which the union was heavily involved (though not so heavily as the T. & G.W.U., since all transport workers were called out) had already cost the union over £100,000, and a steady weekly drain on reserves continued to meet payments to the locked-out colliery surface workers in Yorkshire and elsewhere, and to other members who had come out on strike and had not yet started work.[1] The union had, however, weathered the worst of the storm, had been able to make loans to other unions in greater distress, and still had considerable reserves, so that, although there was much talk of the serious financial position, only one economy measure was taken. The rules were altered to make it clear that no member who was drawing unemployment insurance could qualify for strike or lock-out pay.[2] At the same time the increase in collecting stewards' commission, which had been recognized at the Amalgamation Conference as the first claim on the funds, was granted.

It was not until 1934 that serious attention was given to financial policy again. Then Charles Dukes, giving his first report to Congress as General Secretary, drew attention to the

[1] Strike benefit for the year fell just short of £250,000. It has never since exceeded £10,000 in any one year, except in 1948, when almost £15,000 was paid out.
[2] This decision arose out of a strike of sley-makers at Blackburn. At the time it caused considerable bitterness.

fall in reserves during the second half of 1933. Even J. R. Clynes, renowned for his dislike of the strike, said in his Presidential address:

'These reserves must be carefully guarded, for just as in times of depression we have to fight against reductions and encroachments, and must sometimes compromise or give way, we will find that when conditions substantially improve, little can be obtained by merely asking for it. We are not seeking trouble, but we know from experience that trouble is in store for us, and we must be ready to face it with adequate Union support for our members.'

Dukes pointed out that since the reserves constituted a fighting fund the union could not rely on the interest therefrom to cover management costs. Again no specific economy measures were taken, but a number of proposals for new expenditure, on a union Convalescent Home and on education, were defeated. The excessive management costs of the smaller districts were used as a further argument for reorganization.

In 1936 funds were looking up, and Congress voted in the reorganization scheme, with all the expenditure it involved on officers' superannuation, new Recruitment Officers and so on. A number of proposals for new benefits — accident benefits, a general superannuation scheme, a marriage dowry for women members, put forward at that and subsequent Congresses were cautiously referred to the Executive for consideration. The resultant reports in each case found the schemes too costly. In 1938 Congress, as we have seen, made the conditions under which late entrants might qualify for funeral benefits more stringent. In that year the General Secretary pointed out that unemployment figures had taken a turn for the worse, and that with expenditure at its current level, contributions had only to slip back to the rate of 1935 for the union to lose money.

Costs increased sharply with the war, and at first the union was uncertain about the probable trend of membership. Proposals for increased contributions would have been presented to Congress in 1940, had it not been postponed. The following year the additional 1d. was approved, but only after a long debate, in which it became clear that many members held that the union could not afford to get out of step with competing unions.[1] The main reason given for the increase besides rising costs was the need to accumulate funds for the years of disputes which were thought likely to follow the second world war, as they had the first war. Industrial peace could hardly last for ever. At the same time, the commissions of branch secretaries and collectors were raised by 25 per cent.

During the following years the increase in membership sent the reserves up at a good pace (although, of course — a point which union members often miss — the increase did little more than offset rising prices). Consequently, the union's mood after the war was generous, and in 1947 strike, lock-out and victimization benefit was raised from £1 to £1.10s. and the maximum disablement benefit was raised from £60 to £100. The far more expensive funeral benefit was left untouched. At the 1950 Congress, resolutions from branches seeking an increase in dispute benefit were referred to the Executive which reported the following year in favour of a further increase to £2 a week. This was accepted. Since 1947 costs have continued to rise and there has been a slight decline in membership. The annual increase in reserves is, therefore, declining while the value of money continues to fall. Although the attitude of trade unions to their reserves may have altered to some extent after twenty-five years of industrial peace, they are still likely to feel that it would be unwise to allow employers to know that they could not call a large-scale strike even if they wished. Even £3,000,000, the result of twenty-five years' accumulation, would not support a really large strike for many weeks.

For these reasons the Executive came to the Congress of 1952 with an emergency proposal to alter the rules by increasing the contributions to 9d. and 6d. a week — an increase of 2d. The increase was to take effect in the week after Congress met, on June 29th. Together with this proposal came suggestions that dispute benefit should again be raised — to £3 — and that the total disablement grant should be supplemented by a partial disablement grant. The sum awarded was to be based on the

---

[1] As it happened, the T. & G.W.U. raised its contribution from 6d. to 7d. the following year.

percentage assessment made under the National Insurance (Industrial Injuries) Act, 1946.

The debate at Congress provided the most serious defeat that the National Executive has suffered. Speaker after speaker rose from the floor to attack the proposals, and the only support, with one exception, came from members of the Executive defending their own proposal. The opposition argued that the financial stability of the union could hardly be in danger when its reserves stood at over £3,000,000, and (a point stressed most by delegates from Lancashire, suffering from the textile depression of that year) that the time was inopportune, since most workers were experiencing difficulty in maintaining their earnings while prices continued to rise. There were, of course, answers to both these criticisms. In relation to price increases, the reserves were, in fact, declining; and, as for the occasion, when has it been opportune to increase contributions? The delegates, however, had other reasons for opposition. They had received little warning of the proposal before Congress, and, worse still, they were expected to go back to their branches to collect the increased contributions without an opportunity to explain the need for the change, or to make preparations for it. Fears were expressed about its effect on membership, and the advantages that competing unions might draw from it. Some of these objections might have been met by amending the proposals, but the Chairman ruled that since only the Executive had the right to propose alterations to the rules at other than 'rules revision' Congresses, no amendments from the floor could be accepted.

When it became abundantly clear that Congress was hostile, there was an adjournment. After the delegates had returned, the Chairman suggested that the Executive itself should be allowed to amend its own proposals, but they would not hear of it. A motion to suspend Standing Orders was defeated by 198 to 112, the proposals were put to the vote as they stood and rejected without need to take a count.

In the past, the financial policy of the union has been conservative, and has been determined by the General Secretary and National Executive, who have kept close watch on the reserves. Proposals for new spending — on accident benefits, superannuation for all members, Convalescent Homes and the like — have come from the branches, but reports prepared for the Executive to show the costs involved have almost invariably been sufficient to convince Congress to withhold its approval. Before 1952 strong opposition to the Executive had arisen only when it had attacked the branch officers' commission, or the Congress delegate — by proposing to reduce the number of delegates or to return to biennial Congresses.

At the same time, the Executive's power to spend has been increased. In 1928 it was empowered to make grants for any purpose it considered 'to be in support of Trade Union or working-class objects', up to £500 in any one year. In 1945 the limit, which had, in fact, been considerably exceeded in more than one year, was removed. In its early years the union granted £100 a year each to the Workers' Educational Association and the National Council of Labour Colleges to spend on classes or correspondence courses for members of the union. This sum was gradually increased. In 1950 the Executive was empowered to spend up to £5000 a year on educational purposes. The following year Congress passed a special motion accepting 'the need for intensive education of trade union officers in modern industrial developments' and approving 'the action taken by the National Executive Committee to initiate full-time courses at various educational centres throughout the country'. During the following winter, 435 members of the union attended these courses, at a cost of about £20,000, and it was estimated that, if demand was maintained, the cost might rise to £30,000 a year. This development, and the Executive's proposals for increased contributions suggest that it is no longer entirely correct to describe the union's leaders as financially conservative.

The Political Fund

Since 1913 trade unions have been forced to separate their political fund from their other funds and to allocate to it a stated proportion of the contributions of those members who have given their approval, either by refraining from 'contract-ing-out' or (between 1927 and 1946) by 'contracting-in'. In most unions the political contribution has been an additional amount above the regular contribution. The N.U.G.M.W. has always included it in the normal contribution. Before 1946 the Registrar permitted the union to apportion a sum representing a proportion of the contribution of all the assenting members to its political fund, and to use the full contributions of its other members for its normal purposes. Under the new rules made necessary by the repeal of the 1927 Act in 1946, the Registrar instructed the union that it must allow those who contracted-out to reclaim a portion of the contribution equivalent to the political contribution of the others — 4d. a quarter.

Under the 1927 Act the union paid a commission to branch officers on signatures to the 'contracting-in' form with the result that the union rapidly achieved the very high proportion of over eighty per cent paying the political contribution. The payment was dropped, and the incentive was absent when membership again rose after 1934, and by 1946 the proportion had dropped to 45 per cent. The income of the fund was hardly greater than ten years before, despite increased member-ship.

The income of the fund is divided between the districts and Head Office in a proportion which is fixed by Congress, and which Congress has varied from time to time. The Amalgama-tion Conference fixed it at 80 per cent for Head Office and 20 per cent between the districts. In 1926 the districts pushed their share up to 30 per cent, in 1930 to 40 per cent, and in 1932 to 50 per cent. It was clearly a matter on which the allegiance of district secretaries was likely to be divided. During the debates criticism was heard of the time and money spent on politics by the union. From 1929 to 1931 the General Secretary and General President, Will Thorne and J. R. Clynes, two of the three National Officers, Jack Jones and Miss Bondfield, and the Vice-President, Arthur Hayday, were members of Par-liament. When Charles Dukes stood for the Secretaryship he gave an undertaking that, if elected, he would not stand again for Parliament. New leadership at Head Office was quickly followed by a return to a 60 per cent-40 per cent distribution, but in 1938 an Executive report on the state of the fund failed to persuade Congress to reduce the districts' share to 30 per cent. The General Secretary argued that this would reduce the likelihood of raids by Head Office on the reserves in the political funds of the districts, which would inevitably hurt the economical districts most. His opponents defended the interest of the districts in municipal politics, and criticized the expenditure of too much of the Central Fund on 'safe' Parliamentary seats. They were able to carry the day on this occasion. The change was, however, agreed at the following Congress in 1941.

Expenditure is almost entirely at the discretion of the National Executive and the district committees. The districts spend their share mainly to assist the union's candidates in local government elections, and to pay the district and branch affiliation fees to local and regional Labour Party organizations. The Central Political Fund meets Labour Party affiliation fees, expenses of the union's delegates to the Labour Party Conference, and an agreed proportion of the expenses of official union candidates for Parliament. Large contributions are made to Labour Party election funds (sometimes augmented by calls on the districts' political funds) and considerable assistance is given to the London and Southern districts to make a donation to the London Labour Party for the L.C.C. elections. Part of the union's expenditure on education is also met from the fund.

Financial Control

As in all registered unions, the property of the union is vested in trustees; the N.U.G.M.W.'s trustees are appointed by the General Council, normally from amongst their own number. They act only on the authority of the Council or the National Executive. There is a similar relationship between district committees and the district trustees in whom district reserves are vested.

Two general auditors are elected by ballot every two years — the only regular national ballot the union has retained — and district auditors are elected by the district councils. These posts are regarded as rewards for old and popular members of the union, and for the office of general auditor there is normally a large number of nominations. The holders of the posts fairly naturally need a good deal of expert guidance in their work. In addition, Head Office and some of the districts employ chartered accountants to audit their books.

In the branch, control is more difficult. Throughout the union a large number of men and women with no training for the task are elected or appointed to positions in which, as secretaries or collectors, they have to handle and account for considerable sums of money. It is only natural that a proportion should make mistakes, and that some should give way to temptation. Perhaps the wonder is that the proportion is so low.

Some districts have found it advisable to give an officer or member of the staff full-time responsibilities for teaching new branch secretaries what they need to know about book-keeping and handling money, and for checking branch returns, sometimes by travelling through the district making periodic checks on the books of each branch. Other districts rely on checking weekly with quarterly accounts, income against figures of membership, and on their power to call in the branch books and collectors' books at any time for full investigation.

When errors are found arrangements are usually made for the branch officer concerned to pay off in regular weekly instalments. In cases of flagrant embezzlement, prosecutions are set on foot. In one district, however, no member has been prosecuted since the early 'twenties, when one of their branch secretaries died whilst serving a sentence for misappropriating branch funds. In any event the main object of the districts is to see that they receive their proper income, and not to prosecute their members, and thereby almost inevitably accumulate bad debts.

Optional Funds

Reference has already been made to the funds which are run by union branches. The union's monthly journal, which has a circulation of about 75,000 copies, is printed and distributed at the cost of Head Office. Branches are allowed to charge members 1d. for their copy for the benefit of branch funds. Many branches distribute copies to their members as one of the benefits to which they are entitled for an extra 1d. a week contribution.

The union has always run a National Optional Fund for sick, accident and funeral benefit. For many years it has been its policy to persuade the districts to transfer their members to their own optional funds, or to build up funds of their own, starting with those of their members who have previously contributed to the National Fund, and a *per capita* fee (usually of £1) for the members taken over. Now the National Fund receives contributions from only a few hundred members in the Southern district and Scotland, and some 11,000 in Yorkshire. In recent years the state of the fund's reserves has caused some alarm. Each of these districts has a fund of its own. That of the Scottish district has a very small membership. Scottish officers still oppose the 'friendly benefit' as opposed to the 'fighting' trade union. The Southern district has a fund which pays accident benefit alone for a 1d. a week contribution. The great majority of the members of the district contribute. The Yorkshire district has inherited an 'Auxiliary Fund' from the N.A.U.L. with a membership of some 12,000, which is mainly confined to the Sheffield area. This fund is unique in the union in paying an auxiliary strike benefit as well as sick, accident and funeral benefits. It is not, therefore, protected under the Friendly Societies Acts. For many years these districts claimed that they were unable to persuade the members concerned to abandon the National Fund in favour of their own district fund. Early in 1952, however, plans to wind up the National Fund by allowing its members to be absorbed by the district funds had been almost completed.[1] The balance of the National Fund was to be transferred to the districts on a *per capita* basis.

The other seven districts each have their own fund. The funds are governed by a meeting of delegates from those branches which have contributing members, and by commit-

[1] The scheme was finally approved by Congress in 1953.

tees chosen by these meetings. The actual management is carried out by the financial departments in the district offices, and, under their supervision, by the branch secretaries. Secretaries and collectors are granted a commission on contributions, and in some districts the district office makes a management charge. The rates of contribution and of benefit vary considerably. In each fund members are allowed to pay 1d. for accident benefit alone, and 4d. for sick, accident and funeral benefits. In the Birmingham district double contributions are allowed to qualify for double benefits, and the maximum contribution is 8d. a week. Limits may be placed upon the age of entry. According to the strength of the reserves rates of benefit are raised or lowered and the maximum period for which benefit may be paid is lengthened or shortened. The hold of the funds varies considerably from district to district. The London fund, which started in 1939 with a few thousand National Fund contributors, now has some 13,000 contributors. In Lancashire and the Birmingham districts there are very few members who do not pay at least the 1d. a week accident contribution. The Birmingham fund was taken over from the old Birmingham Gasworkers, and because of its high rates of benefit was guaranteed support from the Central Fund for ten years. As the end of the period approached the district wanted an extension of the guarantee. This was refused on the grounds that the treatment of the district so far had been distinctly generous. Birmingham was forced to reorganize its fund and managed to do so successfully.

Several of the funds go back in this way to the early days of the constituent unions, having been begun through an amalgamation of several branch funds. They show that even in the early days of labourers' unions the policy of 'no benefits but fighting benefits' did not always recommend itself to the members. In the twenties and early thirties Charles Dukes and other leaders of the union gave considerable attention to fostering the optional funds, and spoke of their effect in stabilizing union membership in terms which would have seemed familiar to the champions of the 'New Model' unions of the mid-nineteenth century.

Until it was wound up under the National Insurance Act of 1946 the union, like other unions, had an Approved Society into which had been merged the Approved Societies of the constituent unions. The funds and management of this Society were, by law, entirely separate from those of the union, although many branch secretaries were agents for the Society, and a close liaison was maintained between the two Head Offices. The union (again like other unions) found that only a minority of its members subscribed to its own Society, and from time to time ran a recruiting campaign amongst its members in conjunction with the Society, or arranged a reorganization of methods of work. Congress, on occasion, debated the lack of interest in the Society. For all that it had very little effect on the union. Since those union members who subscribed were likely to be the keenest members the Society had little effect in holding wavering members. The passing of the Society was almost unnoticed in the union.

CHAPTER VIII

THE LEGAL WORK OF THE UNION

THE great bulk of the legal work of trade unions is concerned with injuries at work and industrial diseases. In the past the two main procedures were to claim compensation under the Workmen's Compensation Acts, or to sue for damages at Common Law where it seemed likely that negligence on the part of the employer might be established. The National Insurance (Industrial Injuries) Act of 1946 substituted 'a system of insurance against personal injury caused by accident arising out of and in the course of a person's employment and against prescribed diseases and injuries due to the nature of a person's employment' for the old Compensation Acts. Apart from points of law referred to the High Court by the Minister, or by persons aggrieved by a ministerial decision on legal issue, the Act has removed the determination of claims from the courts. The Act is administered by insurance officers, and appeals may be made to local appeal tribunals, and from them to a Commission. The assessment of disability is carried out by medical boards, and appeals against their decisions may be made to medical appeal tribunals. The doctrine of 'common employment' was abolished, and it was also made possible to claim benefits under the Act and to instigate proceedings for damages at Common Law at the same time.

The immediate effect of the Act was to increase the work of the unions, for most insurance companies became anxious to wind up outstanding cases under the Compensation Acts. It was thought, however, that once this rush of work had been cleared, the task of the unions would be eased, since the bulk of claims would be settled by insurance officers and medical boards, without any need for the union to act. Under the Compensation Acts many claims might be settled out of court, but the union had at the least to start proceedings, and the regular procedure was through the courts. It is, however, doubtful whether the unions' work has been reduced, for there has been a considerable volume of appeals under the scheme, and since lawyers cannot handle cases before departmental tribunals, the whole of the work falls on union officers. They have to attend hearings, plead the case, and keep themselves informed of all relevant decisions of the appeal tribunals and the Commissioner, for a body of case-law is being rapidly built up. Previously the function of the union officer was to form a preliminary judgment of the worth of a case, to set the solicitors in action, and to act as a channel of communication between them and the injured member.

Industrial Injuries and Diseases

The union has long realized that legal work requires specialized knowledge, and in each district an officer, a member of the staff or, in one case, the district secretary himself, is given responsibility for work in this field. The degree of specialization varies. In most districts the person concerned gives his whole time to the task, and handles all cases, whether court cases or appeals under the Act. In others it is a part-time job, and only court cases are exclusively dealt with by the district office, so that it is left to the officer responsible for the branch concerned, or to the whole-time secretary, to handle appeal cases before tribunals.

Each district prints its own 'Accident Form' and distributes copies to its branch secretaries. Members are advised to fill in forms for even the slightest accident, and to return them, through their secretaries, to district office. A good deal of the success of the system, therefore, especially in dealing with minor injuries, depends on the degree to which the branch secretary can make his members and his stewards 'accident conscious'. At district office the returned forms are studied to discover whether there is any likelihood of a claim at Common Law. If not, the case is put aside until the decisions of the insurance officer and medical board are known. If it does appear to be a court case, the form is sent on to the solicitors. Each district employs its firm of solicitors, or in a widespread district perhaps two or three, who are specialists in industrial injuries.

On the solicitors' advice the district secretary decides whether the member should be told that the matter must be dropped, or whether to give instructions to proceed. If he decides to proceed the conduct of the case is left in the hands of the solicitors, but the district office still has work to do, for even if the member concerned is interviewed direct by the solicitors he may want the advice of his union on the way in which the solicitors are handling his affairs, and particularly on the sums suggested as reasonable in any settlement. The degree to which district offices continue to play a part varies. In at least one district the member of the staff in charge of legal matters regularly attends the court to help as a go-between. It is one of the most valuable parts of the union's legal service that it provides the working man, who is naturally scared and suspicious of lawyers, with an adviser who is expert enough to follow the lawyer's reasoning and yet talks the language of the client.

The new Act has brought greater uniformity to district practice in legal matters. In court professionals must be employed.[1] Before the departments' tribunals the union officials must conduct cases themselves. Under the Workmen's Compensation Acts so many cases were settled out of court that some districts encouraged the person responsible to handle cases right up to a settlement, or until it definitely became a court case.

When appeals are made against administrative decisions under the new Act all the work falls on the union officer. He must interview the member, and perhaps his fellow-workers or employer, to make sure of all the details of the case, he must judge whether it is advisable to seek medical advice on decisions of medical boards, and to arrange for medical examination, and he must argue the case before the tribunal or the Commissioner.

The division of responsibility between districts and Head Office in legal cases took some time to clear up. In 1927 it was

---

[1] Owing to the acute shortage of lawyers in the Second World War, one union officer at least pleaded cases until attention was called to the fact that he was unqualified.

decided that legal expenses incurred by the districts should be a charge on district funds 'except in special cases referred for decision to the General Council or National Executive'. There the matter rested for many years until in 1937 Charles Dukes proposed that only Head Office should seek Counsel's opinion. Previously the districts might seek Counsel's opinion and then refer the case to the Executive who would also take advice, and perhaps be differently advised. After some opposition his proposal was accepted the following year, so that now all cases requiring Counsel's opinion are referred to Head Office and become a charge on the Central Fund. The decisions of the Executive, as of district committees, to pursue or drop cases are naturally formal decisions taken on expert advice.

The new Act has added to the functions of Head Office, whose Research Department has undertaken the task of collecting and distributing to the districts important decisions of appeal tribunals or of the Commissioner. Many cases, particularly those which arise out of industrial diseases — almost always far more difficult to settle than straightforward cases of accident — are referred to the Research Department by the districts for expert advice. This Department is responsible for making appeals to the Commissioners.

The legal service of the union is certainly one of the most valuable that it provides.[1] The great majority of workers are ignorant and helpless before the law. If they seek legal advice they are unlikely to be able to meet the costs should the case be lost.[2] They are without the means of judging the course which the lawyer adopts or the suitability of the settlement which he advises them to accept. The union is able to shoulder the ex-

---

[1] In 1927 the union claimed to have recovered £100,037 in 1375 cases of claims under the Workmen's Compensation Acts and at Common Law. In 1937 the figures were £142,713 in 2688 cases, and in 1947, the last full year before the new Act came into effect, £611,758 in 5307 cases. Recent totals have been even higher. In 1947 the total legal expenses of the union were only £9312. Union lawyers have established a high reputation in this field and the low figure for expenses is a reflection of their ability to win cases, and of the effect of their reputation in achieving settlements out of court.

[2] The Legal Aid Act has undoubtedly helped those without resources to obtain legal assistance. No union member would, however, receive assistance under the Act if his union provided legal service, and was willing to take up his case.

pense, to employ the best solicitors, with long experience and a reputation which makes out of court settlement likely, and to provide sound, but acceptable and comprehensible, advice throughout the case. The 1946 Act has indeed taken compensation cases out of the court and supplied more simple and homely procedures, but even here the law is far beyond the average layman. He needs expert advice on whether or not to appeal, and he needs an expert to conduct his appeal for him.

The service is not without its difficulties. Some members are so convinced that the law is a racket that, if union officers advise the member that the amount the solicitor suggests is the best that can be got, or that delay is to his advantage, they suppose the officers must be implicated in the racket. Sometimes the officer concerned has extreme difficulty in getting advice accepted, although rule lays down that a member who refuses advice relieves 'the Union of any further responsibility, financial or otherwise'. On occasion a member has withdrawn his case and found his own solicitors — usually to his regret. The interpretation of the rule that only a member 'in benefit' can receive aid has caused difficulty, particularly in the days of Workmen's Compensation, when a member might feel unable to pay his contribution out of his weekly allowance, or might be without compensation while a case for damages at Common Law was pursued. Branch funds or district contingent funds often help here, the union makes loans (and sometimes finds it extremely difficult to recover loans when a case is won), and sometimes the officer concerned has dipped into his own pocket to keep a member 'in benefit' and his case alive.

Other Legal Work

Although the bulk of the legal work of the union arises out of industrial injuries and diseases, legal departments have to deal with a wide variety of other cases. There are many other hierarchies of ministerial tribunals — unemployment insurance, service pensions — before which the union provides the same kind of service as it does for industrial injuries. In the years between the wars its officers had a large number of cases to plead before Unemployment Insurance Tribunals. Not one of these systems of administrative tribunals has been established by an Act so clear and simple, and not one has devised a procedure so straightforward that expert assistance is not of great value. The social service state inevitably increases the contacts of the ordinary man with government departments and with the law, and increases the number of occasions on which he is in need of the expert advice his union can give him.

The union may help members in cases not connected with their work — street accidents for instance — by offering preliminary advice, by getting the union's lawyer to act, and perhaps persuading him to make the financial burden as light as possible. The union may take up cases which it feels are of general interest to the union. One of the most important of these was *Rex v. Davies* (1932), in which the High Court decided that the defendant, as a County Council roadman, was debarred from sitting on the Abertillery Urban District Council, of which he had been a member since 1928, and was at that time chairman.

The union has been involved in several cases in which dismissed officers have sued for wrongful dismissal,[1] and in a considerable number of cases of defamation. Most of these have been for alleged libel, either against newspapers, or, more often, against competing unions, arising out of leaflets or statements in union journals. It might be thought contrary to the trade union spirit for unions to pursue each other to court, but a glance through the cases in which the N.U.G.M.W. has been concerned shows that almost invariably damages have been awarded or the matter has been settled out of court with an apology, and it may be concluded that unions rarely act against each other without justification. The same record of cases suggest that the N.U.G.M.W. is more sinned against than sinning.[2]

[1] The most famous of these was probably the unsuccessful claim of A. W. J. Lewis, M.P., arising out of his dismissal after the Savoy Dispute. See pp. 128-129.
[2] One recent libel case, N.U.G.M.W. *v.* Gillian (1946), established an important point in trade union law, that 'a registered trade union might sue in its own name for tort, including defamation of its collective reputation, affecting its functions and business as a trade union.'
See N. A. Citrine, *Trade Union Law*, Stevens, 1950, p. 455.

CHAPTER IX

SHOP STEWARDS, UNOFFICIAL MOVEMENTS AND COMMUNISTS

Shop Stewards

THE term 'shop steward' is often used loosely in the trade union movement, and particularly in the N.U.G.M.W. where 'collecting steward' and 'shop steward' are frequently employed as if they were interchangeable. Strictly speaking, the collecting steward is an officer of the branch whose function is to collect union dues, and to keep the members in touch with union affairs; the shop steward is a union member elected by his fellow members in a 'shop' or other place of work to act as their spokesman to the management. In some industries the duties of the shop steward are laid down by collective agreement, either nationally, as in the Engineering Industry, or more frequently, in individual works or companies. The N.U.G.M.W. is a party to some national agreements of this kind, and to a very large number of agreements with individual employers laying down the functions of shop stewards. Until 1951, however, it did not give recognition to shop stewards in its own rules, and its shop stewards were, to this extent, 'unofficial'.

Thus the two posts could be distinguished on paper, but often in practice the distinction was, and still is, blurred. In many industries and undertakings there is no official provision for shop stewards. The need for a spokesman to deal with the management on the many trivial issues which arise is not thereby removed. It is easy to see that matters of this sort are likely to be brought to the attention of the collecting steward, who is probably the only officer of the union on hand, and that he, unless he refuses the task with determination, is likely to become the regular spokesman of his fellows. So in a large number of industrial undertakings the collecting steward comes to have the functions of a shop steward, and is even referred to as a shop steward. Even where the two posts are distinguished

the same union member may well hold both, and, as we have
seen, it is in many branches the accepted policy that he should.
Sometimes the branch secretary makes it his practice to choose
his collectors, as far as possible, from those who have been
elected shop stewards; elsewhere the union may try to ensure
that those who have been appointed collectors shall be nominated and elected shop stewards.

The practice of setting up Works Committees, Works
Councils or Joint Consultative Committees, widespread during
the first world war, and even more popular since 1939, adds a
further complication. Often the Works Committee is the body
of the shop stewards, or a group of representatives elected from
and by the shop stewards, including representatives of the other
unions if there are several unions in the undertaking, which
takes up common problems with representatives of the management. But in other instances, the representatives on a Works
Council or Consultative Committee are elected by the whole
body of workers, regardless of trade union membership, and the
number of shop stewards who sit depends on the strength and
activity of the unions. Consequently in a given shop there may
be a collecting steward, a shop steward and a Council representative; or two, or even all three of these offices may be filled
by the same man. It must also be remembered that too often
before the war, and occasionally even since 1939, committees
or councils of this sort were used by employers as *alternatives* to
trade unions, in order to undermine the unions.

Although shop stewards came into prominence only during
the first world war, they go back much further. As early as
1892 the N.A.U.L. was debating the functions and powers of
its shop stewards. The N.U.G.W. took a more cautious attitude
towards them and preferred to give official recognition only to
its collecting stewards. The war, however, forced the union to
accept shop stewards. In the union's journal of May 1920,
J. R. Clynes wrote:

'Often is the shop steward[1] found performing the most

---

[1] He may, of course, have been referring to collecting stewards. But if the President of the union could use the terms interchangeably, it argues even more
strongly that shop stewards had come to be accepted.

essential, the least respected, though the most serviceable job in the whole range of branch work.'

This was still in the years of war-induced expansion. In depression the union's attitude was coloured by anti-union workshop representatives, and by Communist attempts to work through shop stewards. At the 1942 Congress Charles Dukes opposed a motion for payment of shop stewards:[1]

'Shop stewards in the sense indicated by the mover and seconder of this resolution are not altogether an unmixed blessing, and those of us who have been handling this problem in the set-up of Production Committees for the T.U.C. have had to move very carefully . . . I am very apprehensive when I hear statements which reveal that shop stewards can negotiate inside while organizers are precluded. (Hear, hear.) We had some of that during the last war and within the same district it resulted in the setting up of company unions which we have never been able to break down.'

He went on to suggest that the best solution was that the collecting steward, who already had his commission, should do the shop steward's job.

The resurgence of shop stewards and workshop representative bodies during the second world war forced the Executive to reconsider its attitude. When it became clear in 1941 that government approval was to be given to the setting up of joint consultative committees on production, the General Secretary consulted the National Executive who felt they could approve 'the appointment of shop stewards or Works' Committees . . . on the condition that they were appointed for the sole purpose of stimulating production and would not interfere with the functions of the union'. After a few weeks, however, in which thought was given to 'Communist-dominated' unofficial shop stewards' movements, and the practice of some firms in using 'the committees for purposes which should belong exclusively to the Trade Union Movement' the Executive left the matter in the hands of the General Secretary, with the understanding

---

[1] This is a frequent proposal. The argument is that the shop steward may lose pay, or at least piece-work earnings, in carrying out his job, and that he deserves compensation for the risk of victimization (if not by dismissal) by unfavourable treatment from managements and foremen.

that their attitude was generally unfavourable. The attitude of the Executive was defined by its Chairman, Fred Marshall, M.P., in the union journal for January 1944:

'The war has thrown up many of these [workshop movements] under the various titles of Shop Stewards, Production Councils and Works' Committees . . .' but our union is not 'unduly suffering from their activities. On the contrary we can say that the loyalty of our Branch officials is something to be proud of'.

He noted 'a veritable spate of strikes during the last few months' from which the N.U.G.M.W. had been 'relatively immune'.

'I am bound to say that I cannot dissociate this state of things with [sic!] the existence of a multitude of these Works' and Shop Committees. I have always felt a bit doubtful about the creation of these bodies. It is inevitable in the nature of things that sooner or later they begin to exceed the purposes for which they were set up, and usurp the functions of the Executive Authorities of the Unions. They tend to become an organization within Trade Unionism, possessing power without responsibility. They also give great scope to disruptive elements whose object is certainly not the welfare of Trade Unionism.

'Another sinister possibility is that they can be used by reactionary employers . . . Company unions based on the firm or the company are about the worst and most ineffective form of organization. They can never become really independent. These workshop committees are just the material out of which this form of Union could be created.'

We cannot exonerate the leadership of the union from ostrich-like behaviour in this matter. A different trend had continued to run through discussions about shop stewards. For instance, the recognition of shop stewards by the London Gas, Light and Coke Company in June 1937, had been treated by the journal as an important victory. Then as now, district officers knew that, when a new group of workers had been organized, their two most important tasks were to get some sort of agreement with the employer, and to set up some kind of representation amongst the workers, whether by a properly elected shop steward, or by an understanding that the collector would act. Shop stewards or collectors hold the union together in the places of work, and prevent the task of the district officer from becoming unmanageable, by settling a thousand minor matters with the employer. For many years districts have issued official shop stewards' cards to those who require them in industries in which shop stewards are recognized by agreement.

The knowledge that the union was not immune from unofficial strikes had a sobering effect. The union's committee of inquiry on the 'Cossor Dispute',[1] ended its report with a recommendation that the districts should look into their shop steward system in order to bring about 'rapid handling by the District Office' and 'prompt contact with the Branches'. Shop stewards should only take office when their election had been ratified by the district secretary or committee. They should be issued with an authoritative credential card carrying a concise statement of their duties and obligations 'emphasizing the need for periodical report to the Branch, and through the Branch, if necessary, to the District Office', and the need for immediate report of trouble. The withdrawal of the card should terminate office. This report was given the approval of the National Executive and circulated to the districts, and has been generally acted upon. The attitude of discouragement has been changed radically — and wisely.

At the same time, the leaders of the union showed that they saw a need for limiting the functions of shop stewards. At a meeting of the General Council in September 1947, two branch resolutions on shop stewards were considered.

'The position of shop stewards established under accepted machinery had been ... recognized, but it was impossible to concede to shop stewards the right to conduct major negotiations on wages and conditions. . . .

'Opposition was expressed to the idea of the extension to other industries of the shop stewards' movement as it existed in the engineering trades ... It was thought that any extension of the shop steward system should not be accepted unless accompanied by the most stringent safeguards.

[1] See p. 123.

'The view was expressed that difficulties experienced in one district . . . were not common to every district . . . largely because of the fact that special care was taken in the appointment of shop stewards.'

The same meeting of the Council claimed that shop stewards were doing a fine job in increasing production, and,

'. . . as the question of consultation in industry was a fundamental part of the Government's policy, we should be prepared to see that those who represented the Union in consultation with managements should at least have a clear idea of the duties which they would be expected to perform'.

Subsequently the union's research department prepared a handbook for shop stewards which was approved by the Council and circulated to all the union's shop stewards.

Finally, at the 1950 Congress, the General Secretary suggested that a resolution from the Northern district, proposing the insertion of a new rule 'authorizing the election of shop stewards', should be referred to the Executive. A new rule was accordingly drafted, and approved at the following Congress. Shop stewards are permitted subject to the approval of the Branch Committee, or of the District Secretary 'if more than one branch is involved'. They are to be selected by one of three methods: by show of hands or ballot 'of the members concerned at the place of employment'; by show of hands at the branch; or, with the consent of the members concerned, by the District Secretary. They work 'under the jurisdiction of the District Committee', with due provision for notification of appointment, issue of credentials and termination of office. Their duties are 'as defined in the Shop Stewards' handbook published by the Union'. An undertaking is required from them that they will observe the union's rules, 'and at all times act in conformity with the decisions and policy laid down by the governing authorities of the Union'.

It remains to explain the connection of shop stewards and workshop representative bodies with 'unofficial movements'.[1]

[1] The word is used in two senses. First to signify 'not in the rulebook'. All N.U.G.M.W. shop stewards were until recently unofficial in this sense. Secondly, to signify 'subversive of the rules' and it is in this sense that it is normally used by the press.

The shop steward is notoriously a radical in the trade union movement — he sees the hardships under which he and his fellows work without the opportunity of appreciating the wider industrial and political problems which complicate the settle-ment of his grievances. He is a trade unionist and proud of it — a most essential link in modern trade union organization — but his job is mainly in industry, and not in the branch. Conse-quently he may have common interests with other workers which transcend trade union boundaries. Joint shop stewards' committees may be formed in the works and local or national shop stewards' movements have sprung up from time to time. The first are frequently recognized by the union, the latter rarely, so that they are unofficial. In times of stress extremists — including Communists — often come to the front in such un-official bodies; and in quiet intervals it is the extremists who keep their organization alive.

Communists

The N.U.G.M.W. reacted early and strongly to the difficulties presented to the trade union movement by the Communist Party, in its attempt to create within the unions an opposition which responded to a political leadership wholly outside the unions, and by its use of secretive and often deceitful methods.

The Communists' first large-scale attempt to gain support within the trade union movement began with the foundation of the National Minority Movement in 1924. The N.U.G.M.W. did not react immediately. In February 1925, the Executive, in deciding its policy on resolutions for the Labour Party Con-ference, even formed the view that:

'to exclude nominees of an affiliated body who may not hold strict Labour views was not practicable, and that should a Communist accept and conform to the Labour Party Constitu-tion, there could be no reasonable objection to his endorsement as a candidate'.

In July, however, the London district withdrew from the London Trades Council on the grounds that it had affiliated to the Minority Movement, and in November, after opinion had been sounded in other districts, the General Council decided that all branches should withdraw from all Trades Councils so affiliated.

Opinion hardened further after the General Strike. At the Special Conference of Trade Union Executives which held a post-mortem on that strike Charles Dukes seconded the motion to accept the report of the General Council of the T.U.C. He pointed out[1] that there were 'black spots . . . in huge areas thousands of men — tens of thousands — refused to respond' and that:

'. . . Every day that the strike proceeded the control and authority of that dispute was passing out of the hands of responsible Executives into the hands of men who had no authority, no control, no responsibility, and was wrecking the movement from one end to the other.'

The publication of the Communist documents seized in the Arcos raid, articles (some of them inaccurate) critical of the union in Communist publications, and growing experience of the Minority Movement, particularly in London, also influenced the leadership of the union. In November, 1926, the Executive defined its attitude. No one was debarred from the union on political grounds, but the policies of the Communist Party and Minority Movement were 'directly opposed' to those of the union, and a member who held them 'could not honestly represent the Union or express views on its behalf at . . . conferences'. Furthermore, 'this union agrees with and upholds the policy of the National Labour Party in reference to the Communist Party and Minority Movement and considers that membership in the Communist Party and Minority Movement is inconsistent with loyal attachment to the Union'. The decision on Trades Council affiliation was reiterated, and attendance by officers or other members at conferences of the bodies named was deprecated. If they attended they could express no opinion on behalf of the union. The General Council upheld these decisions with one dissentient, and one or two officers were required to give

[1] *National Strike Special Conference Report,* January 20th-21st, 1927, Central Hall, S.W.1, T.U.C. General Council Publication.

explanations of their connection with the Minority Movement. C. J. Moody, a representative of the London district on the General Council, who openly proclaimed his membership of the Communist Party, was asked to account for the use by the Minority Movement of his name as a representatitve of the union in their organization. In January 1927, a number of London branches were circularized with an invitation to a Minority Movement conference to discuss 'Executive decisions' relating to that body. The union promptly banned the conference, but it was held on February 6th. The London district committee thereupon disqualified six district council members (including Moody), suspended five branches, and disqualified a considerable number of branch officers. The decision was approved by the Executive and by the General Council, to whom S. J. Wright, the London district secretary, pointed out that the Minority Movement had tried to form a general workers' group of the movement, and had 'endeavoured to secure the election of certain individuals for the various offices which were available in the Union, and in some cases were successful, by instructing Branches how and whom to vote for'. Confirmation of the decision automatically debarred Moody from membership of the General Council. The Council clearly stated that 'any person had the right to be a member of the Communist Party or the National Minority Movement and also a member of the Union, but such person could not hold any official position in the Organization'. Several appeals were lodged, but they were all rejected.

At least one district instituted a practice of requiring district council members on election to sign a document denying membership of the Communist Party or the Minority Movement, and of disqualifying those who refused. The National Executive upheld the practice.

The whole matter came up before the 1928 Congress. The Executive reported its actions and decisions and claimed that it had acted strictly within the rules. S. J. Wright moved a resolution adopting the report, and instructing the 'General Council to take every measure consistent with our rules to protect the Union against disruptive forces which seek to operate within the organization'. The Congress was unanimous in its approval.[1]

Here the matter rested for many years. Policy had been affirmed and enforced, and was called to mind whenever occasion arose. Members were warned against Communist articles, against occasional circulars (one issued, for instance, by Tom Mann) and from time to time there were suspensions for activity in the Communist Party. The union gave its full support to the famous 'Black' Circular 16 of the T.U.C. General Council, which instructed Trades Councils to exclude Communist delegates.

During the war, however, the atmosphere of the Russian alliance, the resurgence of workshop organization, and the rapid growth in popularity of the demand for affiliation of the Communist Party to the Labour Party, made the issue come to life once more. Congress began to debate resolutions calling for a 'Second Front' or the raising of the ban on the *Daily Worker*, and between Congresses resolutions suspiciously close to Communist policy came in from the branches, mainly those in the London and Southern districts. As a result, in March, 1943, the Executive reaffirmed all its previous decisions and unanimously rejected proposals for Communist Party affiliation to the Labour Party and attacks on the electoral truce (which were also denounced as a Communist manœuvre). The General Council approved, and at the next Congress J. Cooper moved an Executive resolution reaffirming the 1928 Congress decisions and supporting these actions. He stated that the decisions had been forced on the General Council by 'the constant pressure that we have received from time to time' and referred to trouble 'rarely of an industrial character' in the branches, and pressure on branch secretaries who refused 'to toe the line'. He was opposed by V. Fox, of London, who argued that when the 1928 decision was taken the Communist Party had been 'to the best of my knowledge' immature, and pointed out the unfortunate results of the split in the French and German movements. The

---

[1] We must assume that this unanimity was in part due to the success of the Executive in enforcing its decisions. At the 1926 Congress a resolution to reverse the decision on Trades Council affiliation had been lost, but had mustered eight votes against eighty-five.

resolution secured an 'overwhelming majority'. At the same Congress, Fox moved that the T.U.C. be congratulated on withdrawing Circular 16. The chairman tartly told Congress:

'So far as this Congress is concerned we determine our own internal policy. Frankly I cannot congratulate the Trades Union Congress on withdrawing it. We were against it. The withdrawal of that circular has already caused a considerable amount of controversy in the Trade Union Movement.' The motion was lost.

We may safely assume that the Executive, relying on its 'absolute discretion' to determine standards for full-time officers, and its authority to remove such officers for any reason it 'considers good and sufficient' would not allow any open Communist or sympathizer to obtain a full-time post, and would remove a convert. Practice with part-time officers varies from district to district. In some an open Communist might, if elected, be allowed to serve as branch secretary or as a district council member, so long as he observed the rules of the union. In others party membership would be considered incompatible even with holding a shop steward's post. In others, again, a line would be drawn between a full branch officer and a shop steward elected in a factory.

Whether the rules are strictly applied or not, however, the union cannot be sure of preventing Communists and sympathizers from rising to high position in the union, so long as they keep their affiliations secret. They can be known only by their deeds. So long as they abide by the rules they cannot be touched. That there have been such persons cannot be doubted, but we cannot say who, nor how many. One of the many unfortunate results of their existence is that it so easily leads to the branding of any independently-minded person as a 'fellow-traveller'.

London, *1945-1948*

By the end of the war it was clear that a considerable section of branch officers and district council members in London had adopted a very Left-Wing line on both political and industrial issues. The tone of many branch resolutions to the National Executive or to Congress, and the speeches at Congress of the district chairman, J. Leslie, and of V. Fox, a member of the district committee who was one of the district's two representatives on the General Council in 1946 and 1947, left no doubt about this. In April 1945, the district committee endorsed a resolution from the Edgware branch in favour of electoral unity between the Labour Party and other Left-Wing bodies, and sent it on to the National Executive. Not surprisingly the Executive rejected it and restated its views on the Communist Party. In March 1946, the London district referred to the General Council an invitation it had received to join in a Hyde Park demonstration which had been called by the London Regional Committee of the A.E.U. to protest against delay in the settlement of engineering wages. The General Secretary explained that in his view other more effective and more desirable steps were being taken to deal with production difficulties (for it was alleged that the delay was adversely affecting production) and Fox was persuaded to withdraw his announcement that he intended to lead a contingent of N.U.G.M.W. members to the demonstration. In the following month the Executive received another resolution from the Edgware branch, via the London district, asking for official support for the London Trades Council's May Day Demonstration. Support was refused on the grounds that the London Trades Council was under the influence of Communists.

The Executive, however, made no attempt to interfere with the district's conduct of its own affairs. The nearest approach to interference came during the following summer when the Workers' Side of the Electricity Supply Joint Industrial Council protested to the various unions represented upon it about the actions of a London Electricity Shop Stewards Committee, which had been responsible, it was felt, for a number of unofficial stoppages, and had 'arrogated to itself the powers which normally resided only within the province of the National Executive authority'. The Workers' Side asked the unions 'to consider the circumstances of its own members and shop stewards in the light of its rules and settled policy'. Accordingly the Executive instructed the London and Southern districts to take appropriate disciplinary action.

In the autumn, however, there was a long unofficial strike at Cossor's London factory, where the great majority of the workers were members of the N.U.G.M.W. The Executive felt that the conduct of the strike and several incidents connected with it called for intervention, and decided, with the approval of the General Council, to set up a Committee of Inquiry of two district secretaries, two of its lay members, and the chairman and secretary, to report to the General Council.

The trouble began with an unofficial strike in September on the grounds of alleged victimization of four leading shop stewards (including the N.U.G.M.W. branch secretary, who was also Works Convener of Stewards). This strike was called off in order to allow the industry's negotiating procedure to be used. A Works Conference and a Local Conference were held and registered 'failure to agree'. Meanwhile, further incidents of alleged victimization had taken place, and on October 4th a second strike was called by the strike committee. This time only some 500 out of over 2000 responded. The strike dragged on until the end of November when the union arranged terms for return to work which the strikers, after a long meeting, accepted. The Committee of Inquiry, which reported in May 1947, heard the evidence of a number of witnesses. Its report found that the incidents which had provoked the strikes were the outcome of wanton, if not deliberate, misuse of facilities granted to shop stewards by the firm, that the conduct of the branch secretary had been contrary to the rules and policy of the union, and that his evidence was confused and contradictory. The 'factory committee' had maintained connections with various unofficial bodies. Those who had been concerned in the second strike had made bitter attacks on the members who had obeyed the union's instructions to remain at work, and in this they had the support of the district committee, which had passed and later reaffirmed a resolution recording its opinion that there had, in fact, been victimization. This decision had been the occasion for a leaflet distributed by the strikers claiming official support for the strike and suggesting that those still

at work were 'blacklegs'. Smithfield workers had been pre-
vailed upon to withhold meat supplies for the works' canteen.
Considerable sums had been raised on behalf of the strikers by
unofficial bodies (including the Shop Stewards National Council). A member of the district committee, who was convener
at de Havillands, had taken part in meetings and collections on
the strikers' behalf.

Accordingly the Committee recommended the expulsion of
the branch secretary and recorded its severe censure upon members of the district committee. The district secretary had in one
matter acted injudiciously, but had supported the policy of the
union in the face of his committee throughout the strike, and
the district officer concerned was in no way at fault. The Committee went on to make the recommendations concerning shop
stewards which we have already noted.[1]

Some of the districts felt that the General Council, which
endorsed the report, should have taken firmer disciplinary
action. During September 1947, their view was referred to the
Executive for consideration, but before a decision could be
reached an even more serious series of incidents, in which many
of the same persons were concerned, prevented any further
disciplinary decision on the Cossor report alone.

The N.U.G.M.W. had been party to an agreement with other
unions to divide responsibility for the organization of catering
workers by regions. It had been allocated London and Scotland. After the end of the war there had been a most successful
organizing campaign in London which, despite all the difficulties of a trade in which earnings are largely dependent on
'tips', in which work is seasonal and workers are of many
nationalities, and in which the employers were not favourable
to unions, had swept in some 13,000 workers by March 1947.
The district officer mainly concerned was Arthur Lewis, M.P.,
who had been given special responsibility for supervising the
affairs of the Catering No. 1 branch. Arthur Lewis sought on
many occasions to obtain recognition from the London
Hoteliers, but received no reply to his letters. On October 8th,
1946, an unofficial strike started at the Savoy and spread

[1] See p. 115.

rapidly to other hotels. Although unofficial the strike was not condemned by the union, since it was not in breach of a signed agreement. The Savoy was advised that the strike was illegal[1] and issued a writ claiming an injunction to restrain Messrs. Lewis, Ravera and Piazza[2] from 'counselling, persuading or procuring employees of the Savoy to come out on strike or continue on strike . . .' and were granted an *ex parte* injunction. On October 15th, however, the employers' association and the union agreed on the principle of recognition, and the Savoy — a member of the association — settled its action on terms which included recognition and no victimization. During subsequent months the details of an agreement were worked out and the whole was finally signed in March 1947.

During the same month, however, the management of the Savoy took exception to the part played by Piazza in a minor dispute and suspended him. An unofficial strike followed, but was called off as soon as the strikers heard the decision of an *ad hoc* Council set up by the union and the association to report on the dispute.[3] The Council found that Piazza had been in the wrong and recommended that his suspension should last for fourteen days. The hotel, however, refused to carry out the recommendation of the Council, as it was in law perfectly entitled to do. The parties failed to agree on terms for submission of the dispute to the Industrial Court, and the union accordingly reported the dispute, under the provisions of S.R.&O. 1305, to the Minister of Labour, who referred it to the National Arbitration Tribunal. The Tribunal heard the parties and on July 30th, 1947, issued their award which stated that they had found in favour of the union's claim. The hotel still refused reinstatement and on August 9th Piazza was finally dismissed, and the payment of his wages ceased.

The Executive decided to write once more to the Minister to draw his attention to the gravity of the situation. This was done on August 21st. At the same time, it decided that every

[1] Under the terms of S.R. & O. 1305 of 1940 – 'The Conditions of Employment and National Arbitration Order'.

[2] Ravera was secretary of the branch, and Piazza a prominent member of the branch employed at the Savoy.

[3] There had not been time to constitute an official Council under the agreement of March 3rd.

means of achieving an amicable settlement should be tried, but that if such a settlement was not reached there would be 'no other course available but to authorize a ballot' — of the members concerned in order to sanction an official strike.

Nothing was heard from the Ministry, and on October 14th the Executive sanctioned a ballot in the Savoy group of hotels. The great majority of those voting supported strike action, and on the 28th the union gave notice to the Savoy management that, unless the terms of the tribunal award were accepted, its members would be called out on November 6th. On November 4th the Ministry gave notice to the press of the Minister's decision to set up a Court of Inquiry under the 1919 Act, and notified the union by 'phone the same evening. An emergency meeting of the General Secretary with the London district committee on the following day decided to postpone the strike until the 8th, but a number of workers came out unofficially on the 6th, and the same evening notices were issued to all of them by the management that unless they resumed work on the morning of the 8th they would be dismissed. An emergency meeting of the National Executive was held on the 7th to receive reports on these developments. It recorded its regret that the decision of the Minister had been so belated and resolved that the 'precipitate' action of the Savoy management gave it no option but to call out all its members employed by the Savoy group in an official strike.

The Court, chaired by Sir John Forster, K.C., sat from the 10th to the 24th to hear the parties and to prepare its report, while the strike was in progress. Meanwhile, however, on the 10th the High Court had delivered its judgment in the case of *Rex v. National Arbitration Tribunal* (concerning a case in which the tribunal had awarded in favour of the reinstatement of an employee of Horatio Crowther & Co. Ltd.) holding that the National Arbitration Tribunal had no power under the Order which constituted it to direct the reinstatement of a workman in any circumstances. The central support of the union's case, which had up till that time seemed very strong and had aroused widespread sympathy throughout the trade union movement, was suddenly removed.

The Court issued a long report[1] on the 24th which reviewed the events leading up to the strike in considerable detail. In view of the decision in the Crowther case the Court recommended 'that the Executive Committee of the Union and the Savoy should join in an effort to rehabilitate Mr. Piazza by endeavouring to obtain employment for him on terms reasonably equivalent to those which he had when in the service of the Savoy'. To this they added strictures on the conduct of both sides. They asked the union to 'consider whether their District or Local officials should be permitted to undertake the leadership of strikes which the National Executive has not thought proper to recognize as official', and criticized the conduct of the strike ballot at length. 'In the present case it is significant to note that there was a number of members of the Union in the employ of the Savoy who in the course of the taking of the ballot made complaint to the Union that the ballot was being improperly conducted, and apart from the fact that there were no real facilities for permitting members to record their votes in secret, it was deplorable that Mr. Piazza should have been permitted at any time to be present in close proximity to the ballot box and that no effective steps should have been taken to ensure that only those persons were allowed to vote who were properly entitled to do so.'

The strike continued. Volunteer pickets were used owing to the reluctance of some strikers to be seen in such a role by customers. There were several incidents in which pickets were involved with the police, when they lay in the road to prevent oil lorries gaining access to the hotel. Arrests were made, and amongst those arrested was Arthur Lewis.

On the 28th the Executive decided to concentrate on securing a settlement, and on December 1st it sanctioned the proposed terms (which included 'no victimization', the reinstatement of strikers as soon as possible, and joint action to aid Piazza) and proposed to inquire fully into the actions of the London district and the Catering branch. On the 3rd the London district com-

[1] Report of a Court of Inquiry into the Causes and Circumstances of a Dispute between the Savoy Hotel Limited and Members of the National Union of General and Municipal Workers, Cmd. 7266 of 1947.

mittee asserted its full confidence in Arthur Lewis (who had been relieved of his responsibility for the Catering industry) and passed a resolution 'disapproving of the action of the National Executive and expressing profound disgust at the terms of settlement'. Accordingly, on the 5th the Executive suspended the committee and instructed the district secretary, Watering, to act under the General Secretary's supervision. Lewis was suspended from all industrial activities and similar action was taken with the branch committee and officers of the Catering No. 1 branch.[1] On the 11th, despite the objections of Fox, the General Council endorsed the decision.

Reinstatement took a considerable time, and the union continued financial support for its members until they regained their places or found alternative employment. Fox and Leslie appealed against suspension, but their appeals were rejected. Arthur Lewis started legal proceedings against the union to secure reinstatement, and the report on the dispute for the 1948 Congress was, therefore, privately circulated in order not to prejudice the case (which the union eventually won).

The report to Congress disagreed with the Court's findings on the conduct of the ballot. The presence of Piazza was 'unwise but . . . did not in any way influence the result'. [Trade union ballots are not normally conducted with the same care as parliamentary elections; this ballot seems to have been as fair as most, and the Executive's verdict should probably be accepted.] It suggested that there was a case for inquiry into the actions of the police during the picketing incidents. But its main concern was with the conduct of the strike by the strikers and the London district.

It found that the branch officers and Arthur Lewis had attended a meeting on the evening of November 5th at which it appeared that a decision had been taken to ignore instructions to postpone the strike. Unofficial and misleading leaflets had been distributed. The officially constituted strike committee had found the conduct of the strike taken out of their hands by a 'small section'. The branch had had affiliations

---

[1] The branch was reported to have resolved to ask the T.U.C. to set up a separate union for catering workers.

with organizations proscribed by the union and had 'set up an Action Committee which recommended unofficial strike action in the Corner House restaurants of Messrs. Lyons'. Arthur Lewis's conduct was criticized on several grounds, particularly on his failure to control the branch's conduct before and during the strike, despite his direct responsibility for its affairs. The district committee had exercised no restraint over the strike and had far exceeded the bounds of their authority in passing their resolutions of December 3rd. Leslie and Fox were singled out for particular censure. The district secretary had also failed to exercise proper control and appeared to have 'publicly approved of Brother Lewis's conduct in lying down in front of lorries'.

The report recommended that the suspension of the district committee should continue, but be reviewed at the end of six months. Leslie, Fox and Blair (a prominent member of the branch and a member of the district committee) were banned from all offices in the union and from serving in any representative capacity until otherwise determined by the National Executive. [The Cossor report was taken into account in determining the action taken with Leslie and Fox.] Arthur Lewis was to be dismissed and given three months' salary in lieu of notice. This report had already been adopted and acted upon by the General Council, who had transferred the secretary of the Southern district, J. Cooper, to take temporary control of London's affairs in place of Watering, who had been superannuated.

A resolution deploring the terms of the report and the disciplinary action taken was moved and seconded by delegates from London branches. After a long debate their motion was lost by 289 votes to 36.

Arthur Lewis was later expelled in connection with an unofficial leaflet which was thought to be intended to influence the outcome of the Congress debate. In August the Executive terminated the suspension of the London district committee and allowed the district council to elect new members to the committee and a new representative to the General Council in place of those debarred from office. J. Cooper remained in charge of the district's affairs until after his return to Parliament for Deptford in 1950, when permission was given to the district committee to select a new secretary and one of the district officers, L. J. Wright, was chosen. In September 1950, the General Council lifted the ban on Leslie and Blair. Meanwhile Fox had left the union.

The London branches have continued to pass Left-Wing resolutions, and the speeches of their delegates at Congress have sometimes been in the same vein, and in opposition to the platform's policy. It may then fairly be said that the Executive of the union has acted in accordance with its claim that anyone is permitted to voice his opinion, and to try to change the union's policy by constitutional means, and that it acts only to prevent clear breach of the rules, or open opposition to policy that has been decided. This conclusion is reinforced by the overwhelming evidence in both the Cossor and the Savoy reports showing frequent breach of rule, connection with banned organizations external to the union, and flouting of union decisions.

The strike admittedly presented the union with awkward problems, but for these the employer, the Ministry, and the decision of the High Court must take their share of responsibility. The Executive had a very difficult task to carry out in bringing the strike to an end, but here again it can fairly be said that they took the course which was most in the interest of their members concerned. It is not likely that intransigence would have achieved more favourable terms.

Unofficial Organizations and Unofficial Strikes

The events in London were outstanding in the union's history. It must not be supposed that they were typical. Even Communists are not indiscriminately condemned by the union. Each district has its 'good' Communist of whom it is said: 'He does a good job and would not do anything underhand. He is a party member, of course, and thinks he's a Communist, but he's not a *real* Communist.'

Groupings not provided for by rule have their place in the union, so long as they act openly, and avoid external affiliations.

About 1935 the union organized a great campaign to recover its hold on London gasworkers. To aid the campaign regular meetings of representatives from the gas branches — the London Gas Committee — were arranged, and these meetings were attended by district officers. Their function was advisory. After the formation of the Southern district the gas branches south of the Thames were allowed to continue to send representatives to the Committee. 'Left-Wingers' are always prominent in trade union organizing drives, and the opinions of the Committee showed that this was no exception. After the end of the war the Southern district and the Executive felt that it was desirable to form a separate Committee in the Southern district's London area in order to avoid too close connection with the Left-Wing London district; and the connection was in clear violation of the rules that communication between districts should only be through the district secretaries. Later the South London Committee was disbanded owing to its attempts to instruct branches on the content of resolutions to be submitted to the district office and to its connection with an entirely unofficial joint shop stewards' movement which included shop stewards from the 'red' craft unions. In future, meetings of delegates from the South London gas branches would be allowed when items of general interest arose, but were to be called by the district office and sanctioned by the district committee.

Objections to activities of this kind are understandable, and are reinforced by the practice of industrial block voting in union elections which readily arises when industrial organization of this kind is allowed. The London Gas Committee, for instance, could swing a considerable proportion of the votes of the London district. For these reasons most districts prefer to hold industrial delegate conferences only when occasion arises, and under adequate control. Regular conferences of industrial delegates are, however, permitted in a considerable number of industries in the London district, and also in the gas industry of the Birmingham district. And the officers concerned find they have their value. They maintain interest, and it may be that in a district so prone to radical trade unionism as London, they provide a useful safety-valve. The union could dissolve the London Gas Committee at any time, but that might only strengthen the joint shop stewards' movement.

Unofficial strikes are often condemned in round terms. Speaking in Plymouth on September 1st, 1946, Charles Dukes, having praised the democratic organization of the two general unions, asked: 'In view of the machinery outlined above, how do unofficial strikes occur? They are invariably fomented by dissident elements who are unwilling to accept the majority decisions of elected delegates.'

In 1947, and again in 1949, Congress passed resolutions containing unqualified condemnations of unofficial strikes. Unofficial strikers have been disciplined, not only in London. In 1944 the Northern district replied to an unofficial strike of Newcastle dockers by closing its docks' branch and expelling all the strikers.[1] A new branch was formed and the chastened strikers were re-admitted on condition that they signed a document promising in future to abide by the constitution of the union. In the years since then, famous for their dock strikes, Newcastle has been singularly free. In 1947 the same district committee adopted the same tactics with equal success, when the employees of the Newcastle Economic Bus Company struck unofficially. In 1950 the district secretary refused the contributions of a branch of colliery surface workers who had instituted an unofficial overtime ban, telling them that the decision would stand until they should accept the services for which those contributions were paid.

This, however, is not the whole story. Between 1940 and 1951 no union could wholeheartedly condemn all unofficial strikes, for almost all strikes were illegal and, therefore, necessarily unofficial.[2] The same district secretary, John Yarwood, wrote in the union's journal of April 1948:

'Every union officer knows how these things develop. Every one of them has had the bitter experience of ordering men back to work while feeling that, ethically, they were justified in their

---

[1] The strikers probably thought that this action terminated their employment, since under the wartime scheme, as now, dockers' cards were issued by the unions.

[2] The prohibition of strikes and lock-outs under S.R. & O. 1305 of 1940 ceased when that Order was replaced, in 1951, by S.I. 1376. See p. 144f.

attitude. It is the misuse of the system which causes trouble. . . .

'You know, the democratic system is specifically designed to delay. It offers every opportunity to obstructionists.'

After the Crowther case the union felt itself entitled to call official strikes on issues of victimization, since thereafter no arbitration award could settle them. Thus the Scottish district committee conducted a ballot of the employees of the London Metallic Capsule Company in Hamilton in April 1950, on a case of alleged victimization, and called them out in an official strike, which was successful. Union members thrown out of work by strikes of craft union members — frequently of boiler-makers in the shipyards — have to be supported if they are not entitled to unemployment benefit. In March 1948, the Con-federation of Shipbuilding and Engineering Unions decided to recognize as official a strike which had broken out as a result of a unilateral decision by the Merseyside shipyard employers to end piece-work, and the union honoured the decision and paid benefit to its 1740 members concerned.

Union officials may sometimes inform employers that unless a certain concession is granted 'they cannot be responsible for the actions of their members'. On occasion, officers have been known to suggest to shop stewards that a demonstration of the validity of this kind of statement by their members would be of assistance in negotiations. In some instances the union's conviction that unofficial strikers are sometimes less to blame than their employers has been demonstrated, as it has by other unions, by sanctioning a grant equivalent to strike pay, or a permanent loan without interest. A grant of this sort was made to employees of a large company who came out on strike because the company announced a large increase in profits on the day after it had refused a moderate increase in wages.

Communists, Left-Wingers, unofficial organizations and un-official strikes are too much a part of the modern trade union movement to be dealt with by repression alone. The problem of the N.U.G.M.W., as of other unions, is to find the best means of preventing them getting out of control. The methods of the N.U.G.M.W. have been as successful as those of other unions.

CHAPTER X

THE RULEBOOK

THE union's rulebook has already been frequently mentioned; it is time to take a closer look at it. The rulebook embodies the union's constitution. As with any other constitution, its interpretation often presents difficulties, and it is surrounded by a number of 'constitutional conventions' or accepted practices, through which alone it is made to work. And as with any other carefully drafted constitution, its provisions are almost always drawn into any important conflict within the union, although the conflict may be primarily concerned with matters not included in the constitution.

Rule-Making

Officers of the union are in the habit of saying to members: 'You must keep within the rules. They are *your* rules. You make them at *your* Congress, at which no officer has a vote. If you don't like them, change them. But so long as the rules prohibit what you now propose to do, it is my duty to see that you don't do it.'

This is formally true, but it is certainly not the whole story. Rule-making is legislation and no legislature, least of all a legislature which must get through its annual business in three or four days, could be other than chaotic without a committee to guide its work. Guidance on procedure is provided by the Standing Orders Committee, but this is not enough. Legislative direction comes from the Executive.

Sometimes the making of a rule is left entirely to the Executive and General Council, as, for instance, the new rule on political contributions and political activity required by the repeal of the 1927 Trade Disputes and Trade Unions Act in 1946. More frequently it is left to the Executive to frame a rule to embody the intention of a Congress resolution. The rules of a registered trade union must conform to the standards laid down in the various Trade Unions Acts and to ensure conformity they must be confirmed by the Registrars of Friendly Societies of the United Kingdom and of Northern Ireland. It is the task of the General Secretary and the Executive to submit rules to them, and to see that the wording is in accordance with their requirements.

Of far more importance than this is the fact that the great bulk of new rules or of amendments to rule which have been passed by Congress have been proposals of the National Executive. Before each Congress[1] the Executive considers any proposals which the General Secretary or other members may have to make in the light of experience since the last Congress, and, with legal advice, drafts resolutions for Congress. It also considers the proposals which have come in from the branches and districts and determines its course of action. There have been occasions on which the Executive has accepted branch proposals, as it accepted, in the end, the proposal for equal pay. There have been occasions on which proposals of the Executive, such as the proposals to return to biennial Congresses in 1948, and to raise contributions in 1952, have been defeated by Congress. And there have been occasions on which branch or district proposals have been passed in the face of Executive opposition, as when, in 1928, Congress carried by 37 votes to 35 a proposal that the number of members of the Executive should be increased from 10 to 12 so that each district could have a representative thereon. But these are the exceptions. When rules are under discussion there are usually a number of Executive proposals, all or almost all of which are passed, and a large number of branch proposals, the great bulk of which are defeated after the General Secretary has explained the grounds of the Executive's opposition.

At the Congress of 1936 the rulebook was thoroughly revised, except for the sections dealing with benefits, contributions and political action. Charles Dukes explained to the Congress that the Executive proposed a large number of amendments, deletions and one or two new rules on these grounds:

'Many of the rules as they stood at present were framed forty years ago when we were a relatively small organization and

[1] Or, since the war, and emergencies apart, before each Rules Revision Congress.

when the problem of administration of Trade Union rules was entirely different from what it was today. It was well-known that steps had to be taken to deal with certain elements within the organization who were acting contrary to the general interests of the Union, and whose disruptive methods took up so much time that a high percentage of the administrative staff throughout the country was engaged not in dealing with the members as such, but were occupied in dealing with all the frictional elements whose main objective was not to carry forward the objects for which the Union existed, but to discredit the Union and aim at its disintegration.

'There were phrases used in the proposed amendments which probably no layman would have drafted, but it was necessary to conform to the law and we had been compelled to use legal phraseology. It was not the intention, however, in dealing with the particular members referred to, to use the arbitrary methods which perhaps the language of the amendments inferred. That was not the intention but the fact remained that when we have given to members and officers facilities to state their case to District Executives, District Councils, National Executive and the General Council, they could still go to a lawyer and say that as the rules stood it was no avail and we could not compel them to accept or conform to decisions properly reached.'

His intention to give the national and district governing bodies sufficient powers to deal with any disruptive elements, and to keep the affairs of the union out of the Courts, was thus clearly stated.[1] He had consulted Sir Stafford Cripps, and the long list of Executive proposals which were the result of Cripps' advice gave the General Council, National Executive and District Committees the powers to disband, suspend, dismiss and expel on grounds deemed 'good and sufficient', with discretion to withhold reasons, which have been outlined in Chapters III and IV. Right of appeal to the branches or to Congress was excised, for how could such an appeal stand if the General Council and District Committees could withhold

---

[1] Charles Dukes was fond of quoting the occasion on which he announced to a solicitor his intention to fight a case 'on principle', and was told that he must fight it 'on law'.

the reasons for their action in order to avoid legal proceedings? At the same time, a good deal of loose wording was revised and the sequence of rules and clauses recast into a more logical pattern. The intention was clear. But we may doubt if the danger of disruption was at the time so great as Dukes feared, or the losses to the union caused by a few legal cases so serious as he appeared to think. Now, wise after the event, we can see that the new rules did not prevent the activities of 'disruptive elements' or keep the union entirely out of the Courts; though, of course, the damage might have been more serious without the new rules. The General Secretary's reasoning, however, convinced Congress, and the rules were passed.

Since that time there has been no further thoroughgoing revision. The National Executive has proposed and carried some important amendments. In 1945 members of the union were debarred from attending meetings of other branches without the approval of the district secretary. In 1947 the old Marxist address of 1889 was withdrawn from the rulebook on the grounds that it bore 'no relationship to present-day conditions' and that the objects of the union were set out in clauses 1-4 of Rule 2, which 'could not be improved on'. Tom Williamson explained:

'As a matter of fact we have had cases on the National Joint Industrial Councils where our position has been made exceedingly difficult because of the feeling that has been engendered by certain phrases[1] of this preface which are not in accord with the spirit of the relationship on the National Board.'

Most Executive amendments have, however, been concerned with less important points. In 1950, for instance, it felt that since the General Council was endowed with power to disband a district, it should also be allowed to suspend a district, if that appeared to meet the situation.

The rulebook as it stands today does not please all the members. A number of resolutions at each Rules Congress are

[1] He had in mind such sentences as these:
'. . . today there are only two classes, the producing Working Class and the possessing Master Class. The interests of these two classes are opposed to each other. The Masters have known this for a long time; the Workers are beginning to see it. They are beginning to understand that their own hope lies in themselves, that from the Masters as a class they can expect no help. . . .'

'Left-Wing' amendments intended to 'liberalize' the rules, by increasing the number of lay members on the General Council (lost by only 188 votes to 142 in 1950); by allowing appeals to Congress or to a special 'all-lay Appeals Committee', or by limiting the General Council to action within the rules, instead of allowing it to settle 'any matter not provided for in these rules'. In 1947 one delegate went so far as to say:

'To my mind the constitution of this Union is undemocratic from beginning to end. The constitution is laid down on the assumption that the general worker is incapable of governing himself.'

But this sentiment has been unable to command majorities.

Rule Interpretation

Some person or body *must* interpret and lay down practice in all those matters which are not covered by the rules. The whole complex of procedures for carrying on collective bargaining in two hundred industries has grown up or has been formed by decisions of officers or committees with few specific references in the book.

Interpretations of benefit rules are often required. Does total disablement mean incapacity resulting from industrial diseases — e.g. silicosis — as well as from accidents? Is a member of 'not less than five years' standing' a member with five years continuous membership, or with five years' membership in all? During the war the membership of those in the forces was suspended, largely to avoid heavy funeral benefit claims. Were the relatives of a Home Guard killed on duty to receive benefit or not?

Amongst other rules which cause trouble is that which provides that vacancies occurring during the term of office of a district council 'shall be filled by the next highest on the list of unsuccessful candidates at the last election'. If an election was uncontested, is a new election to be held, or does the place remain vacant? As we have seen the National Executive has interpreted its power to 'direct an elected official to fill' any vacancy or new position as allowing it to appoint any elected district officer to a district secretaryship (usually only confirming the selection of the district committee), but the next clause of the same rule states that: 'District Secretaries and District Organizers shall in the case of a first election be nominated and elected by the Branches and members in the District to which they are attached.' It is evident that there is room for a claim, which has been put forward, that district secretaries should be elected by the branches. The official answer is that when an elected district officer is chosen to be district secretary, it is not a case of 'a first election'.

In the ordinary run of events rules are interpreted by the district secretaries and the General Secretary. In case of doubt they may refer the matter to the district committee or the National Executive, with recourse to the General Council for a final verdict. Any member who disagrees with the General Council's interpretation may either take the matter to Court, in so far as the Courts have jurisdiction over internal union affairs, or get his branch to propose an amendment to the next Congress which will clear up the rule to his satisfaction.

The power to interpret is no mean power. In interpretation of rules important decisions have been taken. Whole-time branch secretaries have been defined as lay members; members of the staff have been deprived of the right to be elected to representative bodies within the union; but more frequently interpretation is mere exposition to branches or to members; that the rules clearly prevent them from expelling a member, calling a strike, or publicly announcing a policy contrary to that of the union. The district committees and the General Council are possessed of great powers, and it is therefore possible for them, in most matters, to decide on the course of action which seems to them best and still to remain clearly within the rules. They have usually no need to try to interpret the rules to suit their purpose, whether or not they would be ready to do so. It must be added that in matters of major importance, such as the Savoy dispute, the General Council submits a full report of its actions to Congress for approval, even though these have been entirely within its powers. On that occasion Congress debated the issue on a motion 'deploring' the Council's disciplinary measures.

PART III

THE N.U.G.M.W. IN INDUSTRY

CHAPTER I

A GENERAL SURVEY OF INDUSTRIAL WORK

IN discussing the organization of the union we have mentioned its industrial work only incidentally, when touching on the duties of officers, on shop stewards, or on strikes. This method of presentation may be justified, but it must not be allowed to obscure the importance of the union's industrial functions. Trade unions originated as organizations of industrial workers whose purpose it was to protect their industrial interests, and the protection of the interests of its members *as industrial workers* remains the central purpose of trade unions. It is certainly the aspect of its work in which the great majority of its members are most interested, and it is the sole concern which many of them have in the union.

The very large number of industries with which the union deals makes it difficult to describe its industrial work, the more so since each industry's collective bargaining procedures and wage structure have developed in their own way, partly influenced by public opinion, government intervention, and development in other industries, but very largely determined by the peculiarities of the industry itself — its industrial processes, its organization, and the character of the employers and the other unions which organize within it. Because of this the only possible method of description seems to be to take a few industries as examples and describe the union's work in them in some detail. For this purpose six industries have been chosen. First, those which cover the three largest sections of the union's members — engineering and shipbuilding (which, although separate industries, are here taken together), gas and 'non-trading'.[1] The rubber industry has been chosen as an example

[1] For the purpose of industrial relations an industry must be defined by its machinery for collective bargaining. The 'engineering' industry is a unit only in this sense, and the same is true of the 'non-trading' departments of local authorities. The shipbuilding industry (in which is included shiprepairing) has separate machinery for collective bargaining, but its affinities with engineering, both in procedures and in wage movements, are so close that the two industries are here treated together.

of a modern industry in which collective bargaining is of comparatively recent origin. And the laundry industry serves as an example of a 'women's industry', and an industry which has not yet developed a complete system for collective bargaining.

Before we turn to these industries, however, we must attempt some general outline of the scope of the union's work in industry — however dangerous such generalizations may be.

National Industries

The great majority of the union's members work in industries which have national machinery for collective bargaining. This machinery may be one of the many Joint Industrial Councils which were set up after the first world war under the influence of the Whitley Report, or have been constituted more recently in the same pattern. It may be one of the traditional procedures which were developed before Whitleyism, and from which the Whitley Report adopted the main elements of its proposals, such as the procedures of the engineering and shipbuilding industries. It may be a statutory Wages Council. And it may be machinery set up to cover the employees of a single large firm or combine which has plants in various parts of the country.

The parties to a Joint Industrial Council or to one of the traditional procedures are an employers' federation, or possibly several federations, and the trade unions concerned in the industry. In practice the difference between the two types of collective bargaining may not be great. There must be a procedural agreement laying down the functions of the joint body, and the methods by which it is to carry out its work. This may provide for outside conciliation or arbitration (by a specially constituted body or by the Industrial Court) to settle deadlocks. From 1940 to 1951 they were all subject to the Conditions of Employment and National Arbitration Order, and, should they fail to solve their differences within the terms of their own procedural agreement, were liable to have them referred to the National Arbitration Tribunal. Since 1951, under the Industrial Disputes Order, reference is made to the

Industrial Disputes Tribunal, a body with powers less wide than the National Arbitration Tribunal.[1]

In those industries in which wages and conditions of employment are subjects of national agreements — and that is now the general rule — there will be a wages agreement and an agreement on conditions. The latter may be broken down into a number of agreements — one on hours of work, one on overtime and nightshift, one on holidays with pay, and so on. The content of these agreements, however, differs widely from industry to industry. Many national joint bodies have set up subsidiary regional or district bodies. Before the war the settlement of wages and conditions of work was often left to them. The national body concerned itself with those topics only if the subsidiary bodies failed to settle a difference and passed it up for national consideration. Even now the subsidiary bodies may have considerable power over wages. The national body may settle only general advances, and leave to its subsidiaries the determination of the base rates and grade differentials to which the general advances must be added. The national body may fix a national minimum rate for the lowest grade of labour, allowing its subsidiaries to settle rates for higher grades, and perhaps to fix a higher minimum. These are but two of the considerable number of variations which are practised. Settlement of the most important conditions of employment is now normally centralized, but even here subsidiary bodies may be permitted to treat national agreements as laying down the minimum, and to agree on better conditions.

In industries in which there are no regional or district bodies agreements must be centralized, and disputes with individual firms must be referred straight to the national body. Otherwise these differences are only so referred if the intermediate body fails to reach agreement on them. In some instances the determination of the methods to be used in such cases is left to the subsidiary bodies who may provide for recognition of shop stewards by their constituents, for setting up Works Councils or Committees, and perhaps also for constituting a

[1] The Industrial Disputes Order (S.I. 1376) is summarized in the *Ministry of Labour Gazette*, August 1951, pp. 309-10.

sub-committee to deal with local disputes. In other industries items of this sort may be determined by the national procedural agreement.

Where no procedure is laid down for dealing with disputes before reference to the joint bodies, some firms have agreed to recognize shop stewards and set up councils or committees. Otherwise the first stage of the procedure is discussion between the firm and a union officer. An employer and his workers are likely to be interested in a large number of matters which are not covered by national or regional agreements, especially where piece-work or bonus systems of payment are in force. Differences on such topics may lead to purely local agreements, which may be as elaborately laid out as agreements of wider application, or may be recorded by exchange of letters alone, or may be merely verbal understandings.

Wages Councils have wider functions than the Trade Boards from which they took over under the Wages Councils Act of 1945, but they are still concerned with laying down a statutory minimum, which applies to all the firms in the industry. Consequently there may be agreements between individual firms and the union, or unions, to pay higher wages and provide better conditions than those laid down. It is thus possible to have a voluntary national bargaining body and a Wages Council side by side in the same industry, as in the rubber industry, and the cocoa and chocolate industry. In such industries voluntary agreements make the pace for the Wages Councils. Some Wages Councils cover sizeable industries, such as those for the rubber and laundry industries. Others deal with small and localized industries which, from the union's point of view, are district rather than national industries.

The most important negotiating machineries which cover the employees of a single firm and may be included in the national industries' group are now those of the nationalized industries, most of which have continued to use procedures of the Joint Industrial Council type, with some modifications. But they are not the only examples. The I.C.I. withdrew from the Chemical J.I.C. in 1936 and has since dealt with the unions through its own machinery. The employers' side of the Sheet and Plate

Glass Joint Industrial Council consists entirely of members of
the management of Pilkington Bros., of St. Helens, and the
workers' side of officers of the N.U.G.M.W. from the four
districts in which Pilkingtons have factories, together with lay
members of the union employed at those factories. The agreements with the British Aluminium Company might be held to
be in the same class. In this group, naturally enough, collective
bargaining is markedly centralized. Procedures to be followed
in each plant are laid down centrally and in detail. It is in this
group also that procedures for joint consultation on 'managerial' matters have been most fully worked out.

Only in one or two national industries — for instance, the
match industry and the sheet and plate glass industry — is the
N.U.G.M.W. the sole representative of the workers. In a
number of industries the T.&G.W.U. and the N.U.G.M.W.
together represent the workers; in a few industries the
N.U.G.M.W. is associated with another single union; and in
many others with two or more unions (usually including the
T.&G.W.U.). In some instances, as in engineering and
shipbuilding, and in building, the unions concerned come together in a trade union federation; more often they settle their
line of action at a 'workers' side' meeting before the joint
body is formally brought together. Representation on the
workers' side is usually arranged roughly in proportion
to membership in the industry concerned. Where the
N.U.G.M.W. has a large proportion, it sends the National
Officer concerned, perhaps one or two district secretaries and
several district officers. On one or two joint bodies its delegation is large enough to include a representative from each
district. Where its membership is small it may have only one
seat — for the National Officer responsible. The National Officer
is the leader of the union's delegation, and if the N.U.G.M.W.
has the largest delegation he will be secretary (and leader) of
the workers' side. Otherwise he may be chairman, and alternate with his opposite number on the employers' side as chairman and vice-chairman of the full body. Where the union's
delegation is by far the largest it may hold both offices. It is

rare for lay members of the union to be chosen to sit on a national joint body.

On regional or district bodies the practice is similar, except that here the district secretary or one of his officers takes the lead, and the representatives of the union are chosen by the district or districts concerned (for the boundaries of regional joint bodies rarely coincide with those of the districts). Some districts try as far as possible to share seats between district officers and lay members who work in the industry concerned. Others rarely include lay representatives. This entails that in a large delegation there must be several officers who are not specialists in the industry concerned.

Full-time officers must take the lead on negotiating bodies. They have the skill and experience required for the work, and the major share of responsibility for decisions taken is theirs. Moreover, district officers are better able to report back to the various branches concerned in any negotiations than are lay members whose experience is often bounded by the place in which they work and the branch to which they belong. Consequently, on national bodies seats not required for the appropriate National Officers are best filled by district officers, and on regional bodies district officers must take precedence in the allocation of seats. Where a number of places are available, however, it is useful to bring in active lay members, both to give them a larger share in the work of the union, and to bring the feelings and experience of working members directly to bear on the problems discussed.

Dealings between the union and a single undertaking are carried on under whatever arrangements exist for shop stewards and works committees, and by the district officer concerned, who may, if he has dealt with the firm over a long period, have become a well-known figure in its affairs. He meets the firm's representative, at the request of the firm or of his members, to deal with issues which are too big or involved to be settled by shop stewards at the works, or when there is failure, or likelihood of failure, to reach an understanding. If he finds it necessary to conclude a formal agreement, he must report it to his district secretary for approval.

District Industries

If an industry is localized and appears within the territory of only one district, bargaining with its employers is normally left to that district. Cotton is confined to the Lancashire district (which includes Derbyshire), and wool to Yorkshire. The 'shift-system' steel agreement applies only in Sheffield and is also left to the Yorkshire district. Whisky distilleries are confined to Scotland. Where a section of a national industry has its own machinery for collective bargaining, as has the Hawick hosiery trade, the union leaves it to the district in the same way.

In these industries working members have usually a far larger share in the conduct of negotiations. This practice was naturally followed by small local unions (such as the Yorkshire Woolcombers), and in some instances it has been safeguarded by an understanding with the workers concerned, when they amalgamated with the N.U.G.M.W., that they should be allowed to take part in all discussions with the employers and that agreements should not be concluded without their approval. Their knowledge of the specialized operations and processes of the industry is an important aid to the officers handling their case. Moreover, local groups of craftsmen are naturally jealous of their independence, and suspicious of the ability of an 'outsider' to manage their affairs.

Although this group contains many of the most colourful and historically interesting sections of the union, it is now of little quantitative importance.

Unattached Firms

Of greater importance in numbers are the unattached firms. Many of these are to be found in the engineering industry, where they are referred to as 'non-federated' firms because they do not belong to the employers' federation. Some firms of this type still refuse to deal with trade unions, but many of them have a long tradition of collective bargaining, and many have begun to deal with the unions since 1940, when S.R.&O. 1305 laid down that all employers must observe the terms of collective agreements which apply to their trade and district. Despite this order, such firms have been free to settle their own procedure and to reach agreements which are very different from national or regional agreements, so long as they do not provide for less favourable conditions of employment. Their agreements, however, may be said to 'follow' the general pattern of engineering agreements. 'Non-federated' firms in other industries are not usually so numerous as in engineering, but almost every industry has some examples.

Sometimes it may be nearly impossible to classify a firm operating a special process, or a number of processes, into any industry. It is then usual for the employer and the union to agree to 'follow' some industry, in order to ensure that the employer shall have no excuse for falling behind other industries. Stories are told of windfall gains or losses due to an employer agreeing to follow a particular industry just before a wage-increase was granted, or just before the industry struck a bad patch. Sometimes the union persuades the employer to operate a 'bastard' agreement, containing the most favourable sections of two or more agreements in related industries.

The unattached firm is the field in which the district officer has greatest freedom. Subject to the approval of the district secretary and committee, which is unlikely to be strongly interested unless there is trouble, he may construct agreements, settle procedures and set up Works Committees to his liking so long as the employer concurs.

CHAPTER II

THE GAS INDUSTRY

THE gas industry is an industry of middling size which, in 1951, employed some 105,000 manual workers and about 30,000 staff workers. Rather more than half of the manual employees work in the gas works themselves. The others, and the great majority of the staff, are engaged outside in sales or service work. Inside the works the main operations are attending the various types of gas-producing plants, supplying the coal to the operators and loading and despatching coke, attending the purifiers, and controlling the output of gas. None of these tasks is regarded as skilled in the sense that an apprenticeship is required, and the more responsible posts are filled by promotion from the yard labourers, seniority being usually the main criterion. In all the larger works engineering maintenance workers — mainly fitters and electricians — are employed on maintenance work, and also building craftsmen, mainly to build and repair the brick linings of the retorts. The most important groups of workers outside are those employed on sales, on meter reading and collecting, on mains and service laying, on gas fitting and on transport. The meter reader and collector has been treated as a manual worker by some undertakings and as a clerical worker by others. The gas fitters are craftsmen, and most of them have served a full apprenticeship. Their job is akin to that of a plumber, but they are specialists in gas-fitting and are, therefore, not normally required to equal his versatility. Their rate has in the past been slightly less than that of the plumber in the building trades. The N.U.G.M.W. has always claimed to represent both these grades, and has included some of the other craftsmen. It has also organized some clerical and administrative workers, but never with the same success as manual workers.

The Origins of Collective Bargaining

Collective bargaining in the gas industry began with the successes of the Gasworkers and General Labourers in achieving the eight-hour day. As we have seen, competing unions were soon in the field, and up to 1914 each dealt with individual companies or local authorities where they could get membership and where the employers were willing to meet them. The awards of the war-time Committee on Production widened the scope of collective agreements in the industry considerably, and at the end of the war a Federation of Gas Employers was formed to deal with the National Federation of General Workers. In 1919 the relationship was formalized by the constitution of a Joint Industrial Council, whose chairman was Sir David Milne-Watson of the London Gas Light and Coke Company, to whom should be given the main credit for persuading the employers to agree to permanent collective bargaining.

The gas industry has provided the most fertile ground in this country for profit-sharing and co-partnership schemes. Many of these have operated in undertakings which have accepted the union and its right to bargain on the workers' behalf, but the union's attitude to them has been strongly influenced by the use to which they have been put by other undertakings. The reaction of the South Metropolitan Gas Company to the union successes of 1889 was to set up such a scheme with the intention of excluding the union and using the co-partners' committee as the spokesmen of the workers in all matters — in brief, a company union. The Company required co-partners to sign individual contracts of service which were 'inconsistent with collective bargaining'.[1] The union was already weakened amongst the employees of the South Metropolitan by the failure of a strike against the reintroduction of the twelve-hour day, and it failed then and for many years afterwards to make headway against the co-partners' committee. Most of the private undertakings south of the Thames followed this lead. Accordingly the strength of the J.I.C. was in North London, and in the municipal undertakings which predominated in the midlands, the north and in Scotland. The South Metropolitan and the companies which followed its lead refused to recognize the union in any way, although at least some of them paid

[1] Webbs, op. cit. p. 403.

wages and provided conditions of employment equal to those settled by the J.I.C.

Wages and Conditions

The great majority of the workers in the industry are on time-rates. In some of the larger undertakings those operations which are suitable, such as unloading coal, purification work, boiler cleaning and demolishing retorts, are performed on piece-work. Otherwise gas workers must rely on shift work, week-end work and overtime for increasing their earnings above their base rates. Their earnings are, therefore, determined by changes in the minimum rate of labourers, by the differential rates carried by more responsible or onerous jobs and by the agreement on conditions which lays down rates for overtime, week-end and holiday work.

During the 1914-18 war the national advances of the Committee on Production (and its special award of 12½ per cent on 1914 base rates to time workers and of 7½ per cent to piece workers) had been applied to the gas industry, and these were continued by the J.I.C. when war-time wage legislation came to an end. The settlement of the rates to which national variations were to apply was left to eleven regional councils. Some of them established a full set of rates to cover all the important grades. Others did little more than settle rates for labourers, stokers and gas fitters, and left the individual undertakings to add rates for other classes as they saw fit. In 1920 the J.I.C. agreed that, rather than grant a general increase in pay, which the employers felt the smaller undertakings could not stand, the regional councils should be instructed to grade undertakings into categories serving industrial, commercial, residential, agricultural and rural districts, with a difference of ½d. an hour between each category. The grading was left entirely to the regions, many of which found annual output of gas the most convenient yardstick. The basic wage of the gasworker thus depended on the rate fixed for his job, the category of his undertaking, and on national wage variations.

The J.I.C. also undertook in its first years to settle the normal working week and overtime, week-end and holiday payments, and in its second year agreed on a week's holiday with pay for all workers. All national and regional agreements, however, included a 'better conditions' clause under which undertakings were to continue to observe any practices which were more favourable to the workers than the clauses of the agreements, and to maintain any differentials above the rates of the regional councils. Besides this it was understood at the beginning that the various undertakings could improve on the terms of national and regional agreements if they wished, and could come to an agreement with the union for this purpose.

In 1921 the industry was hit by the general trade depression and the rapid fall of prices which accompanied it. Wages were twice reduced by 3s. for dayworkers and 3s. 6d. for shift-workers ($+12\frac{1}{2}$ per cent or $7\frac{1}{2}$ per cent) and then, in October, the J.I.C. agreed to regulate variations of wages by the cost of living index, a movement of 6 points to correspond to $\frac{1}{2}$d. an hour (plus percentages). Prices and wages continued their rapid decline through the following year. By the summer the gas labourer had lost 26s. a week in eighteen months, and, the unions claimed, had fallen from the highest to the lowest position within the public utility services. In July the unions persuaded the employers to make 7 points correspond to $\frac{1}{2}$d. an hour, but by this time prices were steadying. In June, 1923, another reduction of $\frac{1}{2}$d. fell due, but the employers agreed to postpone it until September, and thereafter to stabilize wages for six months. In the autumn, however, the cost of living took an upward turn and the employers agreed to waive the stabiliza-tion agreement and to grant a $\frac{1}{2}$d. increase to which, without the agreement, the unions could have laid claim. At the same time the employers revealed their view of the authority of the J.I.C. by expelling from their federation several undertakings which had agreed with the union not to apply the September reduction.

In 1924 trade improved, and the unions urged the extreme discontent of their members to persuade the employers to grant a further modification of the application of the sliding-scale which brought them another $\frac{1}{2}$d. by the end of the year. Thereafter the trend of the index was downwards, and despite claims for 12s. a week, demands for arbitration and a national petition, the best the unions could do was to agree from year to year to a stabilization of wages, on each occasion reminded by the employers of the reductions which were due. As the country began to move towards another trade depression, the employers suggested that they might not be able to maintain their generosity in the regions most hit by the decline of basic exporting industries, and criticized the 'anomaly' of the 'better conditions clauses' which they felt should not apply to workers who were new entrants to the industry.

In June, 1930, the employers refused to agree to further stabilization and demanded a reduction. The unions kept talking and were able to protract the discussions until the following November, when the employers stated their intention of abandoning the J.I.C. and imposing cuts unless agreement was reached on their proposals. They could point to falling profits, further falls in the cost of living, and widespread wage-cuts in other industries. They refused the unions' request to leave the matter to the regions, but finally agreed to apply cuts of 1d. an hour in the three hardest hit regions and of ½d. an hour in three other regions, with no reductions elsewhere. The percentage additions were to be abandoned in all future variations, and the sliding-scale agreement was formally ended. It had previously been agreed that, under the stabilization agreement, the regions would only consider claims for sections of workers in any undertaking if there was an alteration of job, an anomaly could be demonstrated, or local conditions changed, and the J.I.C. now ruled that the regions had not the power to deal with claims for a restoration of these new cuts.

In 1930 the N.U.G.M.W. put up strong opposition to the unemployment which it expected to follow from the passage of a bill to allow Glasgow Corporation to buy bulk gas, and the union was able to secure an agreement on compensation for those who should be dismissed as a result of the scheme. In June of the same year the J.I.C. made a general arrangement for compensation of those dismissed as a result of schemes of rationalization, under which between one and two weeks' pay, according to age, would be granted for each year of service.

The workers' side took great pride in this agreement, which was far in advance of the practice of most other industries.

As unemployment figures slowly fell the union began to press for a restoration of cuts. It was the turn of the employers to stonewall. In October, 1934, partial restoration was granted in four regions. In one South Wales undertaking workers struck unofficially for a restoration of their 1d. cut, and when the matter was submitted to the J.I.C. for settlement, the exact equivalent was awarded as a 16s. monthly bonus rather than allow a formal local variation of a national agreement.

Next year the workers' side presented a detailed case for a 1d. an hour increase, referring to profit increases and to the higher rates paid by the electricity industry. The employers returned with an even more fully elaborated reply. The N.U.G.M.W. thereupon began a large-scale recruiting campaign in the industry, with great success in North London, where the decreases under the sliding-scale in the early twenties had severely reduced union membership. Next year a claim was presented on the grounds that the workers were extremely dissatisfied with lengthy negotiations and were threatening to break away from the J.I.C., and that the union's membership and strength had greatly increased. The employers expressed disappointment that their case had not been answered, but a ½d. an hour increase was agreed in July 1936.

In 1937 the argument returned to statistics. The employers argued that profit figures were misleading, and that sales *per capita* were falling, so that costs were rising. Nevertheless a further increase was agreed. At the same time the employers again attacked the 'better conditions clauses'. It was agreed that each region should set up a sub-committee to consider the application of these clauses and refer any disagreements to the J.I.C. In 1938 claims were presented to two regional councils for better overtime and holiday conditions. The employers made the strongest objection to this, insisting that 'where a matter has been settled nationally it could only be varied by the national body'.

There was a series of advances during the war, two in 1940, two in 1941, and one in each year after that. On almost every occasion the employers were pushed up from their first offer. Reference was made several times to what had been done in the electricity supply industry. The early claims were based on rising prices, but as the cost of living was stabilized more was heard of the discontent of the workers and the attraction of rising wages in the armaments industry. In 1942 the workers' side said:

'They had asked for an increase of 5s. a week — not merely on what one would regard as the cost of living basis, as it was felt that was outmoded, but the people of this country were being urged to save their money and get something laid by for what might happen in the period after the war, and the gas-worker was as much entitled to have that reserve as anyone else.'

Two difficulties cropped up in many of the war-time negotiations. The first was the controls exercised over the industry, under the Acts governing each statutory undertaking, under the general legislation of pre-war years, and under war-time orders. The employers made frequent reference to the obstacles thus put in the way of meeting wage increases, and the workers' side as frequently offered to join them in approaches to the government for relief. The second was the variation in prosperity due to evacuation of coastal areas, and the vast expansion of industry in the midlands and the north. The unions firmly refused to consider any relief in wages or working conditions for the areas which suffered most, and the employers concurred. In the autumn of 1941, however, the workers' side asked for reconsideration of the increase of $\frac{3}{4}$d. an hour granted in September, on the grounds of great discontent with the agreement, and of a resolution passed by the Midland Regional Council (including the employers' representatives) 'to the effect that in their opinion a further advance of $\frac{3}{4}$d. an hour and 6d. a shift should be granted forthwith in the Midland Area.' The employers said it would be most undignified to go back on the decision; the Midland Council passed a resolution confirming their loyalty to the J.I.C.; and the workers' side agreed to uphold the J.I.C.'s original agreement, but hoped that in future employers would not give their men to understand that more should have been awarded than the union had accepted. In 1943 two undertakings were expelled for a time in the Manchester Region for 'conceding unauthorized advances'. Despite this a number of undertakings there and in the midlands did grant unauthorized increases as a means of attracting labour, or retaining it, and managed to avoid a penalty. The union could not complain too loudly of breaches of the agreement in favour of its members.

In the months after the war there were unofficial strikes in several parts of the country. Troops had to be used in gasworks — not because of the disputes, but to meet the acute labour shortages. An increase of 1½d. an hour came in September 1945. In December the J.I.C.'s 'Terms and Conditions of Employment Committee' recommended a change from a 7-shift to a 6-shift week, improvement in overtime rates, and a national sick-pay scheme. The 6-shift week was to operate from April 1946. In 1946 the industry's largest increase, of 2d. an hour, was agreed, and the following March a reduction of hours to forty-four a week came into effect. Agreement was also reached on twelve days' paid holiday. In these negotiations again a good deal was heard of what was being done in the electricity supply industry.

In April 1948 a further increase was agreed, soon after the publication of the White Paper on 'Personal Incomes, Costs and Prices' and after 'consideration' had been given to it. This also was in line with the electricity supply and other public utility industries. Thereafter there was a lull. The industry was waiting to see what nationalization would bring forth. Vesting-day was to be May 1st, 1949.

Other Work of the Joint Industrial Council

From the beginning the J.I.C. took the view that its functions included more than the settlement of wages and conditions; and indeed, the constitutions of all J.I.C.s directs attention to matters other than these. In its second year the Council's representatives took part in the work of a committee set up to make proposals for training in the industry, and both the national and regional councils have given a good deal of

attention to gas-fitters' training and apprenticeship schemes.
The main subject of joint concern has been the prosperity
of the industry. The gas industry has had to meet the competition of the younger and more rapidly developing electricity
supply industry, with its far lower proportion of labour costs
to total costs. It is generally agreed that the industry has faced
that competition successfully, increasing its total output,
exploring possibilities of development in by-products and
residuals, improving its internal efficiency, and increasing the
attractiveness of its equipment and services to its consumers.
The union has left no doubt about its sympathies in the matter.
In 1929 and 1930 it acted with the employers in seeking amendments to the Gas Bill before Parliament. In the Journal, Will
Thorne urged most strongly the case for giving the industry
more chance to compete, and the union's M.P.s and Councillors were instructed to protest against the use of imported
bitumen for road-making. Joint protests with the employers
were made against restrictions on the use of gas in housing
schemes of the L.C.C. and other local authorities. Further
joint action of this sort continued up to the war. At the outbreak of the war the Lancashire district secretary of the
N.U.G.M.W. told the union Executive that the Lancashire
employers were quite unable to grant increases, although they
held them to be justified, and suggested that the only hope for
wages lay in new methods of production. But the war diverted
attention from that problem.

During the war there was joint action on A.R.P., fire-
watching and roof-spotting, on the economic difficulties of the
industry, and especially on the industry's labour shortage.
Joint representations were made to the Ministry of Labour, and
both sides sat on the Gas Labour Supply Committee. Joint
evidence was offered to the Heyworth Committee on the Gas
Industry. In 1943 the J.I.C. took exception to a memorandum
submitted by the Standing Joint Committee of Working
Women's Organizations to the Central Housing Advisory
Committee of the Ministry of Health on Design of Dwellings,
which it thought an 'extremely partial and pro-electric document'. As an affiliated body, the N.U.G.M.W. made

vigorous protest, and succeeded in having the memorandum reworded. Charles Dukes referred to the right of the tenant to 'absolute freedom of choice' of fuels. The workers' side formed a small Standing Committee 'to assist the Employers in the task of educating the public as to the importance of the Gas Industry and the fact that it was essential to the National Interest'.

The J.I.C. has had to give frequent attention, as a conciliating or arbitrating body, to problems in the undertakings or in the regions. As we have seen the employers generally tried to achieve a standardization of practice. The workers' side were successful in maintaining the right of the regions to settle the grading of undertakings within each region, without reference to the J.I.C., and there was a gradual process of adjustment upwards over the whole period. In some of the local disputes which have come before the J.I.C. since 1940, unions outside the J.I.C. have been concerned. But more of that later.

The staple work of the regions was concerned with grading classes of worker and grading establishments, with claims for re-grading and with the settlement of local disputes. [The J.I.C. was concerned with such disputes only when the regional council failed to reach agreement.] The unions from time to time tried to establish in some regions concessions which the J.I.C. could not accept, and the employers succeeded in severely limiting advance by this method. During the war the regions were concerned with the application of national decisions on A.R.P. and on labour supply, and with a host of other matters like food and clothes rationing, lodging allowances, the interpretation of Essential Work Orders, and the incidence of P.A.Y.E. on labourers who worked as stokers for part of the year.

In 1921 the J.I.C. drew up a model constitution for Works Councils, but not many were set up, and the union's view was that the type of representative chosen, and the attempts of the employers to get the Councils to discuss matters which should have been settled with the union, such as wage-rates, made them appear very like Co-partnership Committees. Consequently the few did not prosper. It was not until the development of a few Joint Production Committees or similar bodies in some of the larger works during the war that there were any local joint bodies of which the union could approve. For this reason, although in most municipal undertakings a local shop or collecting steward or branch secretary might act as the workers' spokesman on union matters, and, if acceptable to the management, deal with them, and although in 1937 the union's works representatives were recognized in North London, the N.U.G.M.W. as far as possible kept matters in the hands of the district officers. Certainly it tried to ensure that only its officers should discuss with undertakings, after consultation with the branch, matters affecting wages or conditions of employment.

The Workers' Side

During the first world war and at the outset of the J.I.C. many of the unions affiliated to the General Workers' Federation were directly interested in the gas industry, but amalgamation has reduced the constituent unions of the workers' side to two — the N.U.G.M.W. and the T. & G.W.U. The Birmingham Gasworkers and the M.E.A. brought considerable numbers of gasworkers into the former, and in the late 'twenties the amalgamation of the Workers' Union and the National Union of Enginemen, Firemen, Mechanics and Electrical Workers with the T.&G.W.U. completed the unification. The N.U.E.F.M.E.W. has retained its identity as the 'Power Group' of the T.&G.W.U. and is affiliated separately to the J.I.C., but that does not imply that it pursues an independent policy.

The T.&G.W.U. recognizes the numerical superiority of the N.U.G.M.W. in the industry, and is content to be left in control of the undertakings scattered over each region which have traditionally 'belonged' to it. Its officers deal with the complaints of its members in those undertakings, and when they fail to settle them locally, take them up to the region or to the J.I.C. Then, however, they normally work through the workers' side secretary, who is an officer of the N.U.G.M.W. in all regions but one. If the matter is of general concern, it is considered by the whole of the workers' side, on which the

N.U.G.M.W. has a majority in all the regions. Occasionally, as in other industries, there may be some local poaching by branches or junior officers, but this is never serious, and there is no record of major conflict between the two unions in this industry.

As we have seen, during the 'twenties and early 'thirties, the membership of the N.U.G.M.W. was strong only in the municipal undertakings of the midlands and the north, South Wales and Scotland. It barely included half the manual workers in the industry as a whole. However, it retained enough members in the company areas to keep the J.I.C. machinery in motion, and no other union was able to take advantage of its weakness. From 1935 it carried on its very successful recruiting campaign in North London, and strengthened its grip elsewhere. In the years since 1945 the citadels of non-unionism south of the Thames were stormed. By 1950 the gas membership of the union's Southern district had increased from three or four thousand to a total roughly four times as large. Undertaking after undertaking was persuaded to recognize the union, and before vesting-day even the South Metropolitan was dealing with the union's officers as well as its Co-partners' Committee.

The union's General Secretary is always Chairman of the workers' side of the National Council, and the National Officer dealing with gas is the secretary. A number of district officers (sometimes including the district secretary) sit on each regional council, with the appropriate district officer as secretary. Accordingly the union has little difficulty in controlling the work of the J.I.C. machinery. Decisions have normally been left to the workers' sides. From time to time the districts or Head Office may call a conference of branch or district representatives to discuss particular problems and discover the feeling of the members, and, as we have seen, London and Birmingham hold regular meetings for this purpose. In the 'twenties use was made of an *ad hoc* meeting of the workers' side and two executive representatives from each union to give full authority to policy decisions, but there seemed little purpose in it, and during the troubles of 1930-31 and of 1935-36, when the districts were pressing very hard for action, and the General Secretary was holding back from presenting a claim until he could be sure of greatly improved membership figures, the main decisions were taken by the workers' side or by the National Executive. At Congress questions have frequently been raised on the section of the General Secretary's report dealing with the gas industry, but these have been for information on particular points, except in the years since the war, when Congress has debated several resolutions on topics connected with the nationalization of the industry. In 1939 the London gasworkers, encouraged by the success of their recruiting campaign, were pressing for a 'Gasworkers' Charter' and for a national conference of gas representatives to draw up a scheme for uniform wages and conditions. The General Secretary scoffed at a 'Charter', saying that the difficulty was not to draw up a Charter but to get the employers to accept any of its clauses, and suggested the workers did better by avoiding too much uniformity over the whole country. Tom Williamson, then the National Officer dealing with the industry, added that some undertakings were paying as much as ten shillings above the agreed rates, and any demands of this sort would have the 'better conditions clauses' thrown back at them.

The N.U.G.M.W. is a member of the National Federation of Building Trade Operatives, and as such may not compete with the building craft unions. Consequently the building craftsmen in the Gas Industry are covered by a separate agreement between the Amalgamated Union of Building Trade Workers (bricklayers and masons) and the Employers' Federation, which has been outside the purview of the J.I.C. In 1927 the A.E.U. began to show some interest in its fitters in the industry, but since it had just opened its doors to unskilled workers, the N.U.G.M.W. was opposed to any agreement and wanted to feel sure that the A.E.U. would not be allowed to deal with craftsmen's mates. The matter was, therefore, left for local arrangement. In 1947, however, it was taken up by the Confederation of Shipbuilding and Engineering Unions, of which the N.U.G.M.W. is a member, and which the A.E.U. had recently joined. A general agreement covering engineering craftsmen in the industry was drawn up. The workers' side of the J.I.C. still wished to keep craftsmen's mates within the field of its authority, so that these were excluded from that agreement, and the regional councils continued to lay down rates for that grade. In some areas, particularly South London, the N.U.G.M.W. includes the engineering craftsmen whose wages and conditions are settled by the confederation agreement. Here it organizes not only many electricians and fitters, but even boilermakers, and it was noticeable that in what was probably the major strike in the industry since the J.I.C. was set up, the strike of gas craftsmen in North London in the autumn of 1950,[1] the strikers received very little support from South London.

The National Union of Corporation Workers (now N.U.P.E.) were admitted as members of the Scottish regional council in the early 'twenties because of their just claim to represent the workers in one or two undertakings. Their representative was speedily ejected when the union called a strike without submitting the dispute to the J.I.C. Little more was heard of the union in the industry until the second world war, when it tried to achieve recognition under S.R.&O. 1305 by submitting to the Ministry of Labour 'disputes' in undertakings in Scotland and the north of England in which it could claim some members. The Minister invariably referred these disputes to the J.I.C., whose Emergency Committee heard the parties, and in most instances rejected N.U.P.E.'s case. There is nothing to be surprised at in this, for the content of the claims seemed to be selected more for the purpose of creating a 'dispute' than with an eye on what was likely to be granted. These tactics did N.U.P.E. very little good in the industry. It retained, for a while, a precarious hold in a few scattered undertakings, but in 1951 decided to withdraw from both the gas and electricity industries.

The same tactics were used by National Gasfitters and Allied

---

[1] This unofficial strike was notorious for the arrest of its leaders on a charge under the 1875 Conspiracy and Protection of Property Act, and their subsequent conviction under the 1940 Conditions of Employment and National Arbitration Order. In an unofficial strike at the beginning of the same year at Tottenham, in North London, the members of the N.U.G.M.W. came out with the craftsmen when they struck against their treatment at the hands of a manager, but here the antipathy, which was the overt cause of the strike, was generally shared.

Workers' Trade Union, a small union of gasfitters in the midlands, with even less success. At the end of the war this union
changed its name to the Gas Industrial Union, and with the
aid of an ex-official of the N.U.G.M.W., recently dismissed
from his post in the Birmingham district,[1] made a determined
attempt to expand at the expense of the N.U.G.M.W. For
a while it achieved some success, aided by the undoubted
discontent of gasworkers at that time, but its drive was
weakened by the failure of a 'sit-down' strike in Birmingham,
and of an attempt to attract some support from the militant
London gasworkers. The series of wage-increases and improvements in conditions in 1947 — all the main points, in
fact, of the new union's demands — broke it. In January 1948,
the N.U.G.M.W. Journal reported that the Birmingham gasfitters had joined the union *en bloc*.

Gasfitting has been a source of constant trouble with the
Plumbers' Union. Insofar as the gas industry employs fully-
fledged plumbers for works maintenance, and not as gasfitters,
the position is clear. The N.U.G.M.W. recognizes the authority
of the craft union, and rates are now covered by the Confederation agreement. The N.U.G.M.W. has always claimed to deal
with gasfitters, however, through the J.I.C. machinery, in
which the Plumbers (who also claimed the right to organize
gasfitters) have no part. Besides this the jobs carried out by
plumbers and gasfitters are similar enough for demarcation
disputes to arise. In the 'twenties, disputes arising from the
non-recognition of the Plumbers' Union, or from demarcation
difficulties, demanded the attention of the Union's Executive
more frequently than any other aspect of the gas industry. The
plumbers tried direct approach to the N.U.G.M.W., appealed
to the J.I.C., and called in the Building Operatives' Federation
(which arranged further meetings) but to no avail. The
N.U.G.M.W. stuck by its claim to deal alone with gasfitters.
The difficulty became acute again in Scotland after vesting-day,
when the plumbers came out in a prolonged strike against the
refusal of the new Scottish Area Board to recognize them. The
Scottish problem seems to have been aggravated by the practice

[1] See p. 82.

of some of the undertakings there which have chosen to recruit surplus plumbers as gasfitters, rather than to train gasfitters. The membership of the Plumbers' Union amongst the latter group was, therefore, considerable. The strike, however, failed.

Gas Staffs

The union has always claimed the right to organize clerical and administrative workers in the industry. In the majority of municipal undertakings it has never made great headway against the National and Local Government Officers Association, and in the south, before the war, it was naturally even less able to recruit salaried workers than manual workers, particularly in anti-union undertakings. During the war, however, it began to make some headway in London and in 1944 the London district claimed that the London Regional Council should set up machinery for dealing with the wages and conditions of salaried workers. The employers replied that the staff associations which existed in the larger private undertakings were more representative and adequate for the purpose. The union regarded these associations as no better than company unions. Soon afterwards several members of the associations, together with one or two ex-members of the N.U.G.M.W., brought the staff associations together into a British Gas Staffs Association, and in doing so met no opposition from the employers. The Association claimed to be entirely independent of the employers, and its membership amongst salaried workers in the London area dwarfed that of the N.U.G.M.W. Feeling in London ran high and in 1946 the district claimed great credit for having achieved the reinstatement of a telephone superintendent in North London by calling attention to the feeling of the manual workers and the likelihood that they would strike on her behalf. It was felt that she had been victimized for trade union activity.

In 1947 the B.G.S.A. and N.A.L.G.O. approached the employers to set up a Council for salaried staffs. N.A.L.G.O. was concerned about the future of its members who would cease, on nationalization, to be covered by the agreements for local authority staffs. The employers agreed, and the N.U.G.M.W.

and the T.&G.W.U. decided to claim representation rather than be left without means of acting on behalf of their members in these grades. The London gasworkers protested most strongly against association with the B.G.S.A. in any form. But their objections were overruled. The new Council, which was later joined by other unions catering for groups of staff workers, has set up Regional Councils and has proceeded with the difficult task of getting some uniformity in the salary scales and conditions of employment for salaried workers in the industry. The B.G.S.A. has continued to stress its independence, especially since nationalization, and the unions have worked together as best they could.

The new Council created difficulties for 'intermediate grades' of such workers as meter readers and collectors, or foremen, who had been treated as manual workers in some undertakings and as salaried workers elsewhere, or whose terms of employment had included clauses drawn from each class. The advantages did not all lie in the one direction. Some 'manuals' were determined to keep their position rather than suffer loss, as they saw it, by becoming salaried workers, and some salaried workers thought they would lose from being classed with the manuals. Besides this some keen trade unionists felt they should remain under the manual workers' Council. The only way to cope with the difficulty was to set up national and regional joint committees with representatives from both councils. In 1950 the national Council produced sets of salary scales for these grades, and alternative sets of conditions which would allow each 'intermediate' group to choose whichever seemed to suit it best. The Southern Area, however, chose not to make use of these provisions, but to grade all workers either as 'staff' or 'manual'.

Nationalization

On vesting-day the Employers' Federation was replaced by the new British Gas Council. Compared with the National Coal Board, the Council is a quasi-federal body. Its members, apart from the chairman and his deputy, are the Chairmen of the Area Gas Boards, which are separate statutory bodies, and in many respects independent of the Council's control. Amongst its limited functions, however, the Council has the duty of setting up machinery for settling wages and conditions of employment with the unions. The constitution of the J.I.C. has been slightly revised, but the only important change is that the employers' side is now the Gas Council. The assets of the industry have been vested in the Area Boards who have the responsibility for producing gas, and these boards have become the employers in the regions. The boundaries of the new Areas are very different from the old regions, and the new Area Councils had to be reconstituted to meet this revision. The immediate result was to include workers whose wages had previously been fixed at different levels by different regional councils under the authority of one Area Council. As a temporary measure it was agreed that no employee should suffer by such a transfer, and that those transferred should get the advantage of any increases in pay or better conditions agreed by the new councils. This could be but a stop-gap, and the pressure for radical action was increased by the knowledge that most of the other nationalized industries, and the local authorities 'non-trading' Council, had by this time agreed on national grading systems under which the rate for each grade of worker is fixed nationally.

The difficulties of reaching an agreement were complicated by hostility within the union, influenced by experience in the electricity and 'non-trading' industries, and by the government's wages policy, towards the complete centralization of collective bargaining.

It was not until the summer of 1950 that the outcome of negotiations was announced. The J.I.C. had decided to settle two labourers' rates, with a higher rate for its London area, which is wider than the areas covered by the special London rates of other industries, and in fact includes one-third of all gasworkers. Allocation of the various undertakings between the two new grades was left to the Area Councils, which had also the responsibility for settling the additional rates to be paid to all other grades. The Area Councils were to settle rates for all grades in all undertakings, instead of for the few important grades as before, and any workers already receiving more than the new rate were to keep their old rate as a personal right; but it was to be merged in future increases. The 'better conditions clauses' were at an end.

The Area Councils started on their task. The new rates gave a considerable increase to most grades in most parts of the country. Difficulties there were. One undertaking might find that the rates fixed by the Area Council did not suit the allocation of duties which it thought best fitted to its conditions. Its normal scheme of promotion might be upset by a common rating for two grades previously on different rates because the undertaking had used a differential of ½d. or 1d. an hour to attract labour from the one grade to the other whose work seemed more responsible or more arduous. But it can safely be said that these difficulties have been far less than those caused by national grading in electricity supply or 'non-trading'. The Areas have retained flexibility to meet a number of difficulties. For instance, the rates for most grades in the new southern area are now, as in the past, rather below those of most other areas, but the Southern Council has been able to fix a relatively high rate for its gasfitters to meet the competition of the new oil-refineries, which have a considerable need for pipe-fitters.

The union claims that the new wages structure is a vast improvement, which only nationalization could have made possible. Small undertakings can no longer claim that, squeezed between statutory price regulation and high costs, they must pay wages considerably below the large undertakings, for the financial unit is now the Area Board. For the time being two grades remain, but the second applies only in small undertakings in rural areas.

Since the new scheme came into force there have been further national advances in wages, roughly in line with other industries. In 1952 a new classification scheme for gasfitters was announced. Under it there were only two grades of gasfitters, and their rates were to be fixed nationally, not by the Area Councils. The National Officer responsible told the 1952 Congress that, as a result of this scheme 'gasfitters in the industry recognize that for the first time they have got a rate that stands on a par with any craft carried on anywhere in industry today.'

The Gas Council, like the boards of other nationalized industries, has been charged with the duty of setting up machinery for consulting with the representatives of its workers on matters not included in national agreements which are of concern to them — welfare, education and efficiency. Both sides have decided that this can best be done through the national and regional councils. The N.U.G.M.W. had already had experience of separate hierarchies of committees for different purposes in the British Electricity Authority's undertakings, and preferred a simpler scheme. Both sides felt, however, that it was necessary to set up Works Committees to deal with these matters in the undertakings. Agreement on a model constitution for these Committees was long delayed. The Gas Council wished to have membership of them open to all its employees. The union, very naturally in view of its previous experience, has insisted that only union members should be eligible for nomination. Since non-unionists are a small minority in the industry, and most other nationalized industries have granted this point, its case was very strong, and was finally accepted. A model constitution for Works Committees was finally approved early in 1951, and the Area Councils arranged for the Committees to be set up.

Meanwhile nationalization had raised in every undertaking a large number of problems in which joint action was called for. The war-time production or consultative committees continued to act where they existed, and one area set up its own provisional Works Committees. In other areas it was arranged that, pending an agreed constitution, the managements should meet collecting stewards or shop stewards to settle minor matters. At the 1950 Congress London representatives voiced considerable complaint about the degree of recognition granted to the representatives of the union's staff members by the North Thames Gas Board. The General Secretary promised that the Executive would look into the matter. Despite such shortcomings it could safely be said that there was, even before the Works Committees were set up, far more industrial democracy in the individual undertakings of the industry than at any previous period.

The unions insisted most strongly that nationalization should end co-partnership. After strong representations had been made the Act provided for the winding-up of these schemes. Negotiations with the interested parties took a long time, but finally an agreement was signed in February, 1951. In the Parliamentary debates on the bill Conservatives championed co-partnership, which they (and the Liberals) seemed to think the panacea to all problems of industrial relations. Union feeling on the matter was, however, very strong. The maintenance of the old functions of the Co-partners' Committees would have been incompatible with the setting up of Works Committees. There seems little doubt that the majority of the co-partners were on the side of the unions, partly for these reasons and partly because most of them preferred a relatively large lump sum in settlement to their present small annual payments.

The main criticisms of nationalization voiced within the union have come from the London district. Its representatives at Congress thought nationalization should have come earlier, and strongly criticized appointments to the boards, to consultative councils and to higher administrative posts within the industry. Their speeches have shown that their criticism is not unrelated to their experience with the B.G.S.A. On one occasion the district chairman — a gasworker — referred to 'Gas Light and Cokization' rather than 'Nationalization'. The official policy of the union has radically changed, from 'workers' control' in the early 'thirties to support for the independent public board approved by the T.U.C. in 1944, but it has shown some sympathy with London's resolutions. Tom Williamson said at the 1947 Congress that he thought gas nationalization should have preceded transport nationalization, and in 1949 and 1950 deflected resolutions demanding direct representation of the workers on Area Boards by stating that the T.U.C. General Council itself was not satisfied and had the matter under review. The supporters of these resolutions cannot have derived much comfort from the T.U.C. General Council's report to the T.U.C. of 1950, which roughly reaffirmed the decision of 1944.

Conclusion

It is widely agreed that the industrial relations of the gas industry have been well above the average in British industry. This has often been attributed to its co-partnership and profit-sharing schemes, but relations have been good in those sections of the industry which have preferred trade union negotiations to the use of co-partnership committees as anti-trade union devices, and the former method has now won its victory over the latter throughout the industry. The J.I.C. has an excellent record in freedom from disputes and in its ability to settle its differences without recourse to arbitration. As we have seen the most important strike of recent years has arisen from a group of workers who are outside the J.I.C. — the North London maintenance workers.

Part of the industry's success in avoiding arbitration should be attributed to the readiness of both sides to agree that wages and conditions in the gas industry must follow closely those of the electricity supply industry. In the summer of 1951 the labourers' rate in the great majority of gas undertakings (Grade 1) was the same as the labourers' rate in the electricity industry, and the two rates have remained in step since then. The N.U.G.M.W. has greater representation on the J.I.C. for that industry than any other single union, and many local authorities were, in the past, affiliated to both bodies. The more serious battles were fought there first, and the verdict usually accepted by the gas industry. But we must note that it is to the credit of both industries that over the last twelve years they have maintained their rate of earnings in relation to the national average far more successfully than other so-called 'sheltered industries' of the inter-war period — for instance, road passenger transport — and that the gas industry has succeeded in substantially reducing the gap between its earnings and those of the electricity supply industry, despite the competitive advantages of its younger rival.

We can hardly avoid the conclusion that the union's work in

the industry has been well done. It has shown itself extremely jealous of other unions, and has used all its power to keep them out. This, however, is an attitude common to all unions which 'control' a given industry, and its defence is that a large number of competing unions would not be able to serve the interests of the workers so well. The union has not tried to use the 'closed shop' in order to attain this end.[1]

The union has always supported nationalization in the past and it welcomed the Gas Act and did its best to aid the work of the new boards. Its members have made criticisms of nationalization, but they have shown themselves far less discontented than the workers of some of the other nationalized industries, and, so far, the running of the nationalized gas industry has attracted less general criticism than that of any other, except perhaps the Bank of England.

---

[1] In 1924 the union members at a Manchester undertaking took a ballot on strike action to enforce union membership. The employers objected strongly, and the strike was called off. At the 1948 Congress the General Secretary explained the union's official attitude: 'Yes, the policy of this Union is 100 per cent unionism . . . It has not been the policy of this Union to use force, by strike action, to enforce the closed shop. We believe in voluntary organization.'

CHAPTER III

LOCAL AUTHORITIES NON-TRADING SERVICES

The Joint Industrial Council

UP to 1914 bargaining between the several unions organizing local authority employees and the local authorities had been quite as random and piecemeal as in the gas industry. The awards of the Committee on Production during the war had a similar effect in extending trade union recognition and collective agreements, and in Lancashire and Cheshire many authorities grouped themselves together at the suggestion of officers of the Manchester City Corporation, in order to deal collectively with the unions. At the end of the war the idea of a more permanent and formal institution was canvassed, and a National Joint Council for the Non-Trading Services was set up at the same time as Councils for Gas, for Electricity Supply, for Water Supply and for Tramways. The main credit for the formation of this Council, and of the Electricity Supply Joint Council, must go to Manchester.

The boundaries of the four other industries, which included private undertakings, were fairly clearly defined. Non-Trading was a residuary legatee. The workers whose wages and conditions the new Council proposed to settle were engaged in a bewildering variety of occupations. Even the term 'Non-Trading' was strictly inapplicable, for some of the workers were engaged in trading services, for instance as baths' attendants, and at seaside resorts in a considerable number of services to holiday-makers for which charges were demanded. Perhaps the best description of the Council's coverage was that it aimed to deal with all unskilled manual workers employed by local authorities and not covered by other national joint councils. Even this is not exact; for the boundaries between salaried and manual staffs were ill-defined, and although engineering and building craftsmen were not included in the scope of the Council, some subsidiary councils dealt with craftsmen employed in road-making, such as paviors.

Although public authorities in this country have not suffered from the doctrine of the 'sovereign employer' which has bedevilled industrial relations of federal, state and local authorities in the U.S.A. by making normal collective agreements almost impossible, local authorities have shown a greater need to assert their independence in collective bargaining than have most private employers. This has had several consequences. Firstly, the coverage of the Council was at first far from complete Very many local authorities refused to join the associations for Municipal Corporations, Urban Districts, Rural Districts and County Councils, and the County Councils Association itself remained outside the J.I.C. until 1943. Secondly, there could be no question of national agreements. The maximum centralization which was found to be possible was to concentrate the settlement of wages and conditions upon subsidiary councils, which were known as Provincial Councils, and to reserve for the National Council only the task of dealing with disputes which the Provinces were unable to settle. Even so the payment of rates above those settled by the provincial schemes for grading jobs and for grading authorities — which were very similar to those of the gas industry — was probably even more common than in gas. Thirdly, the course of negotiations with the individual establishments has been rendered more difficult. In a private company it is usually safe to assume that whatever the manager promises or refuses, he will have the support of his board of directors. Whatever differences they may have they will settle in private, and not reveal either to the public or to the union. With local authorities the union officer can rarely have the same assurance. Behind the head of each department is a committee of the council, and they in turn are responsible to the full council. The councillors and the departmental chiefs are unlikely to have so close a common interest as the manager and the board of directors in a private company. The concern of the departmental chief, apart from his individual interests, should be with the efficiency of his department. The councillors share that interest, no doubt, but they are also elected politicians, and they must be concerned with political considerations, whether mundane — such as their own chances

and their party's chances of re-election — or idealistic — such
as their view of the public good, which may well differ from
the departmental chief's view of the good of his own department. The trade union officer knows that his interview with a
council officer is frequently only a preliminary skirmish. He
is likely to have to plead his case again before the committee,
unless the matter is of small account. He may not have a final
answer until the council has considered the matter. And it is
not unknown for the industrial relations of a department, or of
a whole council, to become intertwined with issues of local
party politics.

The close link between the trade unions and the Labour
Party is of importance here. Unions dealing with local authority
employees share with other sections of the Labour Movement
the desire for representation locally as well as in Parliament,
and have also recognized that it is important to have friends
in the Council Chamber. They, and the N.U.G.M.W. amongst
them, have devoted a part of their political funds to fighting
local elections, and, at least until recent years, have encouraged both lay members and full-time officers to stand for
local authority seats. By this means they not only have some
assurance that their claims will receive friendly consideration,
if not downright support, but may also have more knowledge
than usual of the attitudes and possible divisions of opinion on
the other side, and they can alter their approach to suit. There
is considerable evidence that this has been to their advantage.
The Journal of February 1935, attributed the early restoration
of depression cuts by some authorities directly to Labour local
election successes. Labour councils have encouraged union
membership and some of them, except during the years between
1927 and 1946 (when public authorities were by law prevented
from making trade union membership a condition of employment, have agreed to the 'closed shop'. Throughout the period
in which wages were settled by the Provincial Councils the
Northern district maintained the highest rates — even higher
than London's — and the only explanation can be the predominance of Labour on the local authorities of Durham and
Northumberland, for that district is not in general a high wage

area, and was one of the hardest-hit by the unemployment of inter-war years.

The link with the Labour Party has not, however, been without its difficulties. Labour Councillors — especially of Left-Wing opinions — have been known to think that they know better what is good for the workers than does the union. When an agreement is all but signed, and requires only the final approval of the council, a Labour representative may think of his electorate and demand an extra ½d. or 1d. an hour. At best this delays agreement, and at worst it undermines the confidence of the men in the union. They may think: 'If only the union had not been prepared to accept so little, we could have had more.' For instance, John McKenzie, writing in the Journal for February 1932, of the negotiations for a wage-cut of Glasgow City employees, stated that the Labour group had decided to oppose any cut. 'The policy adopted by the Labour Group of opposition was quite good during certain stages of the negotiation, and would have been very helpful if reconsidered when we reached the parting of the ways.' The council's Conditions of Service Committee finally decided on an all-round cut of 4s. a week. The union thereupon approached the 'Moderates' and suggested that this would bear unfairly on the lower paid. The Labour group still opposed any kind of cut. By playing on division of opinion amongst the controlling group of 'Moderates', the union was able to get agreement on a cut of 5 per cent (which reduced the weekly wage of the lowest paid worker by only 2s. 9d.). The continued opposition of the Labour group 'would have been . . . wise . . . if their opposition could have stopped the cut' — but it could not.

The increase in the number of Labour-controlled councils since 1945, and the advocacy of the policy of 'wage restraint' by the Labour Government and the Labour Party, did not help to smooth relations between the union and Labour councillors.

Union officers do not always find Labour councils easier to deal with than Conservative or 'Independent' councils; and as far as the interests of council workers are concerned, there is not now so great a difference between the two parties as there used to be. This experience has tended to strengthen the view held in some districts that the union officer does best to confine himself to industrial matters and not to get too involved in 'politics'.

We have already seen that the union has challenged the legislation which prevents the election of local authority employees to the councils of those authorities.[1] Since 1945 the union has tried to have the disqualification removed by legislation. The General Secretary explained to the 1948 Congress that both the Labour Party and the T.U.C. were sympathetic to the proposal, but that legislation must 'take its place in the queue'. Another difficulty for the union has been to know whether the law requiring councillors to declare their interest, and to withdraw from discussion and voting on proposals in which they have an interest, debars union officers from taking part in discussion on trade union negotiations. The matter has not been tested in the Courts although both the councils' associations and the unions have taken legal advice. In 1934 both sides received the advice they wished. After the war the union understood that the Association of Municipal Corporations had again sought an opinion, and that it had once more been favourable to the Association's view. The union's Executive, however, told an officer who asked for instructions to continue to speak and vote. It was for the council to act if it objected, and the union would support him before the Courts. The position remains obscure, and, despite this advice, at least some officers choose to be discreet in the matter.

Another difficulty peculiar to industrial relations in local government service arises from the power of the District Auditors to surcharge unreasonable expenditure. Rates of pay and conditions of service much above the average may clearly seem to the Auditor to be excessive. The matter was of considerable concern in the days of 'Poplarism'. Auditors have, however, shown themselves willing to accept not only any rates and conditions settled by the Provincial Councils, but also some higher rates. In the famous 'Poplar Wages Case' (*Roberts v. Hopwood, 1925*) the District Auditor surcharged, but surcharged

[1] See discussion of the case of *Rex v. Davies*, p. 110.

only wages which, in his opinion, were *unreasonably* in excess of the J.I.C. rates. The House of Lords upheld his right to do so.[1]

A notion which has occurred to more than one local authority is that all council-employed labourers, whether working in electricity, gas, or water-works, or in the non-trading services, should receive the same rate. It appeared unreasonable for one employer to pay several rates because it operated in several industries governed by different National Councils. In 1923 the Leeds City Council, under the influence of Sir Charles Wilson, averaged the rates of its various groups of labourers. The scheme was clearly subversive of bargaining by industry, and also calculated to undermine the influence of the union. Although it meant that the union had to take on the responsibility of putting some labourers on a lower rate than they had been receiving, the Leeds Council was forced to return to the nationally fixed rates in 1925.

The Workers' Side, Other Unions and New Councils

Amalgamation reduced the number of unions with a large interest in the 'Non-Trading' services to two — the N.U.G.M.W. and the T.&G.W.U. The N.U.G.M.W., having absorbed the M.E.A., was the more important of the two in this field (although its predominance was not so marked as in the gas industry). It took most of the seats on the workers' sides of the Joint Councils, and normally led in the making of policy. The T.&G.W.U. was content to be left to organize those councils to which it could lay claim, and the transport departments of a number of councils otherwise 'controlled' by the N.U.G.M.W.

The structure of the N.U.G.M.W. was well suited to the settlement of wages and conditions by the Provincial Councils. The strategy of negotiations was settled by the district secretaries and their committees. Only rarely were there matters of national concern to be considered by the union's Executive, and the 'Municipal' Department at Head Office gave as much

---

[1] The District Auditors' power extends to local authority trading services. In 1929 the union was constrained to enter into negotiations for the abolition of a 1s. bonus above South Wales' regional rates which had for many years been paid to the Margam and Aberavon gasworkers, when it was legally advised that the Auditor had the power to carry out his threat to surcharge.

attention to gas and electricity supply industries as to the non-trading services.

The strength of the unions was mainly in the L.C.C., in the County Boroughs and in the larger Non-County Boroughs. Organization amongst the employees of the counties and of the smaller boroughs and rural and urban district councils was weak except in heavily industrialized areas such as the north-east and South Wales. Over large tracts of rural England membership was almost nil. Amongst the main sufferers were county council roadmen, whose wages were traditionally fixed in relation to those of agricultural workers. Their lot was considerably worse than that of the borough road-worker and the union had been able to obtain improvements only for those roadmen employed by heavily industrialized counties (with considerable Labour representation) which had been persuaded to affiliate to their Provincial Councils. By 1941 these were Lancashire, Cheshire, Durham, Middlesex, Warwickshire and the West Riding of Yorkshire.

The 1929 Local Government Act transferred the Poor Law Authorities and their staffs (mainly hospital workers) to the County and County Borough Councils. The unions managed to persuade some authorities — such as Lancashire and Cheshire, the L.C.C. and Bristol — to bring these staffs within the scope of the Non-Trading Council, but over the country as a whole this protection was not granted, and union organization was too weak to enforce it.

The strategy of the workers' side was to keep pressing for the inclusion of all local authorities' employees outside the recognized trading services under the one Council. Throughout the 'twenties and the depression years they made but slow progress, and in 1938 they were seriously challenged by the National Union of Public Employees.

Up to 1934 N.U.P.E.[1] had struggled to maintain itself on the fringes of the various councils dealing with local authority employees. The T.&G.W.U. and the N.U.G.M.W. still regarded it as a 'breakaway' union, and in 1925 the N.U.G.M.W. Executive adopted a resolution from the Birmingham district

---

[1] Previously N.U.C.W. See p. 18.

demanding that it 'take such steps as are necessary to refuse to allow our members to sit in conference with any members or officials connected with the N.U.C.W. as we are of the opinion that the Union referred to is simply a dividing and poaching Society'. Despite this attitude N.U.P.E. had managed to hold together a national organization and in 1933 claimed some 12,000 members. It was represented on the National Council and some of the Provincial Councils. In 1934, the union chose a new General Secretary, Bryn Roberts, an ex-miner, who determined to challenge the two general unions, and to do so not so much by assaulting their main citadels of strength, as by organizing in the areas in which they were weak, in the smaller authorities and the counties.

The plan was wise, it was applied with energy (even if some of the methods used might be criticized), and the times were propitious. In 1934 trade union membership began to rise after thirteen years of almost uninterrupted decline. Bryn Roberts was off the mark before the general unions,[1] and, since it was their policy to ignore N.U.P.E. they did not take his efforts seriously until too late. N.U.P.E.'s membership figures mounted rapidly. From 15,000 in 1934, they rose to 30,000 in 1936 and 50,000 in 1939. Having already made a name for himself as a speaker at the T.U.C., Bryn Roberts proposed to the Blackpool Congress of that body in 1938 that it should urge the establishment of 'national machinery in accordance with the main principles of the 1938 Road Haulage Wages (No. 2) Bill'[2] for County Council Employees. He had the support of the unions of hospital workers, but was opposed by spokesmen of the N.U.G.M.W. and the T.&G.W.U., who maintained that the present machinery was adequate for the job, if the trade unionists sitting on County Councils would make sufficient effort to bring their authorities to use it. The resolution was defeated, but N.U.P.E. maintained its efforts, and its rate of recruitment.

The rates and conditions of county roadmen have always

---

[1] It must be remembered that the N.U.G.M.W. was at this time engaged in a large-scale internal reorganization. See pp. 72-75.

[2] This bill proposed a joint wage-fixing authority with powers roughly the same as of a trade board. It was passed.

been closely related to those of agricultural workers, for both types of employment draw on the same labour force. In 1940 Ernest Bevin, soon after his appointment as Minister of Labour, decided that the supply of agricultural labour must be safeguarded by an Act amending the Agricultural Wages (Regulation) Act, 1924, to require the Central Agricultural Wages Board to fix a national minimum wage, below which the rates fixed by the County Committees must not fall. This Act was bound to affect the supply of county roadmen, and in the same year he made public his view that 'the wages of county roadmen, as of other local authority employees, should be fixed for the whole country on an ordered basis'. Discussion between the Non-Trading J.I.C. and the County Councils' Association started almost immediately, and in July 1941, the National Joint Council for County Council Roadmen was set up.[1] The new Council settled wages for groups of counties, which gave considerable advances to many roadmen. In the following year N.U.P.E. claimed a further success when the Joint Council for Land Drainage Employees was set up, although some workers previously on 'Non-Trading' rates lost thereby, and the general unions' policy of bringing all such workers under the main Council might in the long run have yielded better results.

Although N.U.P.E. had concentrated its main drive on county council roadmen, its membership expanded also amongst the employees of local authorities affiliated to the Non-Trading J.I.C. It argued that its exclusion from some of the Non-Trading Councils became more anomalous each year. The N.U.G.M.W. decided that the membership of the provincial councils was a matter for the districts to settle. In some districts relations between the two unions were not openly hostile, but the Birmingham district of the N.U.G.M.W., together with the T.&G.W.U. in that area, steadfastly refused to consider the entry of N.U.P.E. representatives into the West,

[1] N.U.P.E. complained bitterly that the two general unions, although in its view representing a minority of the roadmen, joined together to monopolize all the offices on the new Council and its subsidiary bodies.

The new Council did not include those counties already affiliated to the Non-Trading Council, so that, in fact, the *majority* of county council roadmen are still on the higher roadmen's rates fixed by that Council, and not on the rates of the new Council.

East and South Midlands' provincial councils, in whose areas that union had for long claimed a considerable membership. The conflict here was of long standing. In 1923 the N.U.C.W. had appealed to the T.U.C. Disputes Committee concerning their exclusion from those councils. The Disputes Committee had ruled in its favour, but the general unions had ignored the decision. In 1930 the matter had been raised again, but on this occasion the General Council of the T.U.C. had been persuaded to rule that it was not in its power to settle such a matter. Bryn Roberts approached the general unions on a number of occasions, but they refused to reconsider their decision. In 1940 and 1941 he felt his strength in that area great enough to appeal to the Ministry of Labour and to the employers' side. The Ministry refused to intervene, but he gained a success when the South Midlands' employers resolved that, although the settlement of representation on the workers' side was a matter for the unions, the exclusion of a union having a substantial number of members amongst their employees set aside a fundamental principle of J.I.C. organization. N.U.P.E. representatives then took the law into their own hands and attended meetings of the provincial councils uninvited. The police ejected them. The dispute was achieving notoriety, and Bryn Roberts could have expected considerable support for the motion he placed on the agenda of the T.U.C. of 1942 demanding that the General Council inquire into the whole affair. The day before the motion was to be moved he met the General Secretaries of the two general unions and came to an agreement to grant N.U.P.E. four seats on each of the councils in dispute, and to institute a procedure for handling future differences between the unions and for dealing with those wishing to transfer from one union to another. The Birmingham district secretary was consulted during the discusssions, and objections from the district were overruled.[1] Subsequently arrangements were more easily made for the representation of N.U.P.E., or for increases in representation, on other Provincial Councils.

The opposition to N.U.P.E., and its leaders was supported by

[1] Bryn Roberts' account of these events may be found in Bryn Roberts, *At the T.U.C.*, N.U.P.E., 1947, pp. 136-64.

doubts concerning the accuracy of their claims to membership, by objections to their methods of recruitment, and by dislike for some of their ways of conducting business. It was held that they offended against good trade union practice in accepting into membership those who already held a card of another union, and that they tried to attract such members by promising to do more for them than the general unions. A union cannot take up all the grievances of its members. Some complaints are frivolous, and in many instances there is reasonable doubt as to the value of pursuing a particular grievance. A competing union may offer to take up a case which a workers' own union has refused to handle. Usually it fails to settle it to his satisfaction, but the failures are forgotten and the few successes are widely advertised, and an astute and energetic union may attract members in this way. Besides this, a union with minority representation on a negotiating body may always take its share of the glory when general claims are successful, and, when they fail, seek to show that the fault lies elsewhere.

The hospital employees of the County Councils had no personal satisfaction in the setting up of the J.I.C. for County Council roadmen. N.U.P.E. had taken up their case in 1939 by entering a motion on the agenda for the T.U.C. of that year in favour of national machinery for settling the wages and conditions of nurses and of hospital domestic staffs. Owing to the decision of the T.U.C. to limit its discussions to two days in September 1939, the resolution was never moved. During the war, however, partly owing to pressure from the General Council of the T.U.C., the government set up the Rushcliffe Committee on nurses' salaries in 1941, and the Hetherington Committee on minimum wages and conditions of service for domestic staffs in hospitals and certain other public institutions in 1943. In that year the two general unions, together with N.U.P.E., asked the Minister of Labour to set up national joint machinery in this field. Discussions dragged on until late in 1945, when Aneurin Bevan, as Minister of Health, intervened to call the parties together and stress the urgency of the labour shortage. In November of that year the National Joint Council for Hospital and Institutional Domestic Staffs was set up. The general unions and N.U.P.E. worked together throughout these negotiations. The main beneficiary from the extension of trade unionism amongst hospital staffs has been, however, the Confederation of Health Service Employees, which was formed in 1946 by the amalgamation of the two unions who organized only in this field. If N.U.P.E. can approach local authority employees with the claim that it is a union which specializes in their field, C.O.H.S.E. can approach National Health Service employees with a greater claim to specialism than N.U.P.E. All four unions, however, co-operate on the workers' side of the new Council.

Although the N.U.G.M.W., the T.&G.W.U. and N.U.P.E. claim some membership amongst the clerical, technical and administrative staffs of local authorities, by far the largest union in this field is the National and Local Government Officers Association. A National Council was set up to cover these classes of employee in 1919, but during the following year it broke down over an attempt to fix a national basic salary, and disappeared in the subsequent years of depression. Lancashire and Cheshire, the L.C.C. and the West Riding carried on with a Standing Joint Conference. During the 'thirties first North Wales and then the north-east coast counties were persuaded to set up councils. Other areas followed, and, by 1940, provincial councils covered the country, although they represented only a minority of local authorities. In 1944 a new National Council for Administrative, Professional, Technical and Clerical Services was set up, on which the three predominantly manual workers' unions and C.O.H.S.E. were represented, as well as N.A.L.G.O.

N.A.L.G.O. has so far remained outside the T.U.C. Disagreements between it and the other three unions are likely to arise because all of them claim the right to organize in the same field. N.A.L.G.O. may seem to have a special attraction as a 'white-collar' union. When promoted manual workers feel this attraction disagreement is likely to be acute, and has at times aroused accusations that N.A.L.G.O., being outside the T.U.C., is a mere staff association and not a *bona fide* trade union. The Northern district of the N.U.G.M.W. which has a fair membership amongst clerical and administrative local government servants, has in the past shown considerable hostility to N.A.L.G.O. The union's Head Office, on the other hand, has tried to establish good relations, and when N.U.P.E. asked the 1934 T.U.C. to urge its General Council to take effective steps to counteract 'associations in Local Government Service' Charles Dukes joined with the T.&G.W.U. in opposing the resolution and advocating a working agreement with N.A.L.G.O., which has been achieved and defended by the general unions at later Congresses. There can be little doubt that in this matter the general unions showed more wisdom than N.U.P.E. There was no chance of attracting the bulk of N.A.L.G.O.'s membership away from their allegiance, and to refuse to work with N.A.L.G.O. would have only caused hardship to those local government salaried employees who were members of the other three unions.

Since the new National Council has established national salary scales, the same difficulty as arose in the gas industry over intermediate grades has become apparent, and has had to be met in much the same way by appointing joint committees to work out special scales.

The position of the N.U.G.M.W. in the Non-Trading J.I.C. has considerably changed since the 'twenties. In the Provincial Councils in the north of England it remains the dominant union. In the midlands and the south, and on the National Council, it has a greater number of seats than either of the other unions, but not more than both of them together. It cannot, therefore, determine the policy of the workers' side to the same extent as in the gas industry. The result of this has been rather to increase than to decrease the concern of the union's Executive with the elaboration of policy. Since there is greater likelihood of disagreement on the workers' side, the line to be followed by the N.U.G.M.W. requires more formal consideration. In all the new Councils which have come out of the Non-Trading services the N.U.G.M.W. is one amongst a number of unions, competing and co-operating on roughly equal terms.

Scotland, Ireland, and Glamorgan and Monmouth

The National Councils for both Non-Trading Services and Administrative Professional and Technical Staffs are entitled 'for England and Wales', but the coverage of the first was for many years incomplete. Joint Wages Boards in Glamorgan and Monmouthshire preceded the formation of the National Council and retained their separate identity. The N.U.G.M.W. was the only union recognized by these Boards, until, in 1949, one seat on the Glamorgan Board was granted to the T.&G.W.U. On several occasions the National Council tried to extend its authority to cover their area, but for many years the South Western district of the union asserted that the present arrangements were satisfactory, and the union supported them, holding that it was a matter for the district to settle.

In February 1952, however, a South Wales and Monmouthshire Provincial Council was established by agreement between the union and the other parties concerned. Besides Glamorgan and Monmouth it includes five other counties. The Monmouthshire Board has been kept in being by a few local authorities who refused to accept the new arrangement. On the workers' side of the new Council the N.U.G.M.W. has seven seats, and the T.&G.W.U. and N.U.P.E. three seats each. Now that a Provincial Council has been established, the three unions are agreed in wishing to extend its scope to include the authorities still remaining in the Monmouthshire Board, as well as the authorities who are still outside any agreed negotiating procedure.

There are relatively few local authorities in Northern Ireland and amongst them the County Borough of Belfast is predominant. The authority of the Non-Trading J.I.C. was never extended to cover them. Their two important gas undertakings, at Belfast and Londonderry, were members of the gas employers' association and thus came within the scope of the J.I.C. for that industry, but no separate regional council was set up there. A regional council was, however, set up for the electricity undertakings in Northern Ireland, and when the national machinery of the United Kingdom was remodelled to fit into the scheme of nationalization, it became an autonomous body. The result has been that collective bargaining in Northern Ireland's public utilities has centred on this body, and its agreements are now generally followed in the other services.

Scotland has its own National Councils both for manual and for administrative, etc. employees. There has seemed to be no need for Provincial Councils, and the Scottish National Councils have dealt directly with wages and salaries since they were reconstituted in 1937. Originally councils had been set up in 1920, but they disintegrated to leave unco-ordinated bargaining in the larger towns and the cities and little bargaining at all elsewhere. In 1936 the Ministry of Labour was persuaded to bring the parties together. The following year the two Councils were set up with representatives, on the employers' side, from the Association of Scottish Cities and the Convention of Burghs. As in England and Wales the County Councils' Association refused to come in but six counties affiliated on their own, and later the remaining counties joined to give the Scottish Council a wider coverage than its southern counterpart. On the workers' side the N.U.G.M.W. has the majority of seats. The other representatives are the T.&G.W.U., N.U.P.E. (which has, in general, a less firm hold in Scotland than in the south of England) and the Scottish Horse and Motormen's Association.

Wages and Conditions

The most important general question which arose in the early years of provincial bargaining was whether the unions were entitled to make approaches to individual authorities to grant better wages and conditions than were provided in the provincial agreements. In 1928 the employers suggested that the constitution should be revised to prevent this, and succeeded in getting a sub-committee set up to draft a new clause to that effect. The sub-committee reported during the following year and the clause was accepted, subject only to ratification by the Executives of the unions. It seemed that final acceptance was almost inevitable but at the first meeting of the N.U.G.M.W. Executive which considered the matter there was enough opposition for the matter to be deferred, and by the time it came up again, ten of the twelve districts had declared against it, and it was rejected.

The employers' attitude was akin to that of the gas employers. They felt that the authority of the councils was being undermined by individual approaches. If the unions accepted an agreement on a council, they should not seek to render it inoperative by individual approaches. The reply was obvious; the employers had no power to force authorities which paid below the rate to conform to agreements,[1] so that the unions had every right to try to persuade other authorities to improve on the agreement. Perhaps the unions also feared that if they bound themselves not to press even when a favourable opportunity arose, some Labour councillors would try to steal their thunder, and membership would suffer. The N.U.G.M.W., therefore, also wanted 100 per cent trade unionism before they accepted the new clause, or at least encouragement of trade unionism equivalent to that granted by the gas employers.

The employers professed themselves most hurt by the attitude of the union, and early in 1930 were suggesting that they would have to cease to operate the councils unless their point was met. The union remained firm, and nothing came of it.

The Non-Trading services are almost entirely time-working occupations. Bonus systems have in a few instances been applied to refuse-collection and one or two other jobs, but these cases are exceptional and the earnings of most workers are determined by the rates for their jobs and any extra allowances or provisions for extra payment outside normal hours. In the 'twenties many Provincial Councils tied the rates which they agreed to the cost of living bonus, then, as the cost of living sagged, adopted stabilization as the gas industry had done. During the depression the cost of living scales were finally abandoned. But the depression had its effect on the wages paid by local authorities. In 1930 pressure for reductions became strong. The Non-Trading services suffered almost no direct

---

[1] This was not an idle complaint. Many local councils, as we have seen, were not affiliated to the employers' associations, and from time to time those associations have had great difficulty in persuading economy-minded councils, which were members, to abide by the agreements of the Provincial Councils.

effect from the depression, but many employers thought the rates were pressing unduly hard on private industry in order to maintain the wages of local authority employees above those of workers outside who were suffering from both heavy unemployment and wage-cuts. In April 1931, the West Midlands Council met to consider whether stabilization could be further continued. Before the meeting the Birmingham and Wolverhampton Engineering Employers circulated a statement on 'sheltered wages' and their effect on private industry through the rates. Later that year came the National Government and its cuts in pay for the services and the Civil Service. A Ministry of Health circular (No. 1222) left the local authorities in no doubt as to the government's view of the need for economy in wage-bills. Some authorities had already applied cuts despite stabilization agreements, and further stabilization would only have caused widespread defections from the J.I.C. During 1932 cuts followed generally, although the union resisted as best it could. In Lancashire and Cheshire, for instance, the percentage cut to be applied was reduced. In Belfast the union succeeded in avoiding any cuts for the lowest paid, and for the next group of grades the proposed reduction of 3s. 6d. was reduced to 2s. The West Riding was even persuaded to renew its stabilization agreement. Restoration came in 1934. The General Secretary reported to the 1934 Congress:

'The panic demand of the National Government two years ago for drastic economies in the wages of municipal employees met with only half-hearted approval by the local authorities, and, in so far as cuts were made at all in those wages, there has now been practically complete restoration.'

He was able to report to the 1938 Congress that all Provincial Councils had granted increases. Difficulty, however, arose in London. The advance there had come early, in 1936, but a clause had been inserted in the agreement to prevent reconsideration of its terms except in 'unforeseen and abnormal circumstances'. By 1939 London was becoming restive, but the employers refused to admit that there had been such a change in circumstances. In June the unions appealed to the J.I.C. which upheld the employers' interpretation of events, but recommended that the claim should be considered in view of the general increases granted in the provinces since 1936. Even so the negotiations were prolonged, and it was not until November of that year that an agreement was reached.

It was natural that a second round of increases should come with the general price and wage increases of the first year of the war. The employers became anxious lest individual approaches should result in wage movements getting out of hand, and renewed their demands that all claims should be made through the Provincial Councils. Eventually both sides came to the conclusion that they should fall into line with other industries and grant the National Council the right to agree on national war wage advances which should apply to all the Provincial Councils. The unions claimed that most councils had already granted increases of about 5s. and thought that the first national decision should be to bring all the provinces up to that figure. If this was granted, they were willing to agree that any advances over that figure which had already been granted should be merged in subsequent increases. They also asked for a further immediate national increase. The employers would not agree to this final demand, and the unions proposed to take their case to arbitration. They were also keen that the agreed increase should apply to county council employees under the terms of S.R. & O. 1305. The employers took legal opinion on the application of the order, and were advised that it did not apply to them, on the grounds that the terms agreed by the Provincial Councils could not be said to be in force 'in any district' as provided in the order, and that, since the employers' side on Provincial Councils consisted of individual authorities, and on the National Council of representatives of the provincial employers' sides, they could not be termed 'organizations of employers'. The Ministry of Labour thereupon brought the parties together, and agreement was reached on the 5s. with a further increase of 3s. from February 1941.

London now caused difficulties again. The employers there, who had resented national interference in 1939, had inserted into the agreement of November of that year a clause providing that no alteration should be made to the rates then agreed except by the London Council. They offered the 5s., and 2s. in addition for some workers. The unions appealed to the National Council who awarded the full additional 3s., and the London employers complied.

Thereafter for a time national advances came regularly. The unions claimed particularly on the grounds of increases in the trading services, which were generally ahead in this matter. London on each occasion claimed the right to consider the case on its merits, but granted the national increase after a delay of a few weeks.

Meanwhile the application of the National Arbitration Order was settled. The unions were pressing through the T.U.C. for a declaratory order making clear its application to the local authorities. It was thought that the Minister of Labour, Ernest Bevin, would be sympathetic to such a proposal. The House of Lords, however, determined the matter when they gave judgment in favour of N.A.L.G.O. in a case which that union had brought against Bolton Corporation under the terms of the Order.[1] In July 1941, the Court of Appeal had found against the union but its verdict was unanimously reversed by the Lords in September 1942.

The unions benefited in many ways. Henceforth all authorities, whether affiliated to the Provincial Councils or not, would have to pay the agreed rates. In 1944, for instance, Hexham was forced to pay Grade A rates by a verdict of the National Arbitration Tribunal, although it had left the Provincial Council and the employers' federation in protest against the decision so to grade it. Later in the same year the Tribunal decided that Lancashire and Cheshire authorities who did not operate the sick-pay scheme general in that area must in future do so. More important than these was a decision affecting London. In 1943 the London employers had tired of following national advances. They therefore refused to grant the national advances of 2s. in May 1943 and in January 1944. The unions took the first refusal to the Tribunal on the grounds

---

[1] The point at issue was whether Bolton should follow the general practice of local authorities with regard to making up the pay of employees serving with the forces.

that London should accept the decisions of the National Council. Their case was rejected. They resubmitted the claim on its merits, and were upheld. The employers thereupon, while maintaining their refusal to accept the jurisdiction of the National Council, granted the second 2s. 'in full regard of the circumstances'.

The Lords' decision greatly strengthened the authority of the National Council. Many new authorities joined the Provincial Councils, feeling they had best take part in decisions which would apply to them. In 1943 the National Council decided that it was time for a general review of the system of 'zoning' or 'grading' authorities in order to fix a different rate for each 'zone' — a matter until that time left entirely to the Provincial Councils. It felt that 'the circumstances which bear upon the problem of zoning have changed substantially during past years' and suggested that there should be only three zones. At that time two Provincial Councils had only two zones, and one as many as nine. By April 1944 there had been considerable reductions; only two councils had more than four zones. Thereafter the unions continued to press, with success, for reduction to three. In 1947 it was decided to reduce the number of zones to two.

By this time, however, the National Council had determined on a far greater extension of its powers. After suggesting other means of increasing the control of the Council over provincial and local agreements the employers finally proposed that it should take over from the Provincial Councils the task of determining not only wage advances, but also the actual rates of wages, and the settlement of conditions of employment. The N.U.G.M.W. showed little liking for the proposal. Those of its districts which were well ahead of the national average were vociferous in their protests, particularly the Northern and London districts, and the general feeling was that the national settlement of rates might well be determined on the basis of the ability to pay of the poorest authority. However, the union did not control the voting strength of the workers' side of the National Council. The Journal of March 1947, stated:

'By a majority our own representatives have expressed considerable disfavour with the substitution of national control of wages and conditions of service for the long prevailing method of provincial fixation . . . But as the other two unions wanted it and had a majority we had to fall into line.'

The war bonus was consolidated into the basic rate and two minimum labourers' rates were fixed: 94s. for zone 'A' and 91s. for zone 'B'. The provinces were to continue to grade authorities into the two zones. The National Council was to set to work to erect a national grading system for all additional rates for jobs requiring greater effort or skill. Meanwhile the provinces could adjust the rates for such grades to make allowance for any increase in their basic rate due to the national agreement. Higher rates were for the moment to be safeguarded by a 'better conditions' clause, but were to be merged in subsequent general advances unless special conditions justified the retention of a plus rate. Conditions of service above the national minimum were not, however, protected in this way.

London, as usual, presented difficulties. A higher minimum rate for its workers was to be settled later. Eventually it was agreed, and the London employers gave their consent to the scheme so long as they should have the right of approving any decision under it before it was applied in their area. In practice this saving clause has not amounted to much.

The National Council proceeded with its task of regrading. In June 1948, the Journal announced that at least 324 manual grades of labour had been discovered in the Non-Trading services.

'It was, therefore, decided to legislate for the most important and easily definable occupations, leaving it to the provincial councils to complete the differentials within the wages framework to be adopted nationally.'

Similar difficulties arose over the very varied conditions of service. In the meantime a national increase of 6s. was agreed. Women were to have 75 per cent of the male rates (unless doing a man's job for which the full rate should be paid). A national working week of forty-four hours was agreed, but it should be spread over five, five and a half, or six days by local agreement.

The first national decision on grading followed, classifying thirty-one grades into six groups, five of which received rates above the minimum, the highest being 13s. more. This has been followed by supplementary decisions including further classes of employees in the scheme, and by the national conditions agreement.

These decisions had a mixed reception. Many workers in the area of the Northern Provincial Council gained something from the new grading scheme, but their basic rate was so far ahead of the national rate that much of the subsequent general increases has been absorbed by the merging of their previous advantages. Their attitude requires little elaboration. London workers and workers in other heavily industrialized areas gained little from the new system, and have tended to be critical. Workers in many rural areas, particularly the eastern and southern counties, gained considerably.

Criticisms of the scheme were not confined to its effect on general levels of wages in the previously higher-paid provinces. The standardization of conditions has been of benefit to large numbers of workers, but the lack of a 'better conditions' clause for conditions of service has hit some groups. In some authorities time-and-a-quarter was paid for night-work. The national agreement provides for a plus payment of 3d. an hour for this work, which is considerably less advantageous, but must be applied throughout the country. Moreover jobs with the same title may involve different work in different parts of the country. Refuse collectors themselves say that their job differs materially from area to area, and according to the 'system' of collection adopted by their authority; London collectors, for instance, feel that most provincial collectors have an easier task. All these variations could at one time be dealt with by small differences in pay, but that now is outside the authority's power unless it can make out an acceptable case for special consideration of unusual circumstances.

The work involved in putting the new scheme into practice, and the centralization of decision on many matters previously settled in the provinces, has necessarily led to delay in dealing with local problems and complaints, and this too has added to the volume of criticism of the scheme

Instances of these difficulties could be multiplied. When they are all described, however, it remains true that something far more like rough justice is done between employees of different authorities under the new scheme than before, when higher rates depended so much on ability to pay and on the political affiliations of council majorities. Any case against the scheme must be based on the N.U.G.M.W.'s original objection that the national rates are likely to be lower than the average of rates under the old scheme, because the unions can no longer use the actions of the best authorities and best provinces as an argument for a general wage increase; that the employers will move only when the majority of them are ready to move. A hypothetical argument may continue for ever, but it is probably safe to say that most of the objections which are made arise from teething-troubles, and to predict that in time the new scheme will be as easily accepted as the old.

So long as they existed, the Glamorgan and Monmouthshire Wages Boards fixed labourers' rates which were the same in both counties, and additional rates for other types of work. Before the war these rates were perhaps slightly ahead of the country as a whole, and after 1939 they roughly moved with the advances of the National Council, thus reducing the difficulties of absorption.

In Scotland the rates also have roughly kept pace with those of England and Wales. The workers' side there has frequently based its claims on the grant of a similar sum in the south. The Scottish Council has, however, established far less control over actual rates of wages. It fixes the minimum rates for labourers, and has reduced the number of grades of authority to two,[1] as in England and Wales. In the agreement for an increase of 5s. 6d. in December 1950, which followed some weeks behind the grant of the same amount in the south, it was laid down that any payments to labourers above the minimum were to be merged in the increase, thus making the minima into standard rates. It was also understood that the increase

---

[1] In grade 2, there is a difference of 1s. between labourers in cities and burghs and labourers in the counties.

would apply to higher grades. As yet, however, the individual authorities retain the right to agree with the union to settle the wages of these higher grades. The Council has been considering the establishment of a grading system for the whole of Scotland for some time. It is to be expected that in time such a system will be settled, and that wages in Non-Trading services in Scotland will become as standardized as in the south. The Council has already established a standard schedule of working conditions.

Superannuation rights have long been a matter of importance to local government employees. Under the adoptive Act of 1922 local authorities were empowered to come into a standard contributory scheme for salaried staff. To determine whether an authority should come in, a system of compulsory balloting was laid down. Authorities were also permitted to extend their schemes to cover manual workers. The N.U.G.M.W. from the first urged the advantages of the scheme, pressed authorities and employees to exercise their option, demanded for manual workers the same right to ballot as had been granted to the staffs, and argued for second ballots within as short as possible a period after a first ballot which went against entry. The T.&G.W.U. at first expressed doubts about the wisdom of a compulsory scheme, but later adopted the same attitude. The unions supported with enthusiasm the Act of 1937 which made the scheme compulsory for salaried staff. After 1937 the great majority of authorities extended their schemes to cover all workers.

When the Beveridge Report was published and it was understood that the government intended to introduce a far more comprehensive (and expensive) system of national insurance, local authority employees doubted their ability to maintain their contribution to both schemes. The unions took up their case and, through the T.U.C., pressed for modification. In 1947 it was agreed that when the national insurance scheme came into force, existing local authority employees could opt to maintain their full contribution to the Local Government scheme (and, therefore, also the full contribution of the authority) and to receive their full pension, or to pay a reduced contribution which would reduce their pension proportionately. New entrants would have to enter the modified scheme. The reduction in pension for those who opted for the modified scheme would depend on age (and, therefore, roughly on the period of contribution at the original rate).

Dealings with the Individual Local Authority

We have already discussed the effects of local politics on collective bargaining in the Non-Trading services, and the decline in its influence which has resulted from national wage fixation. The Labour politician has now small opportunity of scoring at the union's expense, and the 'ratepayers' candidate can economize on the wages bill to only a very limited extent. Collective bargaining has become far more a matter of business than of politics.

Throughout this period collective bargaining has remained very much in the hands of the union's officials. The union's leaders have been ready to hold up the Non-Trading services as an example of an industry entirely free from the troubles generated by shop stewards. Collecting stewards there are, and they may sometimes be called shop stewards. They may act as a first line in collective bargaining by taking the complaints of their members to a foreman to see if they can be settled before the union officer is brought in. Some Provincial Councils, such as that of the Southern Home Counties, have drawn up model constitutions for Local Joint Works Committees, or similar institutions. These Works Committees are to be found mainly in London and the south, and many authorities even in those areas have refused to set them up. In some authorities, however, they exist and function well. The workers' representatives may act as shop stewards in all but name, and the functions of the secretary of the workers' side are almost indistinguishable from those of a factory convenor of stewards. In other areas there is little formal industrial democracy of this kind, and official dealings with departments are through the union officer. One reason given for the comparative lack of Joint Councils in local authorities is the scattered nature of most of the work compared with factory production. Another is that in the union's districts in the north of England, the system of dealing with all matters through union officers in close contact with the committees of the local authorities has stood the test of time, and the union's members show no desire for change.

Although the union has on more than one occasion taken a ballot of Non-Trading employers over an area to determine whether to strike on a matter before a Provincial Council, these crises have been settled otherwise, and strikes have invariably been confined to individual authorities or to departments of larger authorities. In the 'twenties several such strikes were authorized by the union as a means of trying to force a local authority to abide by provincial agreements. Since 1940 all strikes in the Non-Trading services have been unofficial. The most considerable was the strike of City of London employees in 1947, which was roundly condemned at the Congress of that year, as one of the worst examples of failure to use the constitutional machinery in a matter with which it was well able to deal. Not all unofficial action by local authority employees has received equal condemnation from the union. In the same year Wimbledon's employees threatened to strike. They complained of admittedly unusually unpleasant conditions for workers on refuse destruction, of their inability to share in the higher rate paid to their neighbours within the area of the London Council, and voiced doubts about the full recognition of the union by the departmental chiefs. Their threats forced the Mayor into the unusual course of calling a meeting of the Council's employees to be addressed by himself and an officer of the N.U.G.M.W. The immediate claims of the men were met, and the Mayor's statements added considerable strength to the union's case for creating a 'special' zone within the province, to consist of authorities within the London area, who should pay the London rate.

Conclusion

The union's record in the Non-Trading services is perhaps not so impressive as in the gas industry.

The earnings of the manual employees of local authorities

have always been relatively low, but this has been due mainly to the lack of piece-work and bonus systems, and to the fact that most of the jobs concerned do not demand great skill or responsibility. The labourers' rate has always compared and still compares reasonably well with labourers' rates in most other industries.[1] Before national wage fixation the N.U.G.M.W. had maintained rates considerably above the national average in the provinces and authorities in which it had greatest strength. It was not able, however, to provide adequately for County employees nor for the employees of many of the smaller authorities, because it could not enrol a sufficient number of them into membership. For the same reason it was unable to bring pressure to bear on their employers to obtain adequate standards for the Poor Law authority employees when these were transferred to the local authorities. It aimed to bring all these workers under the protection of the 'Non-Trading' Council, and argued that this could be done if they could be persuaded to join the union. At a favourable time, however, N.U.P.E. was able to enrol many of them, and to take over some members from the general unions. It used its new strength to further a policy different from that of the N.U.G.M.W. Whichever policy might have brought most benefit in the long run, N.U.P.E. (assisted by the war-time government's attitude to agricultural labour) carried the day, and separate Councils were set up for county roadmen and other groups of workers.

The objections of the N.U.G.M.W. to the system of national wage fixation (which it has loyally accepted and operated) may have been well-founded. That cannot be finally determined. But for its inability to maintain the system which it preferred it is itself partly to blame, in so far as the growth of N.U.P.E., which supported the change to national fixation, may be attributed to its shortcomings.

[1] The Ministry of Labour inquiry for October 1952, gave earnings in local government service for all workers as 128s. 8d. compared with a national average of 151s. 11d.; for all males 138s. 4d. against a national average of 178s. 6d. At that time the labourers' rates of 124s. 4d. in London, 118s. 4d. in Zone A and 115s. 4d. in Zone B may be compared with labourers' rates of 111s.-115s. 8d. in engineering, 114s. in shipbuilding, 122s. 10d.-133s. 10d. in building.

On the other hand, it can be said that the union maintained the tradition of collective bargaining in the Non-Trading services in the difficult years of the 'twenties and the subsequent depression; and that it has continued to deal with the affairs of local government employees sufficiently to their satisfaction to remain the largest single union in the field.

CHAPTER IV

THE ENGINEERING AND SHIP-BUILDING INDUSTRIES

The Engineering Industry

THE engineering industry is defined for our purpose as including firms affiliated to the Engineering and Allied Employers' Federation, and non-federated firms producing the same kind of articles as members of the Federation. This necessarily excludes the large number of engineering workers who carry on maintenance work in almost every other industry, and other groups of engineering workers in Railway Workshops, Royal Ordnance Factories, the Light Metals Industries and so on, whose wages and conditions more or less follow those determined for the engineering industry proper, but who are covered by other joint collective bargaining bodies.

With all these exclusions the industry remains vast, its boundaries ill-defined, and generalizations about it dangerous. It includes heavy engineering, the motor and aeroplane industries, electrical engineering and many other fairly distinct sub-divisions. Within many of these there is a great variety of products. Electrical engineering includes the production of heavy equipment for generating stations and of the smallest coil or most sensitive relay.

It is a commonplace that over the last sixty or seventy years the industry has changed from craft production methods to mass production methods. Craftsmen have been more and more restricted to the tool-room, to 'setting' operations, or to maintenance, and labourers to the yard. There has been a remarkable growth in the number of 'semi-skilled' workers — machine-operators or workers on continuous flow systems of production. Many of the apprenticed turners who work on boring machines or lathes, or apprenticed fitters who work on assembly are not craftsmen in the sense that they may be required to perform a wide variety of tasks, and to make their own tools for those tasks, but workers who are required to perform slightly more difficult jobs than the semi-skilled workers alongside them.

It is also well known that, although some craft unions, particularly the Amalgamated Society of Engineers,[1] had made some alterations in their constitutions prior to 1914 to permit workers other than apprenticed craftsmen to join, these provisions had not been generally operated by the branches — conservatively-minded in this matter — and that the only unions which had opened their doors wide to the growing numbers of semi-skilled workers by that time were the labourers' unions. Before 1914 successful recruitment had been limited to a few areas such as London, South Lancashire and the north-east coast, but the great expansion of the industry and the conditions favourable to union membership provided by the first world war glutted the labourers' (or perhaps now rather general) unions with engineering workers. Even after the collapse of membership in the depression of 1921 and the engineering lock-out of 1922, the general unions retained a far larger number of engineering workers than they had before the war, although admittedly these were a smaller proportion of their total membership than in 1918 or 1920.

While membership of the craft unions is by trade, membership of the general unions is normally by factory. Although from time to time successful raids have been made, or one union has moved into a factory after the membership of another has disappeared, it is generally true that where a works was originally organized by a constituent union of the N.U.G.M.W. it is still organized by them, and where it was originally organized by a constituent of the T.&G.W.U. their control is unchallenged by the N.U.G.M.W. The picture is not completely tidy, however. Some of the craft unions, such as the A.E.U., E.T.U. and Foundryworkers, began seriously to organize outside the ranks of the craftsmen during the 'thirties. Some works may be entirely organized by the A.E.U. In many others the general workers' union competes with the A.E.U. for the mass of production workers, and in some departments with

---

[1] The predecessor of the A.E.U. On this point see James Jefferys, *The Story of the Engineers*, Lawrence and Wishart, 1945, chap. 7.

other 'craft' unions. Especially in the largest works, such as Metro-Vickers in Manchester or Fords in Dagenham, all unions may hold membership. The original task of organization was too vast for any restrictive claims to be successfully upheld.

The procedure agreement or 'York Memorandum' grew out of the settlement of a lock-out in the industry in 1898. Its present form was determined, after many intermediate amendments, in the settlement of another lock-out in 1922. Under it shop stewards are recognized by both sides. They are to discuss with foremen or other supervisors any grievances on which the union member has been unable to obtain satisfaction himself. Federated firms may also set up Works Committees of which the workers' side is chosen by and from the stewards. Grievances may be further discussed on this committee. If agreement is not reached a formal Works Conference may be held and may be attended by the organizer of the union concerned and a representative of the Employers' Federation. If the grievance is not settled by this conference, it is referred to a Local Conference at which members of the Executive Committee of the Local Employers' Association hear and decide on the case as presented by a union officer (assisted by representatives of the workers) and a representative of the firm. If the union is still unsatisfied it may refer the matter to the Central Conference at York where it is heard by the Central Conference Committee of the employers' National Federation, and presented by a national trade union officer and a representative of the National Federation. Local representatives may be in attendance but remain outside the Conference room. All the important unions in the industry are separately parties to this agreement, and may take cases separately, or together if more than one union is concerned. In recent years the Confederation of Shipbuilding and Engineering Unions has acted as co-ordinator where several unions are interested in the same matter.

National wage claims are dealt with directly between the unions and the Federation. A claim is presented by the spokesman of one side at a large gathering of representatives of both employers and unions, and a spokesman of the other side replies, normally at a second meeting. Where serious discussion is felt to be necessary a sub-committee may be appointed. Up to 1940 there was no redress beyond the final answer of the Federation, either on grievances or general wage claims. Since that year the unions have made frequent use of the National Arbitration Tribunal, or, since 1951, of the Industrial Disputes Tribunal.

This procedure has been criticized on the grounds that it is cumbersome, that it encourages delay, that the Central Conference is too remote from the issues discussed, and that it is not really joint machinery. These criticisms have come most of all from the craft unions, but they have been voiced in the N.U.G.M.W. too. In 1924 it was seriously suggested that the union should withdraw entirely and deal on its own with individual employers.

Bargaining with the non-federated firm is direct, and through whatever procedure the firm and the union or unions choose to set up. Shop stewards almost invariably form part of this procedure. Since 1940 the unions have been able to take such firms direct to an arbitration tribunal. It is certainly a criticism of the official machinery for bargaining that it is not only anti-union firms which remain outside the Federation. Some of the most 'enlightened' firms in the country, with long records of dealing with unions, are not members, and the unions exert little pressure to force them in, finding that better results are often achieved through direct dealings with such firms than through the York Memorandum.

The Shipbuilding and Shiprepairing Industry

This industry has been subject to little technological change during the present century. The serious difficulties which arose within it over the introduction of electric welding during the 'thirties illustrate the strength of traditional attitudes to patterns of work. Perhaps the slowness of change can be in part attributed to these attitudes on both sides of the industry, but change must have been gradual to allow traditions of this kind to take root.

Most of the jobs in the industry are craft jobs. There are a few machine operations such as scarfing and drilling, and a few other jobs such as red-leading which are performed entirely by workers who have not served an apprenticeship, but most workers who are not craftsmen are employed in fetching and carrying, or to work directly with craftsmen — as plater's helpers, rivet heaters, riggers and so on.

There is thus a far clearer line of demarcation between the craft unions, which here are indeed craft unions, and the general unions, most of whose shipbuilding members still work as assistants to craftsmen. The only important exception to this rule is the A.E.U. which, at least in some areas, does its best to enrol those working as assistants to fitters. The A.E.U. is, however, by no means in the dominant position which it holds in the engineering industry. The most important single union is the United Boilermakers' and Iron and Steel Shipbuilders' Society, which has remained very decidedly a craft union. Although during the last twenty years the T.&G.W.U. has probably expanded rather faster in this industry than has the N.U.G.M.W., the latter remains the more important of the two in the industry, certainly in those yards which were originally organized by the N.A.U.L.

The procedure for dealing with grievances and with general wage applications is much the same as in the engineering industry. The two important differences are that if the Ship-building Central Conference fails to agree, a further General Conference with an independent chairman may be held (this clause has been inoperative since 1940 when it was agreed to submit Central Conference differences to the Ministry for reference to the Arbitration Tribunal); and, more important, that in some areas there are separate local associations of Shipbuilding and of Shiprepairing Employers, though both are affiliated to the National Federation. In these areas local conferences are concerned either with shipbuilding or with ship-repair. The decisions of local conferences may build up a considerably different set of working rules and of local rates of payment in the two sections of the industry in one centre, as on Merseyside. In the Port of London the only shipbuilding work is a little barge-building and the shiprepair rules cover almost all workers. The relative isolation of shipbuilding centres gives even greater importance to these local rules than to the various district agreements and understandings in the engineering industry.

Over the last twenty or thirty years general wage negotiations, though by no means always straightforward, have caused less difficulty here than in engineering, because claims have normally been made first to the latter industry, and both sides in shipbuilding have shown themselves fairly ready to agree on something close to the final decision there.

The Unions and the Confederation

The Federation of Engineering and Shipbuilding Trades, founded in 1890, was for many years a craftsman's organization which concerned itself mainly with the difficulties of demarcation between the various trades. Gradually it began to acquire other interests, and in 1910 its status was enhanced and its functions extended to collective bargaining by the decision of the shipbuilding industry to introduce national variations in time-rates and piece-work percentages. In 1909 the Federation allowed the N.A.U.L. to join, and the next year the Gasworkers decided that they could not leave the representation of the labourers' case to that union alone. They made application, and were accepted. Both the unions were admitted to the Federation on equal terms with the craft unions provided that they undertook to accept into their ranks no one eligible for membership of those unions.

The Federation's field of activity was enormously increased by the war, which caused a great expansion in both the industries which it covered, introduced national wage awards, and created a thousand problems which the government and the employers had to discuss with all the unions concerned. Its authority was, however, considerably weakened by the A.S.E. which had joined the Federation, without much enthusiasm, in 1905, and had continued to object to its constitution. In the years between 1910 and 1914 the Federation had been canvassing schemes to bring its members into far closer unity in dealing with 'general trade movements' by mutual support, including financial support and sympathetic action. Nothing came of the proposals, but they served to displease the A.S.E., which tended to believe that the best method of achieving unity was for the other unions to amalgamate with it. In 1915 the A.S.E. showed in the negotiations over the 'Treasury Agreement' and the first Munitions of War Act that it was determined to deal with the government on its own, and it continued as it had begun. Consequently the Federation's authority remained much greater in shipbuilding (where the A.S.E. was not the most important union) than in engineering.

Meanwhile growth of membership had added weight to the views of the general unions within the Federation. The views of Will Thorne, of J. N. Bell of the N.A.U.L., and particularly of J. R. Clynes, were heard more and more frequently. In 1917 Clynes made a great protest against the 'Trade Card' agreement under which the craft unions had the right to determine exemptions from military service, and at another meeting he persuaded a spokesman of the Admiralty to accept the principle that unskilled workers should be included in the systems of payment by results which his department wished to introduce into the shipyards.

At the end of the war the A.S.E., finding, as well it might, 'the Federation of little value in negotiation with the Government and of no value in assisting amalgamation'[1] decided to secede once more, and went ahead with its own amalgamation scheme which led to the formation of the A.E.U. in 1920. The Federation meanwhile took up its own pre-war proposals, and by 1923 had drafted a generally acceptable new constitution which somewhat increased the powers of the Federation over general trade movements but denied it any control over demarcation disputes. It also provided that unions should affiliate on the basis not of total membership, but of membership *within* the industries covered by the Federation, and pay an affiliation fee in proportion.[2] The years of depression, of falling wages, of disastrous strikes and even more disastrous

---

[1] James Jefferys, *op. cit.*, p. 192.

[2] Originally there had been a standard affiliation fee for each society however large or small. This rule had been amended in 1922 to allow some variations in fees according to size.

lock-outs, all but destroyed the Federation. The Boilermakers were only prevented from withdrawing in 1922 (when the Federation accepted a national overtime and nightshift agreement in shipbuilding which the Boilermakers felt discriminated against piece-workers who constituted a majority of their membership) by the Federation's decision to expel them. Shortly after, many other important unions — Woodworkers, Shipwrights, Painters, Electricians, Plumbers and Pattern-makers also withdrew, some of them curiously enough on the grounds that their time-working members were not aided by association with unions whose members were employed under piece-work systems! In 1926, six of these unions, including the Boilermakers, formed a Shipbuilding Trades Committee, which negotiated with the Shipbuilding Employers' Federation on equal terms with the Federation. The Federation had now become an association of the newly-formed N.U.G.M.W. and T.&G.W.U. with the smaller craft unions engaged in ship-building. The N.U.G.M.W. was the dominant union. Its affiliation fee in 1925 was £520, against £91 17s. 6d. of the next union, the T.&G.W.U. Will Sherwood, the National Officer of the N.U.G.M.W., became the Federation's spokesman, and chairman from 1925 to 1934. Even so the Executive of the union was presented with a serious resolution from one of its districts in 1928 demanding that the union should withdraw from the Federation, since it was so unrepresentative, and should thus permit its final collapse.

In 1920, before the spate of secessions, the Federation had taken an important decision that, after the end of the war-time system of four-monthly wage reviews, general wage claims should continue in engineering (as since 1911 in shipbuilding), to be for flat-rate advances for all workers, and that there should be no reversion to the pre-war claims for advances for skilled and unskilled workers in proportion to their basic rate. Despite the lack of co-ordination amongst the unions, this decision was honoured, assisted by the employers' determination not to consolidate the national war bonuses with the district base rates, and to make national variations only in the former. As it happened claims were usually reasonably co-ordinated.

In shipbuilding the two groups of unions usually acted together. In engineering, it soon became clear that if one union presented a claim, others would follow suit. The employers would then consider the claims together. Accordingly the unions saw that they would do well to present an agreed claim. The Engineering Joint Trades Movement was thus formed to include the Federation and the unions outside, in particular the A.E.U. Its sole concern was with national claims, although for some time a parallel body in the London area concerned itself with promoting a special claim for the London engineers.

Representation at the meetings of this body caused the N.U.G.M.W. considerable concern. On the Joint Industrial Councils in which it was the major union it normally disposed of enough seats to allow a National Officer and representatives from almost all the districts concerned to attend. In industries in which its membership was small, exclusion of some districts would cause few complaints. The meetings of the new Movement were usually on matters which the Executive would consider as within its sphere, and of sufficient importance for all its members to attend. Yet each district felt itself vitally concerned and wanted to be represented. Various solutions to the problem were adopted from time to time. At one time attendance at meetings where policy was to be decided was confined to Executive representatives. Later delegations were expanded, to please everyone, to twenty-two. This appeared ridiculous beside the general secretary and three or four executive members of other unions. Thereafter numbers were drastically reduced, by stages, and some balance between the rival claims was achieved. A federal structure in a trade union is not without its difficulties.

In 1931 the engineering unions were presented with a demand for drastic alterations in the agreements covering working conditions to which they were all parties. They did their best to improve the terms offered, but the times were not propitious for a fight. On the suggestion of Charles Dukes the N.U.G.M.W. Executive decided to propose that the terms should be unconditionally rejected and that the unions should prepare to stand a local assault in each district when the employers consequently withdrew from the national agreement. The other unions voted down this proposal at a meeting in June. Some of their spokesmen suggested that the N.U.G.M.W. was 'bluffing' since it had already accepted a general reduction in the chemical industry. This suggestion was indignantly repudiated and doubts cast on the ability of some of the craft unions to support their members in a struggle. One cannot, however, entirely rule out the possibility that the N.U.G.M.W. would have been more cautious had it controlled a majority of the Movement's votes.[1]

In 1935 and 1936 improving trade and membership sweetened the tempers of the unions, and in 1936 proposals for a new Confederation of Shipbuilding and Engineering Unions were accepted by the Federation and all the remaining members of the Shipbuilding Trades Committee. (The Shipwrights had returned to the Federation in 1930). The main alteration in the new constitution was the provision for electing, besides a General Executive, two Group Executives which should be responsible for conducting negotiations in the two industries. Other unions rejoined during the subsequent years, and soon only the A.E.U. and the Foundryworkers remained outside. The Confederation's relations with the A.E.U. were no better than those of its predecessor. In 1937 the A.E.U. seceded even from the Joint Trades Movement, and in 1939, before the outbreak of war, entered into a separate dilution agreement with the employers after the Confederation had decided to reject the advances of Sir Thomas Inskip[2] on dilution. For several years the A.E.U. and the Foundryworkers continued to present joint claims, separate from those of the Confederation. In 1941

---

[1] The union took advantage of a minority position elsewhere. At that time it had one representative on the J.I.C. for the Tramways Industry, and organized tramwaymen in Belfast, Liverpool and Sunderland, whose authorities were not affiliated to the J.I.C. (The employees of these three authorities had originally been members of the M.E.A.) The General Secretary reported to the 1932 Congress that:

'As some . . . districts are governed by local agreements our representative [on the J.I.C.] was advised not to agree to any alteration in wages or conditions so that our districts would not be compromised in any way. This was carried out but the larger union, with the employers, carried the motion for altered [i.e. reduced] wages.'

[2] The Minister for the Co-ordination of Defence.

the Confederation complained bitterly when the A.E.U.
referred a claim to the National Arbitration Tribunal and
forced the Confederation to do likewise instead of joining with
it in persuading the employers to set up a special tribunal for
the engineering industry, from which the Confederation felt its
claims would get more sympathetic treatment.

One effect of the foundation of the Confederation was to re-
vitalize the old district committees and to cause new district
committees to be set up. These committees had always played
some part in the shipbuilding areas, but now began to show an
interest in a wider range of topics, including the organization of
the aircraft industry and the co-ordination of the activities of
shop stewards from the various unions. In these activities they
were far more liable to come into conflict with the A.E.U.
district committees than in the shipyards, where the engineers
tended to keep to themselves and often worked under separate
agreements from those of the other unions.

Gradually trade union enthusiasm for 'the war against
fascism', and the influence of the powerful Communist group
within the A.E.U., who favoured the widest possible unity, had
their effect. Not only was the Joint Trades Movement re-
vived, but in 1944 the Confederation reported that its
relations with the A.E.U. were greatly improved. During the
following year the Foundryworkers affiliated and long drawn-
out negotiations commenced with the A.E.U. The A.E.U. was
concerned to secure a position in the Confederation consistent with its numerical strength in the engineering industry,
and the Confederation to avoid domination by the A.E.U.
should it enter. In 1946 the negotiations were complete, an
A.E.U. ballot favoured affiliation, and in December of that
year they were admitted. The Group Executives were replaced by one Executive Council, which was to elect two
chairmen, one to present claims at engineering conferences and
one at shipbuilding conferences. It was understood that the
former would be the president of the A.E.U. The election to
the Council was to be by card vote, and no union was to be
allowed more than nine members.

Everything seemed prepared for the new wages' structure in

the engineering industry, the replacement of the old procedure by a new Joint Industrial Council, the organization of Confederation stewards in the factories, and other reforms proposed by the A.E.U. Such changes were equally acceptable to the older members of the Confederation, and were intended to put industrial relations in the engineering industry on a new basis.

Before we examine the outcome of these proposals, we must turn aside to look at the development of the industry's wage structure.

The N.U.G.M.W. and the Engineering Wage Structure

Before 1914 engineering rates for craftsmen and labourers were settled by districts — that is roughly the area covered by a local employers' association. Piece-work and systems of production bonus payment were being ever more widely applied, despite opposition from the craft unions[1] and in some districts agreements attempted to regulate their application. In some districts and many firms, special rates were laid down for classes of workers who were neither craftsmen nor labourers. The national war bonus was maintained after the war as a national bonus. The time-worker's wage consisted, therefore, of two parts — a district rate plus a national bonus. In 1919 and 1920 systems of payment by result were brought under a degree of national control by fixing a percentage above the basic rate which any system should enable the worker 'of average ability' to earn. 'Basic rate' here means district rate, so that for such a worker the national bonus was a flat addition to his piece-work earnings.

During the war and in the period between the wars payment by results continued to spread, and the variety of incentive systems continued to grow. Several systems are known to the text book,[2] but few of these are applied without modification to suit the needs of a particular works, and the inventiveness of experts has provided new methods of calculating times for particular jobs, or of weighting times by job evaluation, new

---

[1] Debates in the labourers' unions at that time showed a division of opinion between those who opposed payment by results, and those who wanted all labourers to share in the extra earnings.

[2] For instance, the Rowan, Halsey, Emerson, Gantt systems.

methods of converting standard times into basic rates and new formulae for calculating the additional earnings due at each level of production. The consequences are that it is most difficult for the unions to do more than see that earnings do not fall too low in any works, whatever the system there applied; and that there is no possible standard of earnings for a given job. In different works, even in the same area, engineering workers may be earning widely different sums for doing approximately the same job, with approximately the same effort. It follows from this that although some of these workers may be working for sub-standard earnings, many are getting more than the average for the job. Some earn very considerably more than the average. Any attempt to rationalize the engineering wages structure is bound to meet with opposition from these workers if it touches their earnings, and to be exceedingly costly, or ineffective, if it leaves them untouched. One advantage of the national bonus was that any addition or reduction in wages applied as a flat addition or reduction to all workers. The bonus systems, tied to the basic rate, were left untouched.

Especially during the war, and during the 1948-50 period of strict 'wage restraint', earnings have tended to rise faster than time-rates, and the most skilled workers — toolroom craftsmen, maintenance craftsmen, setters and markers — whose work does not allow of easy measurement and is, therefore, not easily brought under any production bonus system, had good grounds for complaint. A few districts, and many individual factories, had made special arrangements for these classes of workers, and in the early years of the second world war national agreements gave some of them the average earnings of the production workers of their factory, and other special additions above the skilled man's time-rate. Labourers have had the same grounds for complaint, especially those labourers who work as direct assistants of operatives paid by result, but if anything has been done to meet their case, it has been only in the individual firms.

The conflicts which arise out of this wage structure cut across trade union boundaries. It may fairly safely be said that almost

all the skilled men working on time-rates are members of the
'craft' unions, and almost all the labourers are members of the
two general unions, but no generalization can be made about
production workers. Many of them are apprenticed craftsmen,
although there may be little or no difference between their
work and work done elsewhere, or even in the same factory,
by a semi-skilled man. If they are apprenticed craftsmen they
will, with few exceptions, be members of the craft unions. If
they are semi-skilled they may be members of the general
unions, of the A.E.U., of the E.T.U. if working with electricians,
or of the Foundryworkers, if working in the foundry.

At the time of the amalgamation the N.U.G.M.W. and the
Workers' Union were by far the largest unions, other than the
craft unions, in the engineering industry. Up to 1924 the
National Federation of General Workers had provided some
common action from the general unions in engineering matters.
It had, for instance, signed an agreement with the employers on
payment by results in 1920, and had agitated for the inclusion
of all labourers in any such schemes. In 1924, however, the
Federation ceased to be of significance, and soon disappeared.
The Workers' Union, as we have seen,[1] was not prone to co-
operative activities, and it was not until after its amalgamation
with the T.&G.W.U. in 1929 — an amalgamation which
made that union undoubtedly the major general union, with
an interest in the engineering industry only slightly less than
that of the N.U.G.M.W. — that any common policy or action
was restored to the non-craft unions.

The two over-riding interests of the N.U.G.M.W. were to
secure a fair share for their members in payment by results
systems, and to settle the question of the manning of machines.
These interests were complicated by the decision of 'craft'
unions to undertake recruitment of semi-skilled and unskilled
workers. The N.U.G.M.W. argued that this was being done by
the old craft unions only to secure a hold over these workers in
order to strengthen the crumbling craft monopoly. The policy
of the union was laid down by Will Sherwood at the 1926
Congress:

[1] See p. 10.

'The attitude of the National Executive was that we should in all National Conferences claim for the labourer the right to progress within the industry in accordance with his ability, and also to demand for him the right to progress to any job to which his abilities may fit him. This cuts across the whole idea of the craft unions . . . and side by side with their antagonism we were confronted with the fact that they were opening out their rules and constitutions to take labourers within their ranks.

'Our National Executive had held meetings with the A.E.U. on the machine question and we were awaiting a further conference, and Brother Sherwood urged that Congress should determine a policy on two points, viz., that where our members engaged in an industry are working with craftsmen who are claiming to be paid on a system of payment by results, we should demand a share in the reward, and where those organizations refuse to have agreements with us as to an implied line of demarcation in their particular industry and open their ranks to compete with us and take in labourers, we should not hesitate to say that we are entitlted to take craftsmen into our society.'

Some delegates wanted to 'strike out on a new line' but most agreed with Charles Dukes that 'the days of craft unionism were over but we could be premature in taking advantage of these circumstances by declaring open warfare which would throw the craft unions together for protection'.

Interest in inclusion in payment by results schemes waned as mass production methods spread, and as bonus systems were applied to the payment of workers engaged in mass production. The result was that more and more unapprenticed production workers benefited from the extra earnings of such systems, and complaints against exclusion became at least as important within the 'craft' unions as in the general unions. There remained the 'machine' problem, which was already an old problem in the 'twenties.

The major conflicts of the A.E.U. (and its predecessor, the A.S.E.) with the employers have been lock-outs in which the union has challenged the employers' rights to determine working conditions — in 1852, during the second year of its existence, over piece-work, in 1898 over hours of work and in 1922 over the right to determine limits to overtime. One of the rights which the union wished to limit, and the employers were determined to uphold, was the right to choose who should man any given machine.

The A.E.U.'s original interest was to restrict certain machines to craftsmen. In this they were opposed by the general unions, whose interest in the matter was equally clear. Both were also interested in the grading of machines,[1] in order to establish higher rates for more difficult or more arduous jobs. In arriving at a settlement of the problem neither the A.E.U. nor the general unions were strong enough to ignore each other. Hence the discussions of 1925, in which the N.U.G.M.W. also raised the question of renewing the transfer agreement of 1916 between the two unions which the A.E.U. had unilaterally cancelled in 1923. During 1926 the A.E.U. changed its rules to open its ranks even more widely to unskilled workers, and the conversations broke down.

By 1930 the A.E.U. had settled a basis for discussions of the machine question with the employers, and met the two general unions, who agreed to come in on the same terms. The discussions fell through when the trade depression deepened and interest was concentrated on the employers' general demand for a worsening of conditions. The same unions took up the question once more in 1936, and the following year again met the employers. The latter rejected their agreed proposals, stated that manning must be left to them, and reiterated their old formula, that the rate paid should take into account the skill of the man, the kind of machine, and the nature of the job. This vague formula contrasts with the union proposals for grading the types of machines and fixing a rate for each grade.

In 1938 the unions tried to reopen the discussions without success. When the question was considered by the N.U.G.M.W. Executive it was stated that the custom in most districts was to

---

[1] There was a conflict within the A.E.U. between the proposal to grade machines and the proposal to grade classes of workers. Both methods of grading presented difficulties.

grant a worker on a machine two shillings above the labourers' rate, with further increases determined on merit, but that the starting rate had become the standard rate.

When dilution was applied during the war the general unions succeeded in obtaining a letter from the Employers' Federation assuring them that the employers' 'first loyalty belongs to the men who belong to the industry', and that these would receive first consideration in any promotion. At the same time the N.U.G.M.W. advised those of its members who might be promoted that they would gain no advantage by transferring to other unions.

In the years before the war the Confederation was pursuing a claim for consolidation of the national bonus into basic rates, a claim in which the A.E.U. took no part. Nothing came of it until 1943 when the Arbitration Tribunal settled a claim in which the unions had demanded consolidation as well as an increase, by granting 6s. on the national bonus[1] to time-workers, and consolidating 20s. of the national bonus in basic rates (which would have given a worker previously earning the old minimum 25 per cent above base rate on a system of payment by results approximately the same increase on the new minimum $27\frac{1}{2}$ per cent above the new base rate).[2]

Trouble followed swiftly. Piece-workers earning more than 25 per cent on the old rates would require a smaller addition to bring them to $27\frac{1}{2}$ per cent on the new. If they had previously earned 40 per cent or more, no increase was needed to fulfil the new conditions. Were these workers to get less advantage than others, or no advantage at all, from the new agreement? Should all piece-work times and prices be recalculated to take the new base rate into account? If so, would workers earning 100 per cent or more above the old basic rate, as some were, be brought down to $27\frac{1}{2}$ per cent of the new? Different employers adopted different interpretations. There were strikes, one at Barrow so troublesome that the A.E.U. was

---

[1] In 1927 time-workers had had an increase of 2s. in the national bonus, not granted to piece-workers, so that after 1943 there was an 8s. difference between the bonus of a time-worker and that of a piece-worker – another complication in the wage structure.
[2] Award 326.

forced to disband its district committee. The parties had to return to the Tribunal to ask for an interpretation of the award. All unions were critical. In his Presidential address to the Confederation, Harry Harrison criticized the Tribunal violently for having given no more than the employers offered, and for failing to make the award retrospective (thus encouraging the employers to prolong proceedings). He said:

'The Tribunal now take the view that the piece-worker should not have war advances to meet the changed living conditions because, due to longer hours, and extra effort on his part, his wages have increased.'

He asked the 1945 Congress of the N.U.G.M.W.:

'How can you insist on an increase being given to people earning 300, 400, 500 per cent? That is the reason why you cannot deal with piece-workers . . . Some people have talked about putting bonuses on to base rates, but if we make an application for an increase in base rates, which means nothing to piece-workers, we cannot expect to get something from the National Arbitration Tribunal. Future applications, if I have anything to do with them, will be for an increase for piece-workers and time-workers, and ignore it on the base rate.'

The system of national bonus had its advantages.

These were the difficulties which the Confederation had to meet in its post-war proposals for a new wage structure. The employers agreed to a joint sub-committee, but no agreement could be reached. In 1948 a claim by the unions for a £5 minimum with proportional advances to skilled workers was submitted by the Minister of Labour to a Court of Inquiry. The Court recommended[1] that a 5s. increase should be granted, that the lowest district base rates should be raised, and that the parties should make a further attempt to reorganize the industry's wage structure. The Confederation settled down to frame new proposals. The A.E.U. wanted to accept the current minimum rate of 92s. for labourers and to build thereon a grading system which would give the most skilled craftsmen 120s. (an advance of 13s.). The general unions who had per-

---

[1] Cmd. 7511 of 1948.

haps not been too serious until then,[1] became alarmed. They could not accept the argument that the craftsman was 'the real Cinderella' of the industry, and moved for a return to the £5 minimum demand. Compromise was reached on 96s, although the general unions remained unsatisfied.

In 1949, however, the A.E.U. proposed that another claim for £1 increase all round should be lodged, and carried the motion through the Confederation, despite strong opposition, led by Jim Matthews of the N.U.G.M.W., who argued that it was a foolish claim, and that they would do better by taking one claim at a time. The employers refused all claims, and in 1950 the A.E.U. carried a proposal that the Confederation should ballot on whether to strike, or whether to refer the matter to arbitration. Again the opposition was led by Jim Matthews, who could use the argument that since strikes were illegal, and arbitration compulsory, the ballot was meaningless, if not subversive. At one time it seemed that the N.U.G.M.W. would withdraw from the Confederation, but its Executive decided to take part in the ballot,[2] which in most unions, including the A.E.U., went heavily in favour of arbitration.

By this time (July 1950) the atmosphere of Government wage policy was changing, and the employers were more ready to reach agreement. In October they offered a *minimum* of 100s. (+ 8s.) to labourers, 118s. (+ 11s.) to craftsmen (other rates to be increased by 8s. if they were related to labourers' rates, by 11s. if related to craftsmen's rates), consolidation of base rates and national bonus to time-workers, and for workers paid by results a conversion of national bonus into a bonus of 9d. an hour, and a new minimum percentage of 45 per cent (intended to give the piece-worker previously on 27½ per cent an increase roughly equivalent to 11s.). Many unions, including the N.U.G.M.W., were willing to accept, but the A.E.U. led the

[1] At the 1946 Congress Charles Dukes had said of the wage structure proposals: 'Many years ago we set up some machinery to try to define what was a machine worker, and then someone asked us to define what was a machine. Well, we are still looking for that definition, so you need not be alarmed at the prospect of these negotiations.'

[2] The administrative problems raised in most unions by the need to carry out the ballot were considerable, and its conduct was not likely to reinstate ballots of this sort in general use as part of regular trade union machinery.

opposition on the grounds that this offer, like Award 326, gave nothing to the higher-paid worker, and carried its motion to refer the matter as a dispute to the Minister of Labour.

The dispute was referred to the National Arbitration Tribunal, and in November 1950, agreement was reached in accordance with its recommendations. The Tribunal accepted, with some modifications, the employers' view that the increases should apply to *minimum* rates. Accordingly all 'additional emoluments such as lieu rates, compensatory rates or other bonuses, or merit rates commonly applied' should be taken into account in granting the 8s. and 11s. increases. No increase should be granted to a labourer which would bring his rate, taking all these other possible payments into account, above 106s. and no increase should be granted to a craftsman to bring his rate above 128s. 2d.

Thus, far from being simplified, the wage structure was made more complicated. Many non-federated firms avoided the difficulties of the agreement by granting increases of 11s. and 8s. to *all* time-workers and altering systems of payment by results to give all workers paid under them an equivalent increase. In some parts of the country, particularly Manchester and the north-east, strikes, ca'canny restrictions, and overtime bans were the result, as anyone acquainted with the history of Award 326 could have predicted. As a result, although the employers' federation officially upheld the agreement, many federated firms also exceeded its terms in order to give every worker an increase in the interests of industrial peace.

The conflict of the A.E.U. and its main supporters (the 'Communist-dominated' E.T.U. and Foundryworkers) with the general unions, which was exacerbated by a considerable volume of local complaints against poaching,[1] arose in part from their general attitude to Government and T.U.C. wages' policy. The A.E.U. was the leading opponent of the policy of the T.U.C. General Council, which was defeated at the T.U.C.

---

[1] Shop stewards and branch secretaries of the N.U.G.M.W. complained that they had to meet 'insidious propaganda from certain quarters that the Union had been opposed to increases in wages'.

of 1950, whereas the general unions were its main supporters. Hostility to Jim Matthews' outspoken attacks on the A.E.U.'s proposals was shown by the loss of his place on the Confederation's Executive at its annual meeting of 1950. Moreover, there is perhaps little to choose between the N.U.G.M.W.'s constant reference to the 'lower paid worker' and the A.E.U.'s assertion that the craftsman was the Cinderella of the industry. Both these simplifications ignored most of the problems of the engineering wage structure which arise from the enormous variety of payment by results systems and the enormous variety between the earnings which are paid under them. When all this is said, however, it is clear that the N.U.G.M.W. followed the more sensible policy throughout these two years of difficult negotiations, and that had their views been accepted the engineering workers would have benefited sooner.

The fears of A.E.U. domination of the Confederation did not prove to be idle. On a number of occasions on which a vote was taken most unions were with the N.U.G.M.W. The A.E.U.'s block vote carried the issue. It is fair to say that no trouble of this kind arose in the long period in which the N.U.G.M.W. was the dominant union in the old Federation.

Since the settlement of 1950 the rifts within the Confederation have been partially healed. In November 1951, a claim which had the support of all the unions was settled by their acceptance of an all-round increase of 11s.; and earlier in the same year Jim Matthews was re-elected to the Confederation's Executive. In 1952 a further claim for a £2 increase led to protracted negotiations in which the employers were unusually recalcitrant. Only after the Confederation had issued instructions for a ban on overtime and piece-work, and the Ministry of Labour had intervened did they make an offer at all. The threat of the ban was then withdrawn, and finally, in November, agreement was reached on a general increase of 7s. 4d. In pursuing these claims the A.E.U. undoubtedly showed more sobriety than during the negotiations of 1949-50. On the other hand, the general unions supported claims for £2 increases which, according to statements of their leaders, they might have been expected to consider 'unreasonable';[1] and, whatever their opinions of the proposed overtime and piece-work ban, they did not refuse to operate it. Early in 1953 the Confederation decided to put forward a differential claim, an application for a 15 per cent increase. Such claims may contain the seeds of future conflict between the unions.

Meanwhile the Confederation has had protracted discussions with the employers concerning a revision of the procedure agreement. In this the general unions, with their experience of Joint Industrial Councils in other industries, are as anxious for reform as are the craft unions.

Women in Engineering

For as far back as figures are available, women have formed the majority of workers in many of the light engineering trades, such as screw and nail making. Before 1914 mass-production was beginning to bring women into general engineering, and in 1914 a Board of Trade estimate put the figure for women in the metal trades at 170,000.[2] During the war women came into the industry in very large numbers, but after the emergency and in the post-war depression so many left that the total fell to little above the pre-war figure. Thereafter numbers grew fairly rapidly throughout the inter-war period,[3] and very rapidly to a new peak during the second world war. Since the war the level has remained considerably higher than in 1939.

The craft unions tolerated labourers, although they would not organize them. Women they would hardly tolerate, except as a temporary necessity under war-time dilution agreements. They regarded them merely as a means by which the employers could reduce men's wages, and thought the best defence was to keep them out of the industry. The growing scale of female employment, which they attributed to the desire for low wage

[1] Jim Matthews told the 1951 Congress that 'there will be a claim coming forward next month for a £1 or £2, £6, or it may be 30s. – this nonsense of a Dutch auction'.

[2] See M. L. Yates, *Wages and Labour Conditions in British Engineering*, MacDonald and Evans, 1937, chap. IX.

[3] In the 1931 census the figure for all metals industries was 276,000.

costs, may have been partly due to that; for women's wages were low, but it was also due to the development of repetitive operations, particularly suited for women. It is difficult to see that the craft unions' method of defence was of much value if the changing nature of the industry itself was undercutting them, but they were slow to appreciate the logic of industrial development. In its early years even the N.A.U.L. had doubts about admitting women to membership. The Gasworkers were more far-sighted, but by 1914 trade unionism was still in its pioneering stage amongst women in the engineering industry. The war had an effect which not even the post-war depression could wipe out, and with the amalgamation of the Women's Federation, the N.U.G.M.W. could claim, along with the Workers' Union, to represent women in the industry, even though the great majority of them remained unorganized.

The attitude of the Employers' Federation to women was at least as reactionary as that of the craft unions. Although the Committee on Production had dealt with the wages of women as well as men, the Federation after the war refused to include women in negotiations on the male rate, or to apply advances in the male rate, or a percentage thereof, to women. The general unions had to bargain separately, and to bargain hard, if women were to get any part of an advance which had already been granted to men. It was not until 1922 that the employers agreed to apply the same overtime conditions to women as to men. It seemed as though the Federation was as conscious of the advantages of low female rates as the craft unions suggested it was. In August 1927, the N.U.G.M.W. Journal complained that the minimum rate for women in engineering was £1, as against a minimum of at least 25s. in most trades governed by Trade Boards, and 37s. in the match trade, which had once been regarded as 'sweated'.

In 1932 the union discovered, in seeking to settle a dispute in a nut and bolt factory at Atherton, Lancashire, that the industry's procedure for avoiding disputes did not apply to women. Together with the T.&G.W.U., which had now inherited the Workers' Union's claims to organize women, they submitted a claim for some procedure for women, and the employers were willing to grant that the York Memorandum should apply to women.

As wages' advances came in the late 'thirties the two unions put in parallel claims for women, and usually succeeded in getting half the male advance. In 1937 the employers wanted to hold an inquiry into women's earnings in the various sections of the industry to see whether an advance was justified. (This is a favourite gambit of the Engineering Employers, who do not admit that one of the most potent reasons for the great difference between wage rates and earnings in the industry is their own policy of keeping wage rates low.) The unions protested vigorously, and in the end a 1s. advance was conceded. In September of that year the employers agreed to include women in the national holidays with pay agreement.

With war women were once more needed in large numbers, and needed on both women's work and work customarily performed by men. In 1940 a dilution agreement was signed with all the unions, to supplement the agreement signed in 1939 by the A.E.U. alone. Under it women introduced on men's work were to have the women's rate for the first eight weeks, then for twelve weeks the women's rate plus one-third of the difference between that and the male rate. Thereafter 75 per cent of the male rate would be paid unless a full man's job was being performed without supervision, in which case, after a further twelve weeks, the full male rate would be paid. This agreement, as a dilution agreement, required the ratification of the craft unions as well as the general unions.

Advances in the male and female rates came either by negotiation or by Tribunal awards. The general unions sought to use the situation to introduce a system of grading for women's work. They argued, as they and the A.E.U. had argued for years on the 'machine' question, that different degrees of skill and effort were required for different jobs, and that this should be recognized in fixing rates, as it already was by the system of 'lead rates' applied in Royal Ordnance Factories. They wanted a grade above the minimum women's rate, and one or more grades above the 75 per cent for women on men's work not doing the full male job. The employers expressed their willingness to discuss the matter, but revision of the dilution agreement required the sanction of the craft unions, and in 1942 the Confederation rejected the proposal.[1]

During the same year the A.E.U. conducted a ballot on the admission of women to the union, which went in favour of the proposal, and by the end of the year their branches were admitting women. The N.U.G.M.W. was understandably annoyed. It held that it had supported the women's case, often in spite of craft opposition, for many years, and now the A.E.U. was competing just when women were flocking into the unions. However, its leaders sensibly saw that they could not prevent women joining the A.E.U. and during 1943 accepted T.U.C. proposals for discussion. In August of that year the A.E.U., the T.&G.W.U., the N.U.G.M.W. and the Iron and Steel Trades Confederation signed an agreement covering transfers of women between unions in the engineering and metals trades and setting up a permanent joint committee.

Henceforward the A.E.U. was associated with the two general unions in all women's claims, and they were soon joined by the E.T.U. and the Foundryworkers. In December 1943 Jack Tanner, President of the A.E.U., put forward a claim for grading of women's rates along with Miss Elliott, National Woman Officer of the N.U.G.M.W. and an officer of the T.&G.W.U. The employers agreed to set up a joint committee to consider the matter. The next move, however, was a reversal of policy by the A.E.U. Their National Committee[2] decided that the grading of women was no more urgent than the question of a national wages policy for men, and that the two were inseparable. The Committee, therefore, resolved to drop the separate claim. The N.U.G.M.W.'s view was given by Harry Harrison at the 1945 Congress:

'I want to say quite frankly and definitely and it cannot be denied, that women members of our union have been deprived of an advance of shillings per week by the deliberate frustrating efforts of the A.E.U.'

[1] The Confederation has no authority over women's questions, which are reserved by the unions concerned. But dilution was also a man's question and, therefore, properly came before the Confederation.
[2] Equivalent to an Annual Congress or Conference.

The unions certainly made use of the war period to bring women's wages up to a more reasonable standard. Between the outbreak of war and December 1945 the inclusive rate of a woman time-worker on a woman's job increased from 30s. to 58s. Over the same period the labourers' inclusive rate increased from 53s. to 76s. 6d. and the craftsman's inclusive rate from 68s. to 91s. 6d. But this increase, although important, did nothing to place women's rates on a permanently more satisfactory footing. If there was a time for the introduction of grading, it was during the war, when women's labour was so important. It is possible that it might have been settled, if it had been kept as a separate issue. To relate the proposal to the revision of the whole wage structure was, in fact, to kill it.[1] Even before the end of the war, with reconversion, women were leaving the industry, and after the war the men returned. Women, though still far more numerous than in 1939, have returned to their pre-war position, moving along behind the men, and trying to get as much as possible of any advance accorded to men.

District and Local Negotiations in the Engineering Industry

Since 1914 district agreements have declined in importance, although many matters are still settled by districts, and many districts have supplementary agreements filling in the details of national settlements, or granting additional benefits. District agreements in Coventry or Sheffield, for instance, are of great importance.

The spread of mass-production methods and systems of payment by results, together with the low-wage policy of the Federation, which has forced the good employer, or the employer short of labour, to find means of paying above national rates, have brought the purely local agreement — the agreement with a single firm — into greater and greater prominence. And these agreements are even more important to the general

[1] During the war, and in subsequent years, women in the engineering industry have been able to draw some advantage from the employers' refusal to include them in general wage claims. On several occasions they have obtained larger increases than would have been possible in those industries in which the women's rate is a fixed percentage (often 75 per cent) of the men's rate.

unions which organize by factory, than to the craft unions, which organize by the area or district.[1]

The two main features of these local agreements are their enormous variety and the vastly better conditions which many of them contain in comparison with national agreements. Some employers, for instance, have granted grading systems for women, perhaps based on job-evaluation studies, which grant experienced women on women's work 15s., 20s., or even more over the national minimum. Piece-rate systems and production bonus schemes are necessarily governed by local agreements. Normally systems of work measurement, and of relating measures to earnings, are worked out by industrial consultants employed by the firm, and presented to the shop stewards and then to the union officer. In 'advanced' firms the shop stewards and the union may be brought into the process of working out a system from the start. Once it is clear that the shop stewards are willing to accept and the union officer is unable to persuade them (if he wishes to do so) that it contains any snags, the scheme must be accepted, although it still requires the formal ratification of the district office. But refusal under such conditions would only serve to lose members.[2]

The same is true of local arrangements for discussing matters of common interest to employers and workers. The national agreement of 1919 allowed Works Committees to be set up, and a further agreement of 1942 provided for the setting up of Joint Production Consultative and Advisory Committees, by local arrangement. J.P.C.s flourished for a while during the war and then mostly disappeared. After the war the Confederation proposed that the awkward distinction between the two types of committees, one a union committee, and the other elected by all workers (although representation is limited to union members) which had frequently led to a boycott of the

---

[1] The A.E.U.'s districts are far smaller than those of the N.U.G.M.W., and cover roughly the same area as a local employers' association.

[2] Production bonuses are still a source of conflict between craft and general unions. Sometimes craftsmen demand a higher percentage than labourers. Sometimes craftsmen refuse to accept a system favoured by the general union representing production workers. More than once craftsmen have refused to come into a scheme accepted by production workers, and afterwards clamoured for a share in the higher earnings obtained.

J.P.C.s by 'militant' stewards, should be overcome by setting up a single committee on which the stewards should represent the workers on all matters.[1] The employers would have none of it. The result is that there exists a wide variety of works councils, works committees, factory committees, joint consultative committees in those firms in which the employer is willing to have them, with a wide variety of constitution, and an even wider variety in success achieved. In the large number of firms in which the employer dislikes such committees the permissive national agreement offers little help to the workers who want one.

The federated firm is to an extent restrained by national agreements. It must not get too far out of line for fear of trouble from the Federation. Certainly if workers insist that their unions take up, through the York procedure, disagreements about additional benefits granted by individual firms, there is nothing to be gained and the employer may be reprimanded for having given so much. The result is that N.U.G.M.W. officials are anxious to deal with the individual firm, and prefer to rely on good relations rather than the sanction of procedure to achieve results. The well-known tendency of the York procedure to produce monotonous 'failures to agree' only strengthens this attitude.

It can be seen that, so long as the union can maintain good relations with the non-federated employer, it may well be able to get more for its workers from him than from federated firms. He can do what he likes, and certainly some of the most favourable wages' agreements and some of the most satisfactory works committees are to be found in such firms. Non-federated firms have also the advantage from the union's point of view, that they can circumvent awkward clauses in national agreements such as that of November 1950. It is, of course, equally true that the most anti-union firms are unfederated, and the union

---

[1] Factory committees of this sort exist by agreement in Royal Ordnance Factories, and were referred to by Confederation spokesmen as models. The Confederation also wished to set up a system of Confederation shop stewards to co-ordinate the work of shop stewards in the factories, but the Federation insisted on dealing only with stewards of separate unions. Many individual employers meet joint shop stewards' committees representative of all the unions concerned. The N.U.G.M.W. has given its support to all these Confederation proposals.

has sometimes called in the good offices of the Federation to try to persuade an employer to join its ranks and to meet the union. It is also true that the officers of the Federation are often of assistance to the union in persuading unyielding employers to see the justice of at least some parts of a union claim.

The nature of the industry's procedure agreement and the attitude of the Employers' Federation has forced initiative on to the individual firms. Thus the district officer and the shop steward have far freer hands than in other industries. The result is some very favourable local agreements and very difficult relations with other firms. Variety is valuable. Whether it is worth the monstrous and growing complexity of the industry's wage-structure and a procedure for avoiding disputes which is so often dilatory, negative and provocative of conflict that union officers will frequently go to great lengths to avoid using it, is doubtful indeed.

The Shipyard Labourer

The tradition of the shipbuilding craftsman differs from that of the engineering craftsman. The members of the Boiler-makers' Union — platers, riveters, boilermakers — have always worked on piece-rate systems, fixed by price-lists. Thus these skilled men became contractors and the direct employers of labourers.[1] The general unions still refer to the day when the labourer had to wait outside the public house hoping for a share in the earnings which the craftsman was about to spend. These days are gone, and the proportion of the wages of the piece-worker's assistant which comes out of the piece-work earnings is agreed and deducted before payment to the craftsman. Customs, however, still have their effect in a traditional industry.

The aim of the general unions has been to obtain a percentage share in these earnings, and at the same time, or alternatively, to have many of the jobs performed by labourers rated as semi-skilled work, with enhanced rates of wages, and to push up the wages of the shipyard labourer in relation to those of the time-

---

[1] There were always certain classes of semi-skilled workers (see p. 206) who were separately treated.

working shipyard craftsman — for traditionally the gap has been wider in shipyards than in engineering.

Two points about the relation between skilled and unskilled workers, not directly connected with earnings, are worthy of note. Labourers working directly with craftsmen are particularly liable to find themselves out of work as a result of a dispute in which they have no concern. The shipyards are prone to demarcation disputes which rarely concern labourers, and the Boilermakers in some areas resort readily to open conflict with the employers. The N.U.G.M.W. has an understanding with their union that it shall be consulted in any strike which is likely to affect its members, but since strikes today are usually unofficial and the union's officers have no part therein, this understanding is of little value. Jim Matthews told the 1951 Congress that 'they have not yet on any occasion consulted us before they have taken such action as has thrown our members on the streets'. Secondly, Boilermakers often try to surmount unemployment by working in pairs, and sharing piece-work earnings equally, thus ensuring that unemployment shall be borne by the labourers. In contrast to the engineering industry, craft methods of self-defence are still effective in the shipyards.

The demands of the N.U.G.M.W. during the 'twenties for a share in piece-work earnings, and for the right of the labourer to progress, referred as much to the shipyards as to the engineering industry, and during those years the union pursued a claim for a share in the earnings on the Boilermakers' price-lists. It was easy for the employers to assure them that platers' helpers and rivet-heaters deserved a rise, but that since the job was already fully paid for, the rise must come out of the piece-work earnings, and for the Boilermakers to assure the union of its goodwill, so long as the employers would increase their prices to cover the extra earnings demanded by the labourers.

During those years the main interest of the unions was concentrated on national variations. These were complicated by the division of wages into base rates and national bonus, as in engineering, and by variations in cuts and advances between various grades of worker. In 1929, however, the industry agreed on a national uniform plain time-rate of 60s. for crafts-

men and 41s. for labourers.[1] The two general unions voted
against acceptance on the grounds that the agreement would
leave the shipyard labourer between 2s. and 5s. below the
engineering labourer, and worse off in relation to the craftsman
than in engineering. The craft unions outvoted them and they
were forced to accept. Ten shillings of each new rate was a
national bonus.

The N.U.G.M.W. then lodged a straight time-rate claim of
4s. for platers' helpers and rivet-heaters, hoping to have them
rated nationally as semi-skilled workers, a status already
achieved by red-leaders and holders-on, and at the end of the
second war by cranemen, but the claim disappeared in the
1931 demands for over-all reductions.

At this time the position of the union and of Will Sherwood
in the Federation gave it some status in the industry as a
whole, and it was included in joint discussions and inquiries on
the sorry position of the industry. In the early 'thirties much
of the attention of the union was concentrated on the operations
of National Shipbuilders' Securities Ltd. — the bank-financed
company set up to close down shipyards — but they were
powerless to do more than voice their discontent; the rationalization schemes brought no compensation to the worker in the
industry.

Attention then turned to the problems of electric welding.
The employers were determined to create a new class of
welders with a rate below that of existing craftsmen and to
train new workers for the job. The craft unions argued that
the new work should be performed by existing craftsmen at their
old rates. They obtained some concessions on the proposed
rates, but this did not satisfy them, and in 1934 the employers
imposed the new scheme without their consent. The unions
were in no position to resist. The general unions took part in
all the discussions, and assented to the majority decisions, but
they were certainly interested that their members should be
eligible for promotion to the new grade, and cannot have been
too disturbed by the imposition of the scheme.

[1] This excluded Cowes and Dundee, which for some years were left, for special
reasons, on a lower rate. In the end this anomaly was rectified. An additional
bonus of 3s. is paid for ship-repair work and certain types of new work.

In 1936 advances began once more and continued throughout
the war and afterwards, following closely on the pattern set
by engineering. Despite claims by the Confederation, the
industry made no experiments until 1950 in transferring sums
from the bonus to the base rate, and thus avoided the difficulties
of Award 326. When, on the appeal of the Minister of Labour
in the interests of production, the traditionally time-working
unions agreed to the application of bonus systems to their
members, the general unions achieved a victory in obtaining
an assurance that their members working *directly with* such
craftsmen would share in any bonus in proportion to the relation of their basic rate to the craftsman's rate. This arrangement
did not include the trades already working on price-lists, and
thus left the plater's helper and rivet-heater unaffected.

In 1948 the shipbuilding industry followed the engineering
industry in agreeing on an advance of 5s. in accordance with
the recommendations of the Court of Inquiry. The raising of
the lowest district rates in engineering left the shipbuilding
labourers' rate of 90s. below the lowest engineering labourers'
rate of 92s. The rate for shipbuilding craftsmen was 109s.,
against 107s. in engineering. The general unions resolved to
pursue a claim for a 92s. minimum in the shipyards. The
agreement had been accepted against the wishes of the general
unions, and the Confederation as a whole refused to support
them. The general unions lodged a separate claim and were
rebuffed by the employers, but the National Arbitration
Tribunal awarded in their favour. The general unions were
understandably jubilant at the expense of the craft unions. Jim
Matthews said at the 1950 Congress:

'Immediately we got that Award, the craft organizations
came forward and said they wanted 2s., although they did not
support us in our application. When we were successful, they
wanted that which we had got for our members.'

In December, 1950, the industry signed an agreement for an
advance in wages which contained clauses very similar to that
of the engineering agreement of the previous month, so that
little or nothing was gained by piece-workers or workers
receiving lieu rates or other plus rates. As in the engineering

industry, the application of the agreement aroused considerable discontent and conflict.

Meanwhile the union had not forgotten the platers' helper and the rivet-heater. During the war the former was granted an extra 8s. as a temporary measure by Central Conference, but this did not compensate him for the relative loss he suffered when craftsmen's mates under the new bonus schemes — sometimes women under dilution agreements — surpassed his earnings, and it made no permanent change in his status. At the end of the war the two general unions sought to take the case to the National Arbitration Tribunal, but it was referred back for the industry to settle. They then sought for a Court of Inquiry and in the end their claim was referred to the Industrial Court which issued an interim award[1] in June 1948 after its members had visited yards in the Tyne and Clyde. The terms of the Award granted semi-skilled status outright to platers' helpers on certain kinds of work, and referred the determination of the status of other classes of work back to the industry, along with the settlements of the rates to be applied. No settlement of the vexed question of sharing in piece-work earnings could be achieved, however, since both employers and Boilermakers refused to meet the cost. In 1952 the general unions submitted another claim to the Court on this point, but the Court ruled that, since the Boilermakers were not a party to the claim they could give no award on a matter which would also affect the Boilermakers' earnings, and decided that the case for a lieu rate had not been established.[2]

Earnings in the industry are dependent on yard and district agreements as well as on national agreements. Districts are of even greater importance than in the engineering industry, since the ports are separate geographical areas. London, Southampton, Bristol, Mersey, Tyne and Clydeside have very different traditions and district rules, built up out of past district agreements and arbitration settlements, and with separate arrangements for construction and repair. The Port of London rules, for instance, provide for double time to be paid for all overtime work and for rates considerably above those of other areas.

[1] Award No. 2160.   [2] Award No. 2397.

Various district arrangements are made for rivet-heaters, platers' helpers, and other similar classes. In several areas rivet-heaters and other members of riveting gangs have a fixed proportion of the piece-work earnings, despite the refusal to grant this nationally. In London platers' helpers and carriers, by agreement with the Boilermakers' Society, get a fixed share in the lieu rates which are normally paid to platers or riveters on repair work. The lieu rates are paid instead of piece-work rates since repair work cannot easily be accurately priced.

These district agreements and rules have something of the same effect as local agreements in engineering. It is almost impossible to arrange national settlements of many problems because some areas would be likely to suffer, so that oil-ship allowances, dirty-work allowances, allowances for work in confined spaces are determined by districts. One of the most important tasks of the general unions has been to obtain these allowances for labourers working with craftsmen who already receive them.

Further extra rates and allowances may be settled by the yard. One common practice is to agree that so many hours' pay will be allowed for a given job regardless of the actual time it takes, and matters of this kind are usually left for the worker or the shop steward to settle with the foreman or manager. Overtime is more important, especially in repair work, than in most other industries. When work is particularly pressing it is common for gangs to continue on the job throughout the night, and then earnings may run to a high figure.

Just as the Confederation has been more important in the shipbuilding than in the engineering industry, its district committees probably have a greater hold here. In the Port of London there is a strongly organized system of Confederation stewards, who are recognized by the local employers, and the general overtime ban of 1936 and 1937, which won some of the special concessions referred to above, was a well-concerted movement in which all unions, including the general unions, played their full part. For all this, and despite the Joint Production Committees set up during the war, the various groups of workers, as is perhaps understandable in a traditional industry, tend to keep to themselves. Within the N.U.G.M.W. red-leaders, rivet-heaters, platers' helpers, riggers and other groups stick tenaciously to their separate small branches, and resist all the union's suggestions that they would have better service if they joined together in the various centres, and thus enabled whole-time secretaries to be supported.

Because of the shipyard tradition that union members who disobey local customs established by the unions should be penalized, the union, at the request of branches in the Port of London, altered its rules in 1947 to allow by-laws imposing fines, and ratified by-laws for the London and Southern districts.

Conclusion

The record of the union in these two industries is one of which it can justly be proud. It has probably lost some ground to the T.&G.W.U. in both, but it remains the most important labourers' union in the shipbuilding industry, and is not far behind the T.&G.W.U. in engineering.

Of shipbuilding and shiprepair work it may safely be said that so long as the industry remains organized on its traditional lines, a separate organization is necessary for the unskilled classes. The whole record, even in recent years, shows that the craftsmen's organizations, naturally enough, put their own interests before those of the labourers. The N.U.G.M.W. has not achieved all it has wished for the unskilled classes, but it has pressed their claims, and considerably improved their lot.

It may well be true that the mass production methods now common in engineering render the present system of union organization unsuitable, and that far more could be done for the workers in the industry, and far better general standards enforced, by an industrial union enrolling all classes of workers. But it does not by any means follow that the A.E.U., on whose committees and in whose offices craftsmen are still predominant, is the organization fitted to do this job. And it is probably true that the general unions' method of organization by factory rather than by area, their concentration on the production worker and their long-standing claim that craft privileges should be disregarded and the worker should be allowed to progress to any job which he is able to perform are better suited to a mass-production industry than the characteristics of the A.E.U. The changes of rules and of heart in the A.E.U. have not eradicated the craft approach to many of the industry's problems, and it has certainly done no better for women, since it admitted them, than have the general unions.

The problem of the general unions has been to protect the interests of the special classes of worker which they organize in their industries without wrecking the chances of co-operation with the other unions on the many general issues on which common action is necessary. On the whole the N.U.G.M.W. has done well. It must receive full credit for bearing the brunt of the burden of the old Federation in its leanest years, and if its spokesmen have led the opposition against the A.E.U. and the majority in the new Confederation, their case has been strong. He would be a brave man who would roundly declare that the course of action which they proposed in the negotiations of 1949-1950 would not have been more advantageous to all engineering workers, not only the lower paid, than the course which the Confederation was in fact persuaded to adopt.

CHAPTER V

THE RUBBER INDUSTRY

THE rubber industry is an industry which has grown very rapidly in size during the present century, and is now one of the country's middling industries, with a labour force of 103,400 in all sections of the industry in December 1952. It is a competitive industry, but the bulk of production is carried on by a small number of large and well-known firms, using modern machinery and mass-production methods in modern, or modernized, factories. There is a fair number of small firms, some of which continue to produce with antiquated methods, and in unsuitable buildings under unpleasant conditions.

The Growth of Collective Bargaining

Before the first world war the labourers' unions had a foothold in a few firms and were recognized for bargaining purposes by one or two. Thereafter comes the familiar tale of the appeal of the unions during the war to the Committee on Production and the issue of awards covering the industry. By 1918 the Committee was determining disputes between the India Rubber Manufacturers' Association and a joint committee of the N.U.G.W., the N.A.U.L. and the Workers' Union. The Birmingham gasworkers organized in the Birmingham Dunlop works, and a small 'industrial' union — the Amalgamated Society of India Rubber, Cable and Asbestos Workers — pursued an independent line.

After the war the parties agreed to set up a Joint Industrial Council, which was originally intended to cover the cable industry, as well as general rubber goods, tyres and waterproof garments. The cable manufacturers, however, wanted a separate Council, on the grounds that they were using less and less rubber and more of other materials. They had their way despite the predominance of the N.U.G.W. in both industries, and the unions owed them gratitude, for the Cable Council stood its ground when collective bargaining collapsed in the rubber industry.

The Rubber Council drew up a model constitution for Works Committees, which were established 'in most of the larger works'.[1] The employers refused to consider national negotiations through the Council on the grounds that 'the wages conditions in the Rubber Trade are totally dissimilar and are dependent upon the wages paid in other industries in the various localities'.[2] Since no regional councils were set up negotiations were confined to the individual works once national wage legislation was withdrawn, and the unions lost most of their interest in the Council.

In the slump of 1921 and succeeding years union membership collapsed and the hold of the Employers' Federation weakened. The Council disappeared, and so little store did the union set by it and so heavy were the series of calamities and losses of that period that its demise went unrecorded by the union at the time. Writing in the Journal of April 1933 the Scottish district secretary, John McKenzie, gave the union's version of the story.

'. . . During that period a serious attempt was made, not only to secure uniform rates of wages, but also to compel an agreement regarding prices. Unfortunately some of the more powerful employers, who did not accept the principle, would not join the Council — nor were the workers sufficiently organized to compel them to do so — with the result that in due course the Whitley Council broke up, and there followed a period of guerrilla warfare resulting in a feverish and stupid policy of price-cutting, and workers had to pay in reduced wages.'

Certainly very low time-rates were paid in the industry throughout the inter-war period. 8d. an hour, 32s. for a 48-hour week, is quoted by union officials as a common *male* rate, and they assert that a 55-hour week was common. At the same time, many of the employers became strongly anti-union. Union membership was discouraged, if not actively prevented, and in some firms entrants were required to sign documents agreeing to accept the rates and conditions of employment as determined by the management. Many of the works committees were main-

[1] *Report on the Establishment and Progress of Joint Industrial Councils*, 1917-1922. H.M.S.O., 1925, p. 75.
[2] *Ibid.*, p. 161.

tained as company unions. Employers used them as means of discussing any proposals they had to make concerning rates or conditions, and the worker representatives could state their view, but with no union behind them. It is true that in one of the largest firms a factory council of this type was chosen in preference to union negotiations by a majority of the workers at a secret ballot. But it is very difficult to persuade workers afraid of dismissal that a ballot held inside a factory is in fact entirely secret.

There were hopes that the imposition of the 10 per cent *ad valorem* tax in 1931 and a subsequent tariff on imported footwear, would be followed by an agreement between domestic producers which would avoid competitive price reductions and therefore also further wage reductions, but in fact further reductions in both prices and wages were made during the depth of the depression. Some firms, particularly the Edinburgh North British Rubber Company, which was the one large company to maintain relations with the union throughout the period, were anxious to re-form the Council and agree on national minimum rates as a means of stopping price cuts, but their attempt to use the opportunity offered by the new tariffs failed, and it became clear that voluntary action was unlikely to achieve success.

In 1933 and 1934 there were two strikes over the introduction of the Bedaux system of time-study in the North British Rubber Company. The system was finally accepted by the union with certain alterations, since it could not be resisted, and the second strike was declared unofficial, with serious results on trade union membership there. But the principle of collective bargaining was preserved, and membership slowly recovered.

Not all strikes were harmful to the unions. In 1933 there were a number of strikes in firms associated with Fords, strikes of mainly unorganized workers often under Communist leadership. One of these broke out in the Firestone Tyre Company, and though it failed to achieve improvements in conditions or union recognition, it offered an opportunity for organization to the T.&G.W.U., who inherited 'rights' from the Workers' Union.[1] In 1936 strikes in the Midlands at the factories of the

[1] *T.&G.W.U. Record*, August 1933.

John Bull Rubber Company and the Michelin Tyre Company, achieved some improvements and a degree of union recognition.[1]

Meanwhile the N.U.G.M.W. was pursuing the same end by different methods. Its Lancashire district officers, having failed to make much impression by direct attempts at organization of the workers in the several large factories of South Lancashire, tried to persuade the Transport Committees of a number of important local authorities to withdraw their contracts from some of these companies under the 'fair wages clause', on the grounds that the wages and conditions had not been accepted by the unions, and were such that no union would accept. They also sought interviews with several of the employers, and found a good deal of sympathy with the desire to improve conditions, but the employers declared themselves unable to act without assurance that their competitors would be forced to follow them. And the only means of applying force without powerful union organization or a strong employers' federation was a Trade Board.

The union's officers had always been lukewarm towards Trade Boards. The Boards might indeed serve a purpose in preventing the worst excesses of sweating, but the wages and conditions remained well below average, and the unions were unable to raise them further because they had insufficient membership. Their membership was weak in these industries, so they argued, because workers thought of the Boards as statutory and, therefore, as government bodies, and supposed that their wages were fixed by the government. If the government fixed their wages, what could a union do for them? There seemed, however, no other way forward in the rubber industry.

During 1937 the union's Head Office took over. Conversations were held with the T.&G.W.U. to define spheres of influence, and also with individual employers. In 1937 the union signed an agreement with the largest Manchester works regulating wages and conditions. Six months' notice of alterations was required, but it was agreed in an exchange of letters that if the union managed to obtain better conditions in com-

[1] *Ibid.*, February and July 1936.

peting factories, it would be allowed to open immediate discussions on amendment of the agreement. Soon afterwards the Liverpool works of the same company, which claimed that its rates were slightly better than those at Manchester, consented to sign an agreement, if the union would accept existing conditions, and take its chance of obtaining an improvement through a similar qualifying clause.

More employers were brought into discussion, and there seemed some likelihood that they would be willing to agree to set up a Joint Industrial Council, if they could first obtain the protection of a Trade Board. Officers were advised to move slowly in the 'fair wages' campaign and the unions collected information in order to present a report to the Ministry of Labour to prove the need for a Board.

In March 1939, the names of the members of the new Trade Board were announced. In November of the same year the first set of rates became effective. One of the main criticisms of Trade Boards was the slowness of the Trade Board procedure, and no further advance should have been granted within six months, but in January 1940 the Board showed its recognition of the rapid rise in prices since the outbreak of war, by recommending to the Ministry a further 4s. increase as an emergency. It was granted in March. A recommendation on holidays with pay followed and in June 1940 a Joint Industrial Council was formed and at its first meeting agreed to an additional 2s. increase. Since then the Council has become the body which determines national wages and conditions, and on the Board (whose title was changed to that of Wages Council under the Wages Council Act, 1945) a group of employers' and workers' representatives, hardly differing from the members of the Council, meet with the independent members to recommend to the Minister that the rates thus voluntarily agreed should be made obligatory on all employers in the industry.

The wages agreement of the Council provides for minimum rates for adult men and women, an age-scale below twenty-one, and additional rates for more skilled work. There is a separate agreement for rubber floor-laying which follows the increases agreed by the Council, and a separate Wages Council for the rubber reclamation industry, which became of great importance during the war, but it, in fact, settles the same rates as the main Council. The industry thus has a wage structure of extreme simplicity compared to those of any of the industries we have so far considered.

Most workers in the industry are paid piece-rates, or under some kind of bonus system. The national agreement lays down that under such systems a worker of 'average ability' should earn at least 25 per cent above his basic rate. In fact, earnings in many factories run to 75 per cent or even 100 per cent. The effect of rapid expansion and technical improvement in the industry on such systems of payment has enabled its workers, whose time-rates are not remarkably high compared with those of other workers, to rise nearly to the top of the industrial earnings' list from a humbler position in 1939.[1]

During the war one complication was introduced into the wages structure by granting some advances as flat rate 'bonuses' not included in the base rate, and, therefore, not included in the calculation of overtime premiums or piece-rate and output bonus prices. Fortunately the total sum involved did not rise to anything like the figure of national bonuses in the engineering and shipbuilding industries, and, therefore, did not cause comparable difficulties. In 1950 it stood at 4d. an hour, and was consolidated in the base rates by national agreement in the autumn of that year.

Industrial Relations Today

Besides the two great general unions the workers' side of the National Council includes the Union of Shop Distributive and

---

[1] In October 1938 the average earnings of all workers in the industry were given as 51s. against a national average of 53. 3d. In October 1952 the figure for all workers was 162s. 6d. aganist a national average of 151s. 11d. Even in 1938 the exceptionally low time rates were somewhat compensated by piece-work and bonus earnings.

In all industry average hours for all workers were 46.5 in October 1938 and average hourly earnings 13.7d. In the rubber industry the average hours worked were 48.6 and the hourly earnings 12.6d. The rubber worker was thus working longer hours than the average, and his hourly earnings compared even less favourably with the national average than his weekly earnings. In October 1952 the national average of hours worked was 46.1, and the rubber industry's 46.5: the gap was reduced. Hourly earnings in rubber at 41.9d. were well above the national average of 39.5d.

Allied Workers, and the United Rubber Workers of Great Britain. The former is a union which has been established over a period of years by amalgamations of unions of co-operative employees, warehousemen and shop assistants. Although it has less than half the members of the N.U.G.M.W. it is now one of the largest unions in the country, and, although its industrial coverage is not nearly so great as that of either the N.U.G.M.W. or the T.&G.W.U., it is so wide that the union can hardly be classified except as a general union. Its relations with the two larger general unions are usually good, and although its control of one factory in the industry is fortuitous — the factory was organized by U.S.D.A.W. before it changed over to rubber manufacture — they have not objected to its having a place on the Council. The United Rubber Workers is the old 'industrial' union under a new name. It competes for membership with the general unions and does not observe any territorial rights, but is, in fact, too small seriously to challenge their hold, and is, therefore, tolerated, though not encouraged. In 1946 there was some talk of amalgamation between the U.R.W. and the Chemical Workers' Union, an industrial union which has made constant and vigorous attempts, without great success, to oust the general unions from the chemicals industry. Because of its origin the general unions treat the C.W.U. as a 'breakaway'; relations are bitter, and more than once differences have been aired before the Courts. Had the amalgamation been carried through the two general unions might have been expected to object most strenuously to the claim of the new union to a seat on the Council. Maintenance workers are organized by the craft unions and do not come under the Council's authority.

The Joint Industrial Council has expanded from 37 firms in 1940 to just under 100 in 1950. The compulsion supplied by the Wages Council and by S.R. & O. 1305, left employers with little incentive to remain outside, and improving trade union organization, and the growing authority of the Employers' Federation, which had been revitalized by these provisions, provided pressure to bring them in. The work of the Council has proceeded easily and without major conflicts. There have been one or two minor unofficial strikes, quickly settled. Disputes arising in individual firms are submitted to Conciliation Panels of four members — two from each side of the Council — which visit the factory to hold an investigation. The Panels are used three or four times each year. Their awards, although not legally binding, are invariably observed. Both sides of the Council are represented on national and international advisory bodies concerned with the industry, and have made joint representations to the Ministry of Labour on such problems as the importation of foreign-produced rubber goods.

The Council has set up no regional bodies, since rates have been national from the first and the number of undertakings is relatively small. Shop representatives are given recognition for 'conducting local negotiations under the terms of N.J.I.C. agreements, and to deal with other local matters', and the Council recommends that 'where no facilities exist at present for joint consultation . . . Joint Works Committees shall be set up'. Their constitution is left to local arrangement, but 'it is recommended that nominees should be members of their appropriate Trade Union'. In fact, many of the old 'company union' factory or works committees were retained, with limited functions, when the firms recognized the unions, and their constitutions were gradually altered to make them more congenial to union eyes. In several works it is arranged that the union stewards shall be the committee representatives, and this is sometimes rendered more simple by 100 per cent, or near 100 per cent, union membership. As a result 'joint consultation' in the factories is considerably more developed than in factories of other industries with a much longer tradition of trade union bargaining. Many of the larger employers have developed considerable welfare facilities and practise the most 'modern' methods of encouraging participation by workers in the running of their enterprises, although in some instances at least their attitude is strongly tinged with paternalism.

One of the proudest achievements of the Joint Industrial Council is its work on the prevention of accidents. In 1949 it decided to proceed with a thoroughly organized campaign. Joint Accident Prevention Committees were set up in the factories, where they did not already exist, and a comprehensive system of recording accidents on punched record cards provides an Accident Prevention Committee set up by the National Council with material for technical analysis of the causes of accidents, and thus enables it to provide the factory committees with expert advice on the best methods of prevention. The results so far are claimed to be encouraging.

The story of the growth of collective bargaining in the rubber industry is very different from that of the development of trade unionism in the country's major industries during the nineteenth century. Even in 1939 the hold of the unions in most sections of the industry was very weak, and trade union membership has been built up with the active encouragement of most of the employers,[1] and *after* collective bargaining machinery had been established.

The exemplary record of the industry's industrial relations since 1939[2] has undoubtedly been aided by the exceptional expansion and prosperity of the industry in a period of general expansion and prosperity. How well good relations would stand up to adversity cannot be estimated. It may be that the attitude of the employers would change, and that, without their encouragement and the regular advances which the unions have managed to obtain without great difficulty, members easily won would be easily lost. However that may be, it seems reasonable to suggest that in concentrating its efforts on securing good relations with the employers the unions have obtained a greater hold within the industry, and done more for their members, than would have been possible by any other strategy.

[1] The employers have given a national undertaking to 'invite' their workers to join their appropriate unions.

[2] One blot on the industry's record is its high labour turnover. However, the interpretation of turnover statistics is not simple, and an industry which is exceptionally short of labour, as rubber has been over most of the period since the war, might expect a very high rate of turnover at the margin which would inflate the over-all figures. Employers in the industry argue that the figure is to be attributed to this and to other unavoidable post-war difficulties rather than to failure to make work attractive to their employees and to develop good relations with them.

CHAPTER VI

THE LAUNDRY INDUSTRY

IN December 1952 the laundry industry employed 174,400 workers, 41,900 males and 132,500 females. A large proportion of the males are employed in the collection and distribution of laundry, so that the vast majority of workers within laundries are female. The industry is distributed over the length and breadth of the country, and is an industry of small units. Many units are as well-equipped and well-conditioned as any modern factory, and, as with other service industries, a good deal of capital was sunk during the period between the wars. But there remain a great number of badly-housed and badly-equipped laundries in which working conditions are poor.

A woman's industry, a widely-scattered industry, and an industry of small units is not one to recommend itself to a trade union organizer, and, indeed, the industry has never been strongly organized. Before 1914 the general unions and unions catering for women had organized a few workers, and their membership expanded during the war, but to nothing like the extent to which it did in those industries we have considered so far. Transport unions had brought in a number of the men. After amalgamation with the Women's Federation the N.U.G.W. had the greatest claim to represent the women, outside the Co-operative laundries where the workers were included in the National Union of Distributive and Allied Workers.[1] But total membership was not impressive, collective bargaining had hardly developed at all, and the unions could clearly do no more than accept the proposal that a Trade Board should be set up under the amending Act of 1918 (which allowed the Minister of Labour considerable powers to set up Boards outside the industries scheduled under the original Act of 1911).

---

[1] Later, by amalgamation, U.S.D.A.W.

The Board was set up, settled minimum wages for men and for women, and from time to time considered proposals to alter the rates. In 1928 the membership of the Board caused trouble between the union and the Ministry of Labour. Due to a number of retirements the union was asked to submit new nominations for the workers' seats. Formerly there had been nine N.U.G.M.W. representatives, four officers and five members working at the trade. The Ministry asked that six of the new nominees should be workers whose wages 'were regulated by the Board', but the union sent in the names of four officers and five lay members once again. Despite repeated objections the Executive refused to alter its decision, and appears to have won its point.

In 1936 the unions established a claim that overtime should be paid on a daily and not on a weekly basis. In an industry in which irregular hours are worked, weekly calculation of overtime may allow employers to avoid any penalty for working long hours on any one day or even on two or three days in succession.[1] During the following year a 4s. increase was granted and the N.U.G.M.W. Journal reported that after a long period of apathy, laundry workers were 'waking up'. This awakening did not, however, provide the union with strength enough to achieve voluntary bargaining machinery in the industry as a whole.

Co-operative laundries form an important section of the trade, and although Co-operatives are not invariably model employers, they have here shown themselves far better than the average of the laundry trade. Many Co-operatives from the earliest days of the Board made agreements to pay higher rates. But this was mainly the field of N.U.D.A.W. Where hospital laundry workers were employed (after 1929) by a local authority prepared to meet the unions on the wages of hospital workers, the N.U.G.M.W. was able to improve on the Trade Board rates, but, as we have seen, such local authorities were exceptional before 1943.

---

[1] This provision became even more important in 1938, when S.R.&O. No. 728 allowed some relaxation of the provisions covering maximum hours for women and young persons in the industry to meet irregular pressure of work.

During the early years of the war launderers suffered from a shortage of labour due to the expansion of war industries which exercised great attraction over low-paid laundry workers. In 1941 the shortage became so acute that the service seemed likely to break down, and the Minister of Labour was asked to issue an Essential Work Order to prevent further loss. This he was only prepared to do if the employers would meet the unions to settle the rate for the guaranteed week, a rate which was the compensation which a worker received under such Orders for the loss of freedom to leave his job. It was *ultra vires* for a Trade Board to fix a guaranteed weekly wage, so the employers and unions met on October 11th of that year and settled a rate of 4s. above the Trade Board rate to apply to all workers covered by the Order. The meeting was recalled from time to time to consider proposals for alteration of the rate, and became known as the 'E.W.O. Conference'.

Since the rate fixed by this conference was technically the outcome of a voluntary agreement, it was subject to the war-time procedure for compulsory arbitration.[1] Accordingly the unions took the employers before both the National Arbitration Tribunal and the Industrial Court to secure advances. In 1944 they were able to secure an agreement for full men's rates to be paid to women doing a full man's job, for instance as drivers, and rates intermediate between men's and women's rates for women doing some part of a man's job. This seemed to the unions a great advance over the Trade Board methods, and they found their membership, though still low, increasing at a greater rate than ever before.

Improvements were, however, dependent on the Essential Work Order, and in 1944 the unions began to press for some more permanent arrangement. Informal meetings were held with the Institution of British Launderers and representatives of the Co-operative laundries, to discuss the union proposal that a J.I.C. should be set up. The Institution proceeded cautiously. Its representatives wanted time to consult their members, and

[1] Since Trade Board rates are confirmed by regulations issued by a government department, arbitration could not apply to rates settled by the boards.

to inquire of other employers' organizations what the effect and value of a J.I.C. would be.

The war ended. During the great changes in manpower distribution of the following months the unions' new membership in the industry began to melt away. They urged the employers to give them a speedy reply, but the employers had no need to hurry, and when the answer came it rejected the proposal, on the grounds that the unions were insufficiently representative to make a J.I.C. possible. The Essential Work Order was withdrawn and nothing took the place of the E.W.O. Conference. The unions appealed to the Ministry of Labour, but the Minister could not force the employers into a voluntary organization. Wages and conditions would once more be fixed by a statutory body.

There was some consolation in that, under the 1945 Act, the Trade Board had now become a Wages Council with considerably wider powers. Besides minimum rates, rates were fixed for women doing men's work, for waiting time, for shift work, for a guaranteed weekly wage and for holidays with pay. The unions maintained, however, that the minimum rates (from 1947 90s. for men, and 60s. for women) were unduly low, and were pursuing a claim for an increase in 1948, when the employer's hand was strengthened by the publication of the White Paper on Personal Incomes, Costs and Prices. The story is told by the Annual Report of 1949.

'. . . on July 23rd, 1948, after a prolonged discussion on the matter, the appointed members voted with the chairman against conceding any increase in wages.

'The trade unions under pressure from their membership again convened a meeting of the Wages Council to discuss this question, and on this occasion also the appointed members voted with the employers against any increase in wages.

'At the workers' side meeting which followed the unions agreed to submit local applications for increases in wages where they had the requisite membership.

'The employers in this industry put forward the claim that they are intending to introduce systems of payment-by-results, and in this way will increase the worker's pay packet. The unions are not opposed to such systems of payment-by-results, but argue that these should not be based on an inadequate wage. . . .'

The unions also felt that the action of the independent members was influenced by a desire to see that rates were no higher than the most inefficient laundry could pay, and argued that the task of a Wages Council, and of Trade Boards before them, was to fix a reasonable rate, and force out of the industry employers who can only survive by 'sweating' labour. They held that in many laundries where they followed up their decision to present individual claims, bonus systems which had nothing to do with production were introduced to avoid meeting the claims. In 1950 two such claims were taken to the National Arbitration Tribunal. One sought an increase for men paid only the 90s. minimum, and the other for women who received a 1s. attendance bonus in addition to their 60s. The Tribunal rejected both claims.

In January 1951 the Wages Council at last agreed on a national increase, and further increases followed in August of the same year and in 1952. Together these increases brought the rates to 108s. 9d. for men, and 75s. for women.

Meanwhile hospital laundry workers had done better. The Council set up for hospital domestic staffs dealt with them as with other hospital workers, and wages were settled in 1947 which gave some hospital laundry workers in some areas almost 20s. over the Wages Council rate.[1] In 1949 the Co-operative Laundry Association signed a national agreement which gave their employees 10s. more than the Wages Council rates in the provinces, and 16s.-18s. more in London.

Despite these higher rates earnings over the whole country are very low. In October 1952 the weekly earnings of all

[1] On February 17th, 1949, Mr. Joynson Hicks asked the Minister of Health 'whether he is aware that female laundry workers aged 18 and employed in laundries doing 75 per cent of hospital work earned £2 8s. 9d. weekly up to 5th July but since that date in the laundries taken over by the South Western Metropolitan Regional Hospital Board their wages have been increased to £3 15s. 11d. weekly; and if he is satisfied that this increase of over 50 per cent has been justified by increased output'. Mr. Bevan replied that the increase was confined to Chichester laundry, and was due to the application of the national agreement for hospital staffs.

It would have been possible to ask if the £2 8s. 9d. was justifiable.

laundry workers were given as 92s. 4d. and compared with a national average of 151s. 11d. The earnings of adult women in the industry, at 81s. 1d., compared with a national average of 96s. 4d.

There is no conflict amongst the unions in the industry. There is room for all to expand their membership. The two unions besides U.S.D.A.W. and the N.U.G.M.W. are the T.&G.W.U. and the United Road Transport Workers' Association, both of which deal mainly with drivers. During the 'twenties a small Laundry Workers' Union held together a few dozen members for some years. The N.U.G.M.W. held that it existed only to give another vote at the T.U.C. to 'Communist-inspired' resolutions, especially to those demanding a reorganization of British trade unions on industrial lines.

In the N.U.G.M.W., membership is scattered and fluctuating, outside the few Co-operative laundries for which the union caters. Union officers say that the industry is almost incapable of organization, on the grounds that workers think the government fixes their wages, on the grounds that turnover of labour is exceptionally high, and on the grounds that the low wages of the industry attract a different type of woman from those who work in the relatively highly paid factory trades, much less amenable than they are to union organization. One officer relates that when he started as an Appointed Officer he returned one day to relate proudly to the district secretary that he had organized 400 laundry workers. The secretary told him that he would have done better to bring in one dustman, for none of his recruits would remain beyond the first week.

In some laundries up and down the country, however, a more stable membership has been recruited, especially where it has been possible to find dependable stewards. In a few laundries organization is encouraged by direct negotiations with the employer and agreements on additional payments. This organization is most patchy, and in 1950 it appeared that the union included more laundry workers in the North of Ireland than in the whole of the London district.

The union's method of attaining its aims by establishing good relations with the employers will only bring results where the employers yield to its blandishments. The Institution of Launderers has stood firm. But this is no criticism of the union's method, for it is hard to see that any other tactics would have brought better results. If the unions have achieved little, they have at least tried. And the refusal of the employers to go beyond a Wages Council places the responsibility for the exceptionally low wages of the industry squarely upon their shoulders.

CHAPTER VII

THE UNION'S INDUSTRIAL METHODS AND ACHIEVEMENTS

THE account of the union's work in industry could be continued through many volumes. Each industry would be seen to have its peculiarities, in the origin of its arrangements for collective bargaining, in the provisions of its procedural agreements, in its wage structure and in its inter-union relationship. Nearly all industries have had their own conflicts and strikes, which can make interesting stories in themselves. Each industry would also be found to have its similarities, in some matters with a few, in others with many other industries. But it is time for us to drop the descriptive method, in order to attempt to show what general principles may be discovered in the industries which we have already described, and to touch on some general questions which affect all, or most of, the industries with which the union deals.

Business Unionism

'Business' unionism is an American expression, but it is a fair description of a great deal of the work of the N.U.G.M.W. As one union officer has put it: 'It is the business of the union to sell labour, and to get as good a price as it can. The union sells different qualities of labour, and in different markets, and it must have regard to this in the bargains it makes. No business-man who wants to stay in business can afford to cheat or to press his advantage fully home on every occasion. The most successful businessmen keep on good terms with their customers, and the union must do so too.'

The N.U.G.M.W. is certainly not unique in adopting such methods. Good relations exist in many firms and industries which it does not touch; good relations existed in industry before the N.U.G.M.W. was founded. But the great extension of the field of collective bargaining in 1919 and 1920 by the constitution of J.I.C.s was due to the N.U.G.W. more than to any other single union, and if any union leader was the spokesman of that movement, J. R. Clynes was the man. The general unions have since raised the establishment of good relations into a general principle, have driven it firmly into the heads of their officers and have applied it over a far wider field than other unions.

In one respect the general unions, and particularly the N.U.G.M.W., are better able to do business than the 'craft' unions, for it is far more easy for the employer, or the employers' federation, to take the decision of an officer of the general unions as final. Once the N.U.G.M.W. spokesmen on a national negotiating body have given their word, it is most unlikely to be repudiated; if they have made sure that the General Secretary and National Executive approve of their action, there is no official means by which it could be repudiated. Once the district officer has settled a point with an employer, and has had the approval of the district secretary for his action, it is almost inconceivable that the district committee would try to change the decision. The members affected, to be sure, may feel aggrieved. It is the job of the good officer to be sure of their wishes and opinions before he acts, and to convince them afterwards that what has been done is the best possible in the circumstances. They may not be convinced; they may take unofficial action. But the employer can rest assured that once he has come to an agreement with the union the whole weight of its authority will be behind observance of the agreement, and that the likelihood of any trouble is not great.

Not so the 'craft' unions. The President of the A.E.U. may pursue a claim to find that the next meeting of the union's National Committee changes its *industrial* policy, and he must follow them. The district secretary[1] of the A.E.U. may deal with an employer, but rarely with absolute assurance that he can settle without reference back to the district committee. When he returns from his committee meeting it may be with a very different draft of an agreement. The officers of the A.E.U. and of many other 'craft' unions are elected, and stand for re-

[1] The district of the A.E.U. is a far smaller area than the N.U.G.M.W.'s district, and the A.E.U. district secretary may serve no more members than some of the N.U.G.M.W.'s whole-time branch secretaries.

election every three or five years. In times in which political differences affect many such unions deeply, elections are fought keenly, and some officers' actions are affected by the knowledge that their security of tenure depends on their popularity. Such an officer may speak to an employer with two voices; one in private, and one when his members are present.

The 'craft' unions, in this respect, can claim to be more democratic. It is doubtful whether they can claim that such methods enable them to serve their members' interests better. Employers and officials of employers' federations stress, time and again, this difference between dealings with general unions and with 'craft' unions, and it is unlikely to make them consider the claims of the latter with any more kindness. Nor is a negotiator likely to do a better job if he is putting forward a case which has been forced upon him against his judgment.

The methods of 'business' unionism are far removed from the theories of class warfare which were written into the original address to the union's rules. The union has found that, at least in some instances, the desire of the employer to be a good employer has been of as much value to them as the strength of their members' support. It must also be said that its officers like best of all to deal with a good employer, *and* to be sure that they have a strongly-organized membership behind them. It is true that business unionism may have been forced on the union because of its lack of any craft monopoly, which would provide the basis for aggressive salesmanship. And it is true that on occasion the N.U.G.M.W. will, like any other good business man, refuse to carry on with a particular deal, and call its members out.

National Negotiations

The same process which has led to 'business' unionism has led, through the establishment of J.I.C.s and the experience of two wars, to a great development of national bargaining and national wage rates. We have seen that employers have supported this at least as strongly as have most unions, and far more strongly than the N.U.G.M.W. Besides its opposition to national rates in the Non-Trading services and in the gas industry, the union was able to enforce a return to regional bargaining in the electricity supply industry for a period in the 'thirties in order to avoid further national reductions, and in 1931 wished to break up the national bargaining machinery in the engineering industry in order to make the best terms it could for its members in each district.

Little more can be definitely said of this than that the union's preference for regional bargaining is clearly influenced by its structure, and that, although national rates seem to offer rough justice, it is impossible to determine whether, on average, workers do better out of regional or out of national bargaining. It may, however, also be true that in an age of centralization, the stand of the N.U.G.M.W. has done a little to ease the burden placed upon industry by centralized administration.

The Closed Shop

The policy of the union on the closed shop became a matter of importance when it became clear that the 1927 Act[1] was to be repealed. Early in 1946 the Executive and General Council announced their opinion that the districts were 'now free to implement the policy of the "closed shop" where and whenever circumstances were favourable'. Later that year Charles Dukes dealt at length with the subject in his Presidential address to the T.U.C., and his views were repeated in the union's Journal for October as union policy.

In his T.U.C. speech Dukes denied that the closed shop in Britain had any of the unpleasant associations of the American version which turns a union into an employing agency, and supported it on these grounds:

'The non-unionist often seeks to justify his position on the ground of personal freedom; but no consideration either of ethics or expediency can justify a man or woman taking without return the benefit of sacrifices made by their fellow workers in building up a Union. But I apply this principle more strictly in defining the responsibilities of management. It is logically indefensible for an employing authority, for instance in local government, to disown responsibilities about the Trade Union

[1] See p. 176.

status of the workers in its service. Where Trade Union standards have to be maintained by local authorities, where they have to be observed by managements, it is likewise their duty to see that their workers join the appropriate Union.'

For all the apparent definiteness of policy, it is not easy to give an exact statement of the union's position in this matter. The closed shop in local authorities, which was directly raised by the repeal of the 1927 Act, is not typical, since the attitude taken by various authorities is deeply affected by their politics, and may be changed by an election. In this, as with wage rates, it is difficult for the union to appear less ardent than the Labour councillor, although in 1951 Durham provided an example of a council more wedded to the closed shop than most of its employees.

In other industries the matter is not normally raised in the same way. National, regional and local agreements do not usually cover the point. The union's policy is against pursuit of the closed shop by 'aggressive' tactics,[1] and even sympathetic employers' organizations are not normally ready to do more than recommend to their employees that they should join their union, as in the rubber industry.

The question is usually settled in the individual place of work. Sometimes there may be a formal agreement between the employer and the district officer. More often there is an understanding between the management and the shop stewards that new entrants will be told to join the union on the grounds that the management does not want trouble and will certainly find trouble unless the recruit conforms. In fact, local 'militants' are far more ready to be excited about working with a non-unionist than are union officers, and officers are content to leave them to settle the question for themselves. Only if a dispute threatens or breaks out does the officer intervene to try to get a formal agreement in the union's favour, or some compromise which his members will accept. Even then, as we have seen,[2] permission for a strike to enforce the closed shop may be refused.

Accordingly the union's policy on the closed shop is not one

[1] See p. 173.   [2] See p. 173.

which greatly affects its activities in industry, and in conversation officers treat it as an open question. Some of them feel that national negotiations and government wages' policies make it necessary for unions to seek for assurances that their loyalty to agreements shall not lose them members. Others feel that they would rather dispense with members thus recruited.

In his speech to the 1946 T.U.C. Charles Dukes went on to say: 'But there is a larger and more complicated problem involved in the closed shop controversy . . . It is the problem arising from the existence of organizations outside the affiliations of our Congress.'

He suggested that the solution lay in inter-union agreements and the spread of unionism to higher grades. Here he certainly over-simplified as far as his own union is concerned. The exclusion of unions from bargaining rights does raise problems when those unions are not affiliated to the T.U.C. But these problems are sometimes soluble, as in the case of N.A.L.G.O., and the problem raised by the exclusion of unions which *are* affiliated to the T.U.C. is at least no more easily solved, and affects the N.U.G.M.W. more closely.

Although in the cotton industry, the mining industry and the iron and steel industry the union has been prevented from establishing the bargaining rights which it would like by unions which are stronger in those fields, the union is as much the aggressor as the victim in this matter of exclusion. The extreme cases are represented by N.U.P.E. which has forced its way through nearly all barriers put in its way in the Non-Trading services, and by the Rubber Workers who are not powerful enough to inspire fear. Between those extremes there are a number of unions which do inspire fear, but are not strong enough to break down barriers. In 1950 the Chemical Workers' Union affiliated to the T.U.C. on a membership of over 20,000, but it has been unable to secure recognition in the bargaining procedures of the various sections of the chemicals industry except in a few individual firms. N.U.P.E. has been excluded from the councils of the gas and electricity supply industries. The Plumbers have been refused recognition as spokesmen of some of the gasfitters.

It must first be pointed out that there are no large unions in the country who could not be accused on similar grounds, if they are grounds for a charge. The T.&G.W.U. has been associated with the N.U.G.M.W. in almost all the cases of exclusion we have mentioned, and so-called 'craft', 'industrial' and 'employmental' unions usually have something to answer for.

Secondly, solid reasons can be given for exclusion. Unions must guard against 'break-aways'. All unions have to reach agreements and take decisions unpopular with many of their members. If sections can break away to form new unions, and then receive recognition on the same terms as the original union, discipline is weakened and union leaders are unlikely to show courage or foresight when they disagree with their members. The work of negotiating bodies is only likely to succeed if the various unions affiliated stand by their agreements with the employers and their understandings with each other. Unions which fail to observe this code are liable to exclusion. The N.U.G.M.W. considers both N.U.P.E. and the C.W.U. to be break-away unions, and claims that they had broken understandings or agreements.

Thirdly we must remember that the general unions are perhaps particularly sensitive on this point. They have some claims to control by industry, even a few claims to control by craft, but in many industries their bargaining rights depend on the number of their members alone, without any obvious demarcation lines behind which they can stand, sure of at least a part of the territory to which they lay claim. If they lose members they may lose bargaining rights. If they allow competing unions to share their bargaining rights, they may lose members. If the Miners or the Post Office Engineers have to fear competition, how much more the general workers' unions?

National Arbitration and Government Wages Policy

The N.U.G.M.W. accepted the National Arbitration Order in 1940, as did other unions, and continued to support it up to the last moment, when many other unions thought it had outlived its purpose. The Order had several advantages for the union. Under Clynes's leadership it had become strongly opposed to the use of the strike except as the very last resort, and before the war would on many occasions have welcomed an arbitration tribunal as an alternative to acceptance of an employer's offer, or a strike. The union is spread over many industries, some of them only weakly organized, and general provision for arbitration prevented the most strongly organized unions using their strength, in a period of full employment, at the expense of the weak. The procedures under the Order enabled a union struggling to make headway in badly organized industries to bring before the Tribunal an employer who would not meet them voluntarily, and to bring some outside sanction to bear on an employer who would not accept the discipline of an employers' organization. The union had good grounds for its support for the Order besides its outstanding loyalty to the decisions of the T.U.C. and the Labour Party.

In the early years of the second world war, the union was strongly opposed, as was the T.U.C., to any suggestion of a government wages policy. Compulsory arbitration was to complete the system of bargaining machinery voluntarily built up; it must not be allowed to change its nature. Every few months from January 1940 on, Charles Dukes wrote in the *Journal* to oppose a wages policy, and in the intervening months other officers frequently took his place. The arguments were several: 'the method of voluntary agreements free from State regulation was the best method yet devised of maintaining a healthy public opinion and voluntary co-operation'[1]; no one 'outside Government circles' had any confidence in the cost of living index;[2] the profit motive remained and prevented adequate price control;[3] workers were now being taxed by the Chancellor, if their wages were kept down at the same time they would be paying twice for the war;[4] before the war there were flagrant inequalities, and many households had to expand their expenditure to avoid real want before they could be expected to contribute to the war effort.[5]

[1] Charles Dukes, *Journal*, February 1940.
[2] Charles Dukes, *Journal*, January 1940.
[3] John McKenzie, *Journal*, April 1940.
[4] H. L. Bullock, *Journal*, January 1941.
[5] Charles Dukes, *Journal*, August 1941.

At this time it was felt that 'there is clear evidence of government interference behind the general method whereby wages are being dealt with'.[1] From 1941 onwards prices were fairly successfully pegged and wages continued to rise, and the union turned its attention to other problems, although there was a further outbreak of complaints over Award 326.[2]

After the war, during the first years of the Labour Government, the union maintained the same attitude. If inflation threatened, 'the mere clamping down of wage negotiations only tends to aggravate the situation', and the solution was to be found in greater production of consumer goods and continued support for national savings.[3] The first statement of government policy on 'Economic considerations affecting relations between Employers and Workers' prompted the comment that 'the "honeymoon" has indeed ended, and the Trade Unions will need all their vigilance to keep intact these improvements which have already been secured'.[4]

The government's balance of payments' difficulties were driven home by the events of the summer of 1947 and the stronger statement of policy of February 1948[5] was given qualified support by a special conference of trade union executives, at which the union's representatives spoke and voted with the majority. Thereafter the union continued to defend the policies of the government and of the T.U.C. General Council in its *Journal*, at its own conferences, and at further T.U.C.s and Executive Conferences. It voted with the minority when the General Council's policy was rejected at the T.U.C. of 1950.

There is no need to discover contradictions in this development. Many unions moved along the same path. The freedom of collective bargaining was not overtly challenged in the 1948 to 1950 period, and the restraint which the unions then pledged themselves to exercise was no more than a more severe application of a policy which they claimed to have followed since 1940.

---

[1] Charles Dukes, *Journal*, February 1941.
[2] See p. 218.
[3] Charles Dukes, *Journal*, January 1946.
[4] Miss Horan, *Journal*, March 1947.
[5] The White Paper on *Personal Incomes, Costs and Prices*, Cmd. 7321 of 1948.

The new General Secretary, Tom Williamson, showed that he was prepared to go further than this. He wrote in the *Journal* for March 1948 recommending the Government White Paper to the serious attention of his readers, and went on to say:

'. . . I think we must turn our attention to the possibility of creating some form of machinery which, while preserving the present system of voluntary collective bargaining, would provide for a responsible, impartial and properly constituted wage authority or Commission with authority to examine agreements arrived at by direct negotiations and advise how such agreement can be given effect to, having regard to all the relevant circumstances of the industrial and national situation.

'We are obviously entering upon a new chapter in industrial negotiations. The old pull-devil-pull-baker method of deciding wage claims is inconsistent with a policy of full employment. Instead of unions competing with one another in pressing wage claims we must have a common policy.

'I want to see this accomplished by the trade unions voluntarily. . . .'

During the following two years he wrote further articles on the same subject, but seeking control of wage movements rather through the T.U.C. than by an independent authority. The proposal was not worked out in detail, however, either by him or by his union, and found little favour with the movement as a whole.

Trade union interest in the problems of national wages policy declined after the defeat of the General Council at the 1950 T.U.C., and after the return of a Conservative Government in 1951. Thereafter the union's leaders continued to favour 'reasonable' as opposed to 'unreasonable' wage claims, and forcefully rejected suggestions that the union should not carry on with the practice of full consultation with the new government as with the old.[1]

[1] At the 1952 Congress two motions criticizing 'co-operation' with the Conservative Government failed to find movers. Tom Williamson explained that consultation did not entail co-operation. The T.U.C., he said, 'expected the same measure of consultation from this Government with regard to Orders and legislation affecting the interests of trade unionists as they had had from the Labour Government . . . The T.U.C. is not co-operating with the Government in anti-labour policy or in anti-Trade Union policy'.

It is not easy to assess the union's part in the period of wage restraint. It certainly did a great deal to maintain the policy of extreme restraint in the counsels of the T.U.C. by placing its moral support and its huge vote behind that policy. It is not at all clear that the union's attitude has radically affected the outcome of the bargaining in which it has been concerned during the past few years.

Government policy undoubtedly spread its shadow over these bargains, and over all industrial negotiations. After the publication of the White Paper in 1948 there were a large number of wage increases, on the principle that if anything was to be had it must be got quickly. In these the N.U.G.M.W. took its share, in electricity, gas, the Non-Trading services, in a host of other industries, and finally, through a Court of Inquiry, in engineering and shipbuilding. Thereafter wage restraint held largely because there were no increases in the major industries — mining, engineering, the railways — either because the unions presented no major claims, as in mining, or because of inter-union difficulties, as in engineering, or because, as in railways, the employers and tribunals stood firm. The N.U.G.M.W. played its part. It withheld some claims, as in the gas industry and the Non-Trading services. It pursued others in industries, such as laundries, whose workers it felt came within the category of under-paid. When restraint was 're-laxed', in the summer of 1950, it went ahead as much as any other union, on the sensible grounds that if there was to be a scramble, the members of the N.U.G.M.W. must not be left behind.

'Productivity'

Over the years the union's attitude to problems of industrial management has changed, and the change has not been un-related to its policies of good relations and of wage restraint.

During the first world war and the two following years the union's leaders, particularly J. R. Clynes, recommended that their members should give attention to increasing industrial output, but during the following period of unemployment and industrial unrest, whatever interest the unions had in increasing output was dissipated. After the General Strike and the 1927 Act the union, along with most other unions, supported the more conciliatory attitude which the T.U.C. then adopted, and its representatives played their part in the Mond-Turner conferences. Although the conferences raised some hopes of a better industrial future inaugurated by co-operation between unions and employers, interest was not great, and achievement was almost nothing. The subject was debated at the 1928 Congress. Will Thorne and J. R. Clynes argued that the T.U.C. representatives could be trusted and would do nothing to compromise trade unionism, and Charles Dukes seconded the motion supporting the actions of the T.U.C. General Council on the grounds that 'he did not expect any real agreement because both parties had differing principles and viewpoints. The more we met the employers the more plain would become the fundamental difference between us, and the more would it be made clear to the workers that their only hope lies in Trade Union organization and in the labour programme for the national ownership and control of industry'.

The attitude of the union can perhaps be better gauged in other ways. It organized the workers of many of the employers who made the most conspicuous advances in 'progressive management' during the period between the wars — Rowntrees at York, Renolds at Manchester, the I.C.I. and Unilever. It played its part in those experiments. It did so with caution. It needed a good deal of assurance that the I.C.I. scheme for representative committees would not be used as an anti-trade union device, and would not usurp any functions properly belonging to the unions. Once assured on this point, and convinced that these employers would help it to recruit members, the union co-operated. It is clear, however, that it regarded such employers as rare, if not strange, exceptions. During the 1929-33 depression the union was the foremost advocate of 'workers' control' at the T.U.C. and was deeply concerned with the industrial problems raised by 'rationalization' and the Bedaux system of time and motion study. The reaction to the first was to strive for compensation for displaced workers, and to the second to stop it if possible. Of the Bedaux system,

Charles Dukes wrote 'from information already compiled, we know that the system has a harmful effect on the general health of the workers ... It is believed that tuberculosis is a consequence in many cases of such systems'.[1] There was a number of short bitter strikes over the introduction of the system in a number of industries. The strike in the North British Rubber Company we have already mentioned.[2] Another occurred in the I.C.I. lime quarries in Derbyshire in 1933. Since the union could not prevent its introduction most of these strikes were sensibly ended by a modification of the earnings which the system provided in favour of the workers.

Bedaux remained a bad joke throughout the 'thirties. War-time experience of joint production drives, joint production committees and full employment affected attitudes in all unions, and perhaps in the N.U.G.M.W. more than most. A branch secretary wrote in the *Journal* of June 1945:

'When [motion study was] first introduced into filling factories, it was viewed with very great suspicion by shop stewards, workers, and a great majority of the supervisory grades. That there was a catch in it everybody was sure ... However, with the most helpful co-operation of Time Study Engineers, and most members of the management, the method of assessing payments has now been accepted in principle. What are the views of the workers now, after a fair trial? Well, I should say, and there I risk a few brickbats, 75 per cent. of the workers would not willingly lose their bonus.'

In his address to the 1946 T.U.C. Charles Dukes said:

'There have been good reasons for the reluctance of Unions to countenance the piece-work system, and those techniques of time-and-motion study, and methods of scientific management, associated with capitalist industry. But I suggest that in the new situation resulting from socializing legislation and the closer association of Unions with these problems of industrial management the Unions will have to reconsider their attitude towards many of the restrictive methods and practices.'

In this there is perhaps nothing that cannot be paralleled in the experience and pronouncements of other unions. And

---

[1] *Journal*, October 1934.   [2] See p. 240.

subsequent Executive pronouncements and Congress resolutions on productivity did no more than show that the union
was keeping in line with most of its fellows behind T.U.C. and
Government policy. In 1948, however, the union's research
department was instructed to conduct an inquiry to discover
the extent to which the districts of the union were affected by
time and motion studies, and in 1949 as a result arranged for
selected officers and shop stewards to attend full-time courses
of one month's duration on 'current practice in the techniques
of time study, motion study and job evaluation' held by the Department of Industrial Administration of Birmingham Central
Technical College.

This course was accounted a success, and at the 1951 Congress a Special Resolution gave the Executive unlimited power
to expand 'education of trade union members in modern industrial techniques'. Arrangements were made with eleven outstanding Technical Colleges and two Universities to provide
courses of the same duration for shop stewards and branch
officers. The syllabus was arranged in consultation with the
union, and in most instances gave about equal weight to education in the institutions of industrial relations and to training in
the principles of work study. Part of the time was also given to
training the students in self-expression both on paper and in
speech. By the end of the winter session 1952-53 nearly ninety
courses had been held, attended altogether by almost a thousand
members of the union. Members of some other unions, particularly the T.&G.W.U. and the Union of Shop Distributive and
Allied Workers, had joined in some of the courses.

At the same time the union continued to take advantage of
courses provided for union officers by the T.U.C., and several
officers had been sent on longer courses arranged in the United
States or by firms of industrial consultants in this country. In
1953 the union was considering plans for further training for
the best of the students who had attended the technical college
courses, and also for extending training in these subjects to
wider groups of its members.

Perhaps most of these courses teach little to the experienced
trade union official, who knows he cannot beat the work study

engineer at his own game and is prepared to give any system of payment by results a trial to see if speeds and earnings satisfy his members. But if they do no more than show those with less experience that the stop-watch *can* be used to relieve a worker's load and to increase his earnings without causing strain, and that if any time and motion study is to be introduced, workers should insist on the best industrial consultants and the most reputable methods, they will have served a purpose. It is currently held that such work studies are not likely to be successful without trade union co-operation, and that co-operation is likely to be of more value if it is better informed.

At the same time practices of 'progressive management' have spread more widely in British industry and the union's response of co-operation is not, therefore, as exceptional as it would have appeared to be before the war. It is true, however, that in this wider field, as with time and motion study, it has been prepared to go a little further than most unions, both in public and private industry, and a good deal further than many 'craft' unions.

Too much could be read into these changes of attitude. In at least several instances during the period of extreme wages' restraint officers of the union persuaded firms to introduce payment by results and to have recourse to industrial consultants, but there has been no revolution which has made the union a main driving force for improvements in industrial techniques. The union has co-operated in experiments with new managerial methods, but its officers remain highly and rightly suspicious of any experiments which seem likely to exclude the unions, or which are not accompanied by direct encouragement of trade unionism. It is probably fair to say, in conclusion, that in so far as trade union methods and attitudes have changed, the N.U.G.M.W. has been, at least since 1948, one of the leaders of change.

PART IV

THE N.U.G.M.W.
IN THE LABOUR MOVEMENT

CHAPTER I

RELATIONS WITH OTHER UNIONS

W E have already in the last section discussed some aspects
of relations between the N.U.G.M.W. and other
unions, for in almost every industry in which it has
members the union must co-operate or compete with other
unions. There remain, however, a number of aspects with
which we must now deal.

The Transport and General Workers' Union

Relations with the other great general union are of the
greatest importance. Since the two unions meet in over a
hundred industries and sit together as the two major unions on
so many 'workers' sides' an open conflict between them would
be disastrous to trade unionism and to good industrial relations
in this country.

For all that, relations have not always been sweet. Early in
1922 the old N.U.G.W. announced that the new amalgamated
union of transport workers was recruiting its transport members.
It therefore stated that the Dockers' Union had refused 'conditions of solid organization . . . offered . . . by this society' and
appealed to all transport workers to join 'the largest union
catering for transport workers'.[1] Later in the same year the
Journal reported:[2]

'Our Head Office has received many complaints from our
District Secretaries about the poaching of members by the new
organization and their very unfair tactics towards us. They
have been very active recently in various industrial centres with
a view to strengthening their organization, and in some cases
have held meetings in towns where they never had a single
member, but where we have had the workers in various industries well organized.'

The N.U.G.W. was also indignant at the large number of
officers appointed by the new union at relatively low salaries

[1] *Journal*, January-February 1922.   [2] *Journal*, July-August 1922.

for recruitment work. It felt that this recruitment was often at its expense.

It is, therefore, with some surprise that we discover that soon after the formation of the N.U.G.M.W. there were proposals for amalgamation into one great general union, and discussions were proceeding between the two Executives. They ceased before the General Strike, and were not renewed. One outcome of the discussions, however, was a joint committee of the two unions, established early in 1925. It consisted of six members from each union and was intended to avoid 'internecine warfare' and to deal with the recognition of union cards and with transfers.

These arrangements may be taken as a sign of improved relations, but not of the end of all conflict. In 1927 the N.U.G.M.W. was complaining that in several undertakings in which the T.&G.W.U. held a majority, its members were refusing to work with N.U.G.M.W. members as if they were non-unionists. An agreement was reached to give the union with a majority the right to negotiate, but not without first consulting the minority, whose trade union membership should be respected. When a dispute arose in Glasgow during the following year the National Executive ruled that the settlement of particular problems within the terms of the agreement was a matter for local autonomy. Difficulties continued to arise, for instance over T.&G.W.U. attempts to seduce Liverpool transport workers from their allegiance, and were usually settled by some local arrangement. It was by such an arrangement that tramway workers in Liverpool were allocated to the N.U.G.M.W. and busmen to the T.&G.W.U. In a large Nottingham brewery the N.U.G.M.W. was to organize the production workers and the T.&G.W.U. the transport workers.

During the depression the most pressing problem of the unions was to retain and not to gain members, and no important difficulties were reported, but in 1935 a particularly awkward problem arose. The Norwich busmen had been organized by the N.U.G.M.W. The company was purchased by a combine. The N.U.G.M.W. refused to accept the terms offered by the new employer, but the T.&G.W.U., which had a few members there, was trying to win negotiating rights over the country with this combine by signing agreements even on disadvantageous terms in the first instance, in order to be in a position to apply pressure thereafter. For this reason it accepted the terms offered on behalf of its members. The N.U.G.M.W. was understandably aggrieved. Meetings took place and eventually a new agreement was drawn up between G. P. Dean and Harold Clay of the T.&G.W.U. The main point in the agreement was that the major union in any industry should have the right to recruit, but must respect the rights of existing members of the other union. It was ratified after further discussion, and when it was announced by Charles Dukes to the 1938 Congress a resolution for amalgamation was withdrawn.

During 1936 the two unions took a dispute which arose at the Warren Cement Works to the Disputes Committee of the T.U.C. and in subsequent years difficulties arose over recruitment of I.C.I. employees, and South Wales tinplate and aluminium workers. The N.U.G.M.W. was not always the aggrieved party. In 1938 the Southern district secretary had to take disciplinary measures against the Plymouth branch secretary who refused to return to the T.&G.W.U. four members whom he had 'poached'.

At the outbreak of war the T.U.C. tried to persuade unions to enter into agreements for the recognition of cards to avoid disputes over membership of transferred workers. An agreement was signed between the two general unions, and district discussions were commenced in order to achieve closer collaboration. At a dinner held by the union at the 1942 T.U.C. Charles Dukes was reported to have said 'that for many years the two General Workers Unions have pursued a policy of cutthroat competition which was always distasteful to many. A year or two ago both organizations set to work in an endeavour to eliminate that suicidal form of competition which had occupied so much of the time of their officials, and had proved wasteful to each organization. Ultimately a joint relationship committee of the N.U.G.M.W. and the T.&G.W.U. was established, to which any kind of difference between these two big organizations was immediately referred for adjustment, and in a large majority of cases accommodation was reached.'[1]

Whether as a result of this agreement or not, no conflicts were reported for several years. In 1948 when T.&G.W.U. members refused to work with a N.U.G.M.W. member in the Leeds Industrial Co-operative Society, agreement was only reached after the N.U.G.M.W. had reported the case to the T.U.C. Disputes Committee, but a satisfactory agreement on the retention of rights was reached when Liverpool Corporation decided to replace all trams by buses.

The explanation of the tale as told by the records is probably this. National agreements between the two unions cannot solve all problems. Since the earliest years the two Head Offices have worked together without difficulty, and co-operation on national negotiating bodies has been exemplary. 'Poaching' and local conflicts arise out of branch competition which has always existed and will persist. It can only be satisfactorily settled between the N.U.G.M.W. District Secretaries and the equivalent Area Secretaries of the T.&.G.W.U. Over the years these have made arrangements to cover most of the difficulties likely to arise, but the arrangements depend mainly upon personal co-operation. New personalities can renew conflicts and bring the local competition to the notice of the Head Offices. The leaders then discuss and perhaps make a new national agreement, which may be an improvement on the last, but is no substitute for the good relations in the districts, which may well have grown again in the meantime.

At the 1948 Congress a further resolution on amalgamation was withdrawn when the General Secretary explained what had occurred in the past. No student of trade unions could look with equanimity on the proposal. Working in reasonable co-operation the two great general unions check each other fairly well. Amalgamation would bring a concentration of power in the trade union world which many trade unionists, perhaps even the members of those two unions, would have good reason to fear. But the danger is made remote by the difference in structure between the regionally decentralized N.U.G.M.W. and

---

[1] *Journal*, October 1942.

the industrially decentralized T.&.G.W.U., and by the great difficulties which would be raised over finding suitable posts for the leaders of both organizations in any amalgamated body.

Industrial Unionism

We have already described something of the relations with 'industrial' unions like N.U.P.E., C.O.H.S.E. and the C.W.U., and with 'craft' unions which claim they have become industrial unions, such as the A.E.U. and the E.T.U. These are but a sample. The union took many years in arriving at an understanding with the Foundryworkers. In 1926 the Tobacco Workers' Union left the T.U.C. rather than accept the findings of the Disputes Committee, which decided that it was poaching N.U.G.M.W. members in Godfrey Phillips' factory. From 1945 to 1947 the union was in conflict with the Wire Drawers, who wanted to exclude it, despite its considerable membership in the industry, from bargaining rights, and ultimately an official Court of Inquiry[1] was set up to investigate. The union came into conflict with the N.U.R. in South Wales in the 'thirties when the latter began to organize the employees of railway-owned bus companies and the conflict ran on through the war.

This list might be continued, but two conflicts perhaps deserve slightly fuller treatment.

Already before the 1914-18 war miners in many areas had ceased to regard surface-workers as a class apart, and the membership of the craft unions and of the N.A.U.L. amongst them caused difficulty. Then the miners became consciously imbued with industrial unionism. Perhaps also the decline in the proportion of face-workers to total workers 'in and about collieries' had some effect. The miners sought to bring all colliery workers within their federation, and serious conflict ensued. It has not been satisfactorily settled to this day. Disagreements over the General Strike made matters no easier, and from 1927 on, discussions continued between individual unions and the miners or between all interested unions and the miners. They were patiently and persistently fostered by the T.U.C. and con-

[1] Cmd. 7097 of 1947.

tinued off and on for almost twenty years without reaching any satisfactory agreement. There could be no compromise between the miners' desire to be rid of other unions, and the other unions' desire to maintain their position. The N.U.G.M.W.'s attitude was complicated by the varying interests of its districts in the industry. It showed a preference for district agreements, and in some satisfactory settlements were reached. The Welsh district in fact decided in 1933 that it would be best to transfer its membership amongst surface workers to the South Wales Miners' Federation.

At the end of the war came the transformation of the Miners' Federation into the National Union of Mineworkers followed soon afterwards by nationalization. A further effort was made, and the new union agreed with the various national organizations representing manual surfaceworkers to respect their membership, so long as they would agree to allow all industrial negotiations with the new Board to be conducted by the N.U.M. and to pay a capitation fee for that service. To safeguard the position of their members, officers of the other unions were to sit on the governing bodies of the N.U.M. and to attend its Conferences. With some misgiving the agreement was accepted.[1] Almost at once complaints began to come in from the N.U.G.M.W. branches that the miners' lodges, particularly in Lancashire and Yorkshire, were telling N.U.GM.W. members that they must join the N.U.M. Protests were made, and complaints on that score ceased, but the union's colliery branches still voiced the view that they were not being. fairly treated in negotiations, particularly in local settlements, and officers of the union say that, despite the capitation fee, they now have to give more time than ever to the industrial grievances of their members in the collieries if these are not to be overlooked.

It appears that national arrangements with the N.U.M., as with the T.&G.W.U., work tolerably smoothly, and the friction is local. Each year questions are asked at Congress, or

[1] The N.U.G.M.W. also achieved a settlement over coke-oven workers. It was to transfer its members in N.C.B.-owned coke works to the N.U.M. and to respect N.U.M. members in other coke works.

resolutions are moved, and the National Officer explains the arrangements which the Head Offices of the two unions are making to surmount the latest conflicts between the branches. It is not always the N.U.M. which is at fault. In 1952 it was reported that in some colliery coke ovens in Yorkshire which had previously been organized entirely by the N.U.G.M.W., the union had continued to recruit new entrants to the coke ovens, and, despite the 1947 agreement, the leaders of the N.U.M. were willing to make a new arrangement to allow this to continue in some of the plants concerned.

At the time of the amalgamation the union included some thousands of iron and steelworkers. Other workers in the industry were organized mainly by the Blastfurnacemen's Union or by the Iron and Steel Trades Confederation, which had been formed by amalgamation during the war. (Because of the method chosen to effect the amalgamation, the union is also known as the British Iron, Steel and Kindred Trades Association.) There have been conflicts between the N.U.G.M.W. and the Blastfurnacemen, and a joint working agreement made between the two unions just before the war did not give much satisfaction, but in most areas where both unions have members there are local arrangements that they shall conduct negotiations jointly. It is with the larger union, the I.S.T.C., that there has been most difficulty.

No iron and steel production workers are apprenticed craftsmen, although some jobs require considerable skill, entail heavy responsibility, and are very highly paid. Accordingly the I.S.T.C., which drew its main strength from the higher paid workers, was nevertheless by no means a craft union. The N.U.G.M.W., on the other hand, recruited mainly amongst the lower paid, but retained its members when promoted, and refused to be only a labourers' union within the industry. Thus the two unions competed for all grades. Without recognizing its exclusive jurisdiction in any section of the industry, the Iron and Steel Trades' Employers' Association signed an agreement with the N.U.G.M.W. in March 1925 giving it full recognition and complete bargaining rights on behalf of its members in the industry. The I.S.T.C., however, did claim exclusive and sole jurisdiction and refused to join together with the N.U.G.M.W. in negotiations. The latter's Executive debated the problem in the subsequent months, and opened discussions with the I.S.T.C.; but the most the latter would offer was to respect existing members in return for a per capita payment and complete control of negotiations. This offer was rejected. Largely because of disagreement between the districts, the N.U.G.M.W. left the matter to the districts, and various arrangements have been adopted. In Scotland, for instance, the district committee entered into a local agreement to recruit only labourers, and thereby gained exclusive rights to organize the largest group of labourers in the industry — the builders' labourers. In Sheffield the union has a considerable membership and is able to retain it the more easily because the steel industry there operates under the 'Sheffield shift system' which regulates wages in relation to engineering agreements and apart from the rest of the industry. In these, and one or two other districts, the union has retained a considerable membership in face of the challenge of the industrial union, but it has not been able to increase its strength sufficiently to force its rival to come to terms. The national agreement of 1925 remains in force, and regulates the settlement of local disputes in which the N.U.G.M.W. is concerned, and the conduct of national negotiations. In the latter, however, because of the far greater strength of the I.S.T.C. within the industry, the N.U.G.M.W. is usually meeting the employers to discuss the application to its members of agreements already under discussion between the employers and the I.S.T.C.

The N.U.G.M.W. has not been driven out of the iron and steel industry, but its position there is more precarious than if it was recognized by the I.S.T.C. as a partner, and its experience in the industry has given it no reason for friendly feelings towards the doctrine of organization by industry.

During the early 'twenties the two general unions had to face an onslaught of the industrial unions in the T.U.C., backed by the Communists and the Minority Movement, whose trade union theories were uncompromisingly in support of organization by industry. Earlier conflicts had been between industrial unions and craft unions,[1] but from 1922 on a series of industrial unionist resolutions at the T.U.C. seemed to be aimed at the general unions, and were accepted by them as a challenge. The main arguments of the general unions were that new industrial unionism was but a device of the craftsmen to maintain the subjection of the labourer, and that the boundaries of an industry could not be defined. In addition the leaders of the N.U.G.M.W. took up, in answer to the revolutionary slogan of industrial unionism, the ultra-revolutionary slogan of the One Big Union. The contrast between the American syndicalists, the Industrial Workers of the World, who invented the slogan, and our respectable general unions was so great that the union had to apologize for the doctrine's disreputable past.

In 1924 the Miners' Federation proposed that the General Council should inquire into the possibilities of organization by industry. Jack Jones defended the One Big Union in debate, but the miners' resolution was carried.[2] Next year the General Council gave a cautious interim opinion arguing amongst other things that:

' . . . One big union cannot be regarded as a practicable proposition at present . . . Nevertheless the conception of its structure might usefully be borne in mind as the direction in which future efforts towards developing Trade Union organization should be made.'[3]

Thereupon Charles Dukes moved a resolution in favour of working towards the O.B.U., which was lost by 2,138,000 votes to 1,787,000.[4] Immediately afterwards a resolution from the tiny Laundryworkers' Union recommending that all laundryworkers should be in one union received 1,291,000 votes against 1,655,000.[5] Next year Charles Dukes moved a resolution decrying organization on industrial lines, and in favour of the O.B.U., arguing that capitalism was not organized on industrial lines and could not be fought on those lines. An industrial unionist amendment was carried.[6]

---

[1] In 1915 the conflict between the National Union of Railwaymen and the craft unions over railway shopmen almost split the T.U.C.
[2] *56th Report of the T.U.C.*, 1924, Hull, p. 442.
[3] *57th Report of the T.U.C.*, 1925, Scarborough, p. 232.
[4] *Ibid*, p. 425.   [5] *Ibid.*, p. 435.
[6] *58th Report of the T.U.C.*, 1926, Bournemouth, p. 327.

In 1927 came the General Council's final report. A thorough review of union organization led to the conclusion that 'it is impracticable to formulate a scheme of reorganization by industry that can be made applicable to all industries'. A spokesman of the A.E.U. moved the 'reference back' of this section of the Council's report, but his motion was lost by 2,062,000 votes to 1,809,000 and the N.U.G.M.W. thereupon withdrew its own resolution.[1] Thereafter for many years the issue was dormant. An industrial unionist resolution was passed at the 1928 Congress, but it was clear that the General Council had made up its mind that nothing could be done.

During the second world war the Left-Wing trend of trade union opinion brought industrial unionism back into favour. So much support did the doctrine win that the N.U.G.M.W. found it necessary to issue a booklet to instruct its officers on the details of the controversy and to return to it in the pages of its Journal. At the T.U.C. the conflict came to a head on two proposals, first that the Chemical Workers' Union should be allowed to affiliate, and secondly that the General Council should consider whether the trade union movement would not have to remodel itself on industrial lines to fit in to the brave new world which so many committees were busily planning. The major spokesman for both resolutions was Bryn Roberts of N.U.P.E. who met with determined opposition from a majority of the General Council, including the general unions' representatives. In 1941 and 1942 resolutions on both topics were opposed mainly by Citrine and general union spokesmen. In 1943, however, the resolution recommending that the Chemical Workers' Union be allowed to affiliate was carried by 3,258,000 votes to 2,451,000 despite the speeches of the general union representatives on its character and record.[2] Moreover, a resolution asking for an examination of trade union structure, moved by N.U.D.A.W. and carefully phrased to avoid any reference to industrial unionism, was allowed to pass without opposition.[3]

If this was a victory for the industrial unionists it was of little

[1] *59th Report of the T.U.C.*, 1927, Edinburgh, p. 293f.
[2] *75th Report of the T.U.C.*, 1943, Southport, p. 162.   [3] *Ibid*, p. 169.

practical value. Affiliation to the T.U.C. did not give the C.W.U. any bargaining rights in industry, and the report of the General Council on 'Trade Union Structure and Closer Unity', which was published during the following year, found the solution to inter-union difficulties in better working agreements and federal organization. 'Basic alteration of Trade Union structure is impracticable.' The newly-admitted C.W.U. moved a resolution which was treated as an amendment to the report, but it was defeated, and the report accepted.[1] No one knows better than the members of the General Council of the T.U.C. that its authority rests on the co-operation of affiliated unions. It has no power to carve them up into new organizations without their consent, even if it wished to do so, and since the solid votes of the two general unions are almost invariably cast behind General Council proposals it would not be likely to wish it. The matter was allowed to rest again.

Amalgamation

One method of settling inter-union relations is by amalgamation. In this the policies of the two general unions have been very different. From its origin the T.&G.W.U. under Ernest Bevin was prepared to amalgamate on almost any terms in order to build up the strength of the union. Even if a union was on the verge of bankruptcy the T.&G.W.U. was prepared to take risks. If its officers wished to be assured of some status and its members of freedom to manage affairs in their own industry, it might well be possible to form a new trade group in which there would be posts for its general secretary as national trade group secretary, for its district secretaries as area secretaries and for its executive committee as the national trade group committee. It is largely to amalgamation with the 'Power Group' and the Workers' Union in this way that the T.&G.W.U. owes its numerical superiority over the N.U.G.M.W.

The N.U.G.M.W.'s structure did not lend itself so easily to amalgamation. It was only possible for an amalgamating union to preserve some of its identity if it was a local union and could join a single district. Consequently most amalgamations were

[1] *76th Report of the T.U.C.*, 1944, Blackpool, pp. 221f.

of this kind. The officers and Executive of the N.U.G.M.W. took a much more conservative attitude to the financial problems of amalgamation than the T.&G.W.U., and had far more regard for the liabilities which might be incurred than for the organizing opportunities which would be acquired. Consequently most amalgamations were with small unions, having considerable bank balances, but ageing officials and a declining membership, and, therefore, looking for some means by which provision could be made for the future. One or two of these organizations were, however, national unions, and as an example we may choose the largest amalgamating union, the Amalgamated National Union of Quarryworkers and Settmakers.

The A.N.U.Q.&S. was an old union, itself the outcome of an amalgamation. Its branches were spread thinly over the country, from the Channel Islands to Scotland, with half its members in North Wales and the Midlands. Its headquarters were at Leicester, where its two full-time officers, Slevin, the President, and Bennett, the Secretary, worked. They were both over sixty-five years old. In addition there was a clerk, and a full-time branch secretary, Ozanne, in the Channel Islands. Exact membership figures were not easily obtained. The union claimed some 8000 members but, since its rules allowed unemployed members to keep their names on the books until they could once more contribute, the figure proved to be inflated. It was financially strong, for besides property at Leicester and Guernsey its funds were well over £50,000.

In 1932 the A.N.U.Q.&S. executive came to the conclusion that its future, despite its financial strength, was not rosy, for membership had been declining over a considerable period. Should they be required to make provision for their present officers and to find new ones, they would be making a serious addition to their expenses. If they amalgamated with a larger union, however, their future would be more certain; and if they were to amalgamate the time to do so was before choosing new officers. The North Wales' Quarrymen had amalgamated with the T.&G.W.U. some years before. The A.N.U.Q.&S. considered both the general unions, for there were now no other considerable unions in the industry, and concluded that the

N.U.G.M.W. was more to their liking. Discussions accordingly opened in November of that year.

Fortunately the contributions and benefits of the two unions were very much the same. The A.N.U.Q.&S. supplied the N.U.G.M.W. with its balance sheets and membership figures, and the latter's financial department then calculated what benefits would have to be met if the Quarryworkers were admitted at once as full members, making various assumptions about the age of members and the incidence of death. To this had to be added the cost of making provision for the two officers, and of bringing in Ozanne as an officer of the N.U.G.M.W. (and, therefore, a contributor to the N.U.G.M.W. superannuation fund). Against the total had to be set the probable future contributions of the Quarryworkers, should they join (again on various assumptions about age and expectation of life). The calculations made, an offer was put to the A.N.U.Q.&S. executive at a further meeting. It was accepted as satisfactory in outline. The unemployed members of the A.N.U.Q.&S. would be admitted to the N.U.G.M.W. if they paid the twopence contribution laid down by the N.U.G.M.W. rules for such persons. Two special classes of members — the survivors of the old Settmakers' Union and a small group of 'final card holders' — would have their rights and interests respected. The amount required to cover the liabilities foreseen by the N.U.G.M.W. fell far short of the total assets possessed by the A.N.U.Q.&S. and it was accordingly proposed that its executive should continue to function after amalgamation to administer the remainder as a fund to provide free benefits to its old members so long as it lasted.

The officers of the A.N.U.Q.&S. toured the branches speaking in favour of the scheme, which was accepted by a sufficient majority in a ballot. A special delegate meeting in October, 1933, then authorized a second ballot to dissolve the union, and decided, subject to that vote, to transfer its engagements from the following January. The arrangements went through. After a further tour of the branches to settle all details, the two national officers retired the following summer. Ozanne became an officer of the London district. The clerk refused a transfer to an office of the N.U.G.M.W. The distribution of branches assured the Quarryworkers of representation on some of the district councils, but no special arrangement was made to give them national representation. The N.U.G.M.W. inherited an unsettled dispute in Alderney, and carried on paying strike benefit for a number of months.

The amalgamation was accomplished with tact, and with accommodation on both sides. It appears to have given general satisfaction. The N.U.G.M.W. may continue to draw in small societies in the industries with which it deals in the same way. But that will not provide any solution to the major problems of inter-union relations and co-operation.

Federations and Working Arrangements

If organization by industry and amalgamation are rejected as means of securing improvements in trade union structure, we must fall back, as did the General Council of the T.U.C., on the devices of federation and working arrangements.

We have described in some detail the work of the Confederation of Shipbuilding and Engineering Unions. The other great federation to which the union belongs[1] — the National Federation of Building Trade Operatives — has in the past had a less stormy history and has given greater general satisfaction. Since the industry retains the traditional processes carried on by craftsmen and their assistants, many of the troubles of the engineering industry do not arise. Once having accepted the obligation to confine itself to labourers, which it has generally observed,[2] the N.U.G.M.W. has been a loyal member of the Federation, although it has been opposed to an extension of its powers, either by increasing its authority within the industry, for instance by increasing contributions to support more Federation officers, or by extending its authority outside the industry, for instance by allowing it to settle disputes between gasfitters and plumbers.

---

[1] The National Transport Workers' Federation and the General Workers' Federation ceased to have any important function after the formation of the two great general unions, and disappeared in the middle 'twenties.

[2] The Perth agreement. Trouble arises from time to time over building craftsmen employed by local authorities.

In 1952, however, the Amalgamated Union of Building Trade Workers (bricklayers and stonemasons) amalgamated with the small National Builders' Labourers' and Constructional Workers' Union, which had previously made efforts to amalgamate with the one or the other of the two general unions. The new union was thus open to both craftsmen and labourers. In the same year both the Amalgamated Society of Woodworkers and the Plumbing Trade Union made alterations in their constitutions in order to permit the recruitment of craftsmen's mates and other unapprenticed workers. The N.U.G.M.W. Congress debated the issue (along with its current disagreements with the A.E.U. over a 'relaxation' agreement) and decided to retaliate if need be. There are here the seeds of violent conflict within the Federation.

The working arrangements to which the union is a party are many and various. Some go no further than an understanding to co-operate in collective bargaining. Others allocate plants, or even departments within plants, between unions. Others are transfer arrangements to allow members to move from one union to another on a change of employer or occupation which seems to justify it. It may fairly be said that the N.U.G.M.W. has respected such agreements at least as loyally as most unions, and has been more ready than many to make them.[1]

If the N.U.G.M.W. is to be criticized in these matters the criticism must be based on the grounds that it has been conservative in altering joint arrangements to suit altered circumstances, such as changes in representation to suit alterations in the relative size of unions. It must, however, also be pointed out that, despite this reluctance to make changes, such working arrangements are far more flexible than other proposed methods of altering trade union structure. Industrial unions might replace the almost incomprehensible tangle of present British trade union structure by a far neater pattern, but once established that pattern would be even more likely to ossify than present arrangements.

[1] Many 'craft' unions were most unwilling to accept the T.U.C. scheme for 'recognition of cards' during the second world war.

CHAPTER II

THE N.U.G.M.W. IN TRADES COUNCILS AND IN THE TRADES UNION CONGRESS

THE Trades Union Congress is an annual gathering of trade unions. Its members include all the large, and many of the small, unions which organize manual workers, and many of the unions organizing clerical, professional and administrative workers. Since 1921 it has elected a General Council to carry on its work between Congresses, and this Council controls a fairly large full-time staff in Transport House. Most of the work of the Council is carried on by subcommittees which deal by subject with the matters in which the Council is interested — for instance, organization, education, Wages Councils or research and economic affairs. Neither the Congress nor the Council have authority over affiliated trade unions except in so far as these are willing to accept advice or comply with resolutions on any particular issue. Consequently the Conferences of Trade Union Executives which the General Council has from time to time convened are in some ways more authoritative than the Congress itself; if the executives agree to a certain course of action it can be carried out forthwith. The power of the General Council rests on its standing with the trade unions and its recognition by the government and the public as the representative spokesman of the unions.

Trades Councils are local bodies to which trade union branches, or, in the largest cities, trade union districts, may affiliate. Originally they were recognized by the T.U.C. as of equal status with the national unions, but direct representation of Trades Councils at Congress was ended in the 'nineties, and in 1924 the General Council took over control of the Trades Councils by setting up a Trades Councils' Joint Consultative Committee of six General Council Representatives and six Trades Council representatives to supervise the work of the Councils. A registration scheme was instituted whereby official recognition could be withheld from Councils whose actions were not approved. The Councils thus have little authority. They can decide only matters within the competence of trade union branches under the constitutions of the various unions; they have little power to enforce even those decisions on recalcitrant branches; and they are subject to far closer control by the General Council of the T.U.C. than are the national unions. The General Council is quite unable to prevent individual unions from choosing Communist officers, affiliating to 'proscribed' organizations, and even sending Communist delegates to Congress. In the 'thirties, however, Communists were ejected from the Trades Councils under Circular 16. Councils which would not comply were refused recognition, and the General Council set up new Trades Councils which were certain to gain the affiliations of the majority of unions which supported the General Council's policy. The General Council has such considerable powers over Trades Councils largely because the national unions wish them kept in their place. In recent years the functions of Trades Councils have been expanded by the recognition accorded to them by government departments as the proper bodies to nominate trade union representatives to local tribunals, advisory bodies, planning bodies, hospital boards, and so on. Most Trades Councils are affiliated to Regional Federations, and an Annual Conference of their delegates passes resolutions which are regarded as advisory to the T.U.C. Since most Trades Council delegates come from the middle and lower levels of the trade union hierarchy they are frequently more radical and Left-Wing than the T.U.C. itself — even at times when open Communist delegates have been excluded.

The N.U.G.M.W. sends a large delegation to the T.U.C., consisting of most of its national officers, General Council members, district officers by rota, and lay delegates chosen by the district councils. Its importance there, however, is due not to the strength of its delegation, but to its voting strength, for decisions are usually made by 'block' votes of the total affiliated strength of each union. Over the period since the amalgamation the union has been amongst the half-dozen largest affiliated unions, and is now second only to the T.&G.W.U.

The N.U.G.M.W. decides its line on the business of Congress before it meets, or at emergency meetings during the week, and briefs its speakers. Congress itself recognizes the right of each delegate to state his own view, even if it is opposed to that of the majority of his delegation, and miners' delegates or engineers have frequently urged Congress to vote against the line taken by their own union. The N.U.G.M.W., however, has maintained a disciplined front, which was broken only in 1942, when one of its delegates supported an industrial unionist resolution. The leaders of the union openly revealed their disapproval, and the delegate was not chosen to represent the union again.

The members of the T.U.C. General Council are chosen by the whole Congress, but places are allocated to eighteen industrial groupings, with two extra places reserved for women. Only unions within each group can send in nominations for the allocated places. The N.U.G.M.W. is by far the largest union in the General Workers' group, since the T.&G.W.U. is placed in the Transport (other than Railways) group. Owing to the amalgamation of the Workers' Union and smaller labourers' unions with the T.&.G.W.U., N.U.G.M.W. nominees have, except for one brief period, held all three seats allocated to the General Workers' group since 1934. The growth of the T.&G.W.U. has meant that the representatives of the Transport group have a considerably larger constituency than the N.U.G.M.W. representatives. As far as the two general unions are concerned, however, there has been no alteration in the allocation of seats since, on the amalgamation of the Workers' Union with the T.&G.W.U., one of the previous four General Workers' seats was transferred to the Transport group to give it three seats. One of the Transport group seats has been held by a representative of the National Union of Seamen since 1931, but the T.&G.W.U. have normally had four representatives on the General Council, for the miners allow a representative of the North Wales' Quarrymen (an affiliate of the T.&G.W.U.) to sit for one of the seats in their group, and one of the two women's representatives has for many years been from the T.&G.W.U. In the 'twenties Miss Bondfield held one of these seats, but no woman member of the N.U.G.M.W. has been elected since then.

Prior to 1948 the custom was that when a member of the General Council died or resigned during the year he was replaced by the candidate who had received the next highest vote in his group. Since the large unions do not put forward more nominees than the number of seats, the man thus chosen was likely to be a member of a small union, and since the most persistent opponents of the Council in office are the Communists, he might well have had the support of the Left-Wing vote. Under this rule the secretary of the tiny United Rubber Workers succeeded to a seat on the General Council on the death of Harry Harrison, National Officer of the N.U.G.M.W., in January 1948. He was elected against a N.U.G.M.W. nominee at the following Congress, but did not stand in 1949. At the 1948 Congress the rule was changed, partly to meet this case, and partly, it was thought, to avoid a Communist succeeding to the place of George Gibson, when he was appointed Chairman of the North-Western Electricity Board. Now the General Council asks for further nominations from the unions in the group concerned, and selects a member from amongst them.

The General Secretary of the N.U.G.M.W. has always had a seat on the General Council. Most of the other representatives of the union have been National Officers — Miss Bondfield, Will Sherwood, Harry Harrison, H. L. Bullock and Fred Hayday. Up to 1936, Arthur Hayday, Midland district secretary, held one place, and in 1949, Tom Eccles, Lancashire district secretary, joined Tom Williamson and H. L. Bullock[1] as the union's third representative.

Union branches can choose for themselves whether to affiliate to Trades Councils. Unless there is no Council available, they normally do affiliate, but where Councils are dominated by Left-Wingers, branches may prefer to remain outside.

The union's rules lay down that districts shall not pay more than £8 in any one year to a Trades Council as the affiliation fee of any one branch. The T.&G.W.U. has a similar rule.

---

[1] H. L. Bullock retired in 1950, at the end of his term as Chairman of the T.U.C. His place was taken by Fred Hayday.

Consequently the large branches of the two general unions are normally affiliated to Councils on a figure well below their total membership. Other Trades Council delegates complain of this, but their criticism is largely misplaced. There is nothing to prevent a branch paying a larger fee out of any branch fund which it may raise; some branches do. More important than this is the excuse that it is general practice throughout the labour movement for bodies to affiliate, in order to conserve funds, at less than their full strength. Only where great importance is attached to voting strength, as at the T.U.C., is the practice uncommon. Many large branches of many other unions which have no such statutory limitation affiliate to Trades Councils for a fee well below the N.U.G.M.W.'s £8 maximum.

The Union's Work in the Trades Union Congress

From 1926 the two most important men at the T.U.C. were its General Secretary, Walter (later Lord) Citrine, and Ernest Bevin. Will Thorne cut no great figure outside his own union. J. R. Clynes was thought of more as a parliamentary leader than as a trade union leader in the movement. Arthur Hayday was well to the fore amongst the second rank at the T.U.C., being the leader of many of its international delegations, especially to the I.L.O., and its leading authority on social insurance matters. He often acted as spokesman of the trade union group in the House of Commons, most of all under the Second Labour Government. Miss Bondfield was the leading woman trade unionist of the 'twenties, but gradually her interest shifted to political activities. Jack Jones was the movement's main humorist both in the Commons and at the T.U.C. It was Charles Dukes who usually put the union's policy from the floor of Congress.

The position of the general unions at the T.U.C. was not fully assured during the 'twenties. Their struggle against the industrial unionists has already been described. Gradually, however, their spokesmen came to the fore as consistent defenders of the policy of the General Council, and their strength in the Council was enhanced by the knowledge that their leaders were far more sure of the support of their members than those of some of the other large unions. In 1927 Miss Bondfield was in trouble. A motion of censure on her for signing the 'despicable Blanesburgh Report' on unemployment insurance was passed by the Congress of that year, despite her defence that she had only gone along with the majority of the committee in order to ensure that its report was as favourable as possible to the workers.[1] In 1930 Charles Dukes moved the 'reference back' of the Economic Committee's report (largely the work of Ernest Bevin) on the grounds that it tied the T.U.C. to 'economic nationalization'. His motion was defeated by 1,878,000 votes to 1,401,000.[2] But such differences were exceptional.

The weight of the union was usually cast against the most radical proposals. After early support for the legal enforcement of collective agreements the T.U.C. and the union turned against it for a time. Both were opposed to family allowances on the grounds that they would be used to cut wages, despite the support which the Labour Party gave to the proposal in 1929. The union was opposed to further extensions of General Council powers, and argued against any separate organizations for unemployed workers on the grounds that the unions were perfectly capable of looking after their own unemployed. It gave the General Council its complete support in its opposition to Communists and 'disruptive elements'.

In the early 'thirties, however, the union became the foremost supporter of the radical demand for 'workers' control'. The brief popularity of guild socialism had left the unions with a strong but ill-defined feeling that unions should be represented on the boards of nationalized industries. In 1930 battle was joined over Herbert Morrison's London Passenger Transport Bill, which made no direct provision for union representation. Morrison argued that boards should be independent, and that their members should be chosen solely on their merits. At first the protagonists were Morrison and the T.&G.W.U., the union most concerned with London Transport. By 1933, how-

---

[1] *59th Report of the T.U.C.*, Edinburgh, 1927, pp. 283ff.
[2] *62nd Report of the T.U.C.*, Nottingham, 1930, pp. 276ff.

ever, the General Council had gone very far towards accepting Morrison's view, and the T.&G.W.U. was losing interest.

Meanwhile the N.U.G.M.W. had taken up the cause. Its Executive had set up a sub-committee which, after long deliberation, drew up a report in favour of a large measure of workers' control. The Journal carried articles and letters on the subject throughout 1933 and 1934, many couched in the strongest possible syndicalist terms. At the 1933 T.U.C. Charles Dukes moved a resolution demanding that at least 50 per cent of the members of boards of nationalized industries should be union representatives. It was taken as an amendment to the General Council's report, and defeated, after a vigorous speech in support of the General Council's attitude from Citrine.[1] In 1935 the union, without showing any consciousness of a change of heart, was trying to further its claims to recognition from the new British Sugar Corporation by moving a resolution asking that Whitley Committees should be set up in all nationalized industries.[2]

During the 'thirties the N.U.G.M.W. consistently opposed the extension of the authority of the T.U.C. Although it supported the general demand for a forty-hour week without loss of pay as a remedy for unemployment, it protested vigorously in 1933 against a T.U.C. circular to Trades Councils asking for local action on the matter, on the grounds that it was a matter for collective bargaining by the unions concerned. It made special reference to the municipal services, for it was no more keen on Trades Council than on Labour Party interference in its own territory. The General Council was forced to ask the Councils to defer action. In 1934 the union opposed T.U.C. plans for a campaign for trade union recruitment through the Trades Councils and their federations, on the grounds that the unions could carry on their own recruitment. In 1935 it opposed the reorganization of the London Trades Council on the grounds that it had been carried out for the express purpose of assisting recruitment, and in 1936 it opposed the General Council's demand for an increase in T.U.C. affiliation fees, on the grounds

[1] *65th Report of the T.U.C.*, Brighton, 1933, pp. 370ff.
[2] *67th Report of the T,U,C,*, Margate, 1935, p. 402.

that one of the purposes for which the T.U.C. wanted the money was recruitment. Recruitment through the federations was again opposed in 1938, and in the same year the union opposed any scheme for a general insurance fund for disputes on the grounds that it would encourage irresponsible organizations to strike. The N.U.G.M.W. was, of course, not alone in its opposition to these proposals. Its peculiar antipathy to Trades Council or T.U.C. recruitment arose from its fear that the recruits thus obtained might be diverted into 'industrial' unions, especially by Left-Wing Trades Councils.

During the later 'thirties the union played a smaller part in T.U.C. debates. J. R. Clynes, Arthur Hayday, Will Sherwood and Miss Bondfield were gone. Charles Dukes intervened rarely. Miss Elliott spoke annually on the resolution on women's work. H. L. Bullock and Harry Harrison spoke perhaps once at each Congress. For the rest the union's delegates were usually silent.

In 1940 Ernest Bevin became Minister of Labour. Thereafter Charles Dukes naturally became second only to Citrine as the General Council's strong man. But the war period was perhaps not the most favourable occasion for his leadership. After the invasion of the Soviet Union the unions became steadily more Left-Wing and more tolerant of Communism, as indeed did the British people as a whole. With this trend Charles Dukes and the N.U.G.M.W. Executive were out of sympathy. It brought support to the motions for the admission of the C.W.U. and for the reorganization of the trade union structure. It brought support to the campaign against the ban on the *Daily Worker*, and to the campaign for the withdrawal of the 'black' Circular 16 forbidding Trades Councils to accept Communist delegates from affiliated trade unions. In one respect, however, the N.U.G.M.W. was closer to Communist and Soviet policy than the majority of Congress. At the 1943 T.U.C. Charles Dukes moved a resolution on the same lines as one which had received the support of the N.U.G.M.W. Congress earlier in 1942, demanding that 'all those responsible for the atrocities committed during the war, whatever the rank and position, shall be brought to justice' and attributing responsibility to the 'German nation'. A delegate of the Railway Clerks' Association moved an amendment to substitute 'Nazis' for 'German nation', and this was carried. The N.U.G.M.W. motion was dubbed the 'Vansittart resolution' and in Charles Dukes' view it was this, rather than any well-thought-out opposition, which killed it.[1]

During the war Charles Dukes had moved many of Congress's most important resolutions. In 1945 he moved the 'Transition to Peace and Demobilization' resolution in which the slowness of demobilization was criticized. During 1945-46 he served as Chairman of the General Council, and thus was President of the 1946 T.U.C., to which he delivered one of the more memorable of Presidential addresses. For all that, the N.U.G.M.W. was not in sympathy with the immediate post-war atmosphere of the T.U.C. It must have seemed strange to its representatives on the General Council that one of their colleagues, sent by their fellow general union, should be a Communist — A. F. Papworth. And although the union gave its support to the proposals to set up a new trade union international embracing the Soviet trade unions, it was not happy about the World Federation of Trade Unions. Its uneasiness was increased by the bitter opposition of several of the international trade secretariats of which it was a staunch member to inclusion in the Communist-dominated W.F.T.U.

The 'popular front' period was not, however, destined to last. In 1947 the refusal of Marshall Aid and the new 'Cominform' put an end to it. At home the General Council came to depend more and more on the votes of the general workers' unions for support for its economic policy and for 'wage restraint', to which the Left-Wing was now bitterly opposed. The General Council found it necessary once more to threaten penalties on Trades Councils which indulged in 'disruption'. The N.U.G.M.W. Executive can hardly have avoided a smile when the T.&G.W.U. leaders found themselves obliged to purge their union of Communist officers — full-time and lay. It was perhaps fitting that it should be Mark Hewitson, National Officer of the N.U.G.M.W., who at the T.U.C. of 1949 moved

---

[1] *75th Report of the T.U.C.*, Southport, 1943, pp. 329-33.

the resolution approving the action of the General Council in withdrawing from the W.F.T.U. and endorsing its proposals to explore the possibilities of setting up an international of 'free' trade unions.[1] The N.U.G.M.W. might fairly regard all this as a justification of its long opposition to the extreme Left, and of its caution and doubts during the later years of the war and the immediate post-war period.

The new policies of the T.U.C. and the General Council did not win unanimous support, nor did they strengthen the hold of the General Council over the unions. Wage restraint and compulsory arbitration had always had their opponents in the unions. After the devaluation of the pound in the autumn of 1949 the General Council tried to evolve a more strict formula for the limitation of wage advances. The formula which they suggested was killed by the smallness of the majority which passed the resolution in which it was embodied at a Conference of Executives in January 1950. At the T.U.C. of 1950 their wages policy was finally interred when it was formally rejected by a majority, and soon afterwards the round of increases which had already begun spread throughout industry. During the following months the National Arbitration Order was used for selective prosecution of persons supposed to have led unofficial strikes — amongst gas maintenance workers, and dockers. It became clear that the large minority opposed to the Order would soon become a majority and at the beginning of March 1951 the General Council declared itself in favour of modification of the Order.

Both wage restraint and compulsory arbitration found in the general unions their most steadfast supporters, and were attacked mainly by the Left, so that these changes in policy were a defeat for the leadership of the general unions and a victory for the Left. If, however, the leadership of Arthur Deakin and Tom Williamson was repudiated thereby, the Left could not replace them. Except perhaps for the years of 1942-1947, the majority of the General Council has been opposed to the Left on most controversial issues since 1927, and the strongest support for the General Council has been provided

[1] *81st Report of the T.U.C.*, Bridlington, 1949, p. 327.

by the consistent and authoritative leaders of the two general unions. Victories of the Left are bound, therefore, to exercise a disintegrating influence, and these particular Left-Wing victories undid a great deal of the patient and careful work by which Citrine built up the authority of the T.U.C. and the General Council.

The part taken by the union in the counsels of the T.U.C. is determined by its leaders. Each year the Executive either selects one or two of the resolutions passed by the union's Congress which it considers most suitable and submits them to the T.U.C., or, more rarely, frames a resolution of its own. (The latter course was necessary in the period of biennial Congresses.) The line to be taken on the main business of the T.U.C. is determined by meetings of the Executive before Congress, or by emergency meetings of the Executive, or of the whole delegation, during Congress. The union's representatives on the General Council are not normally briefed for its meetings, or for the meetings of its sub-committees on which they serve. From time to time the General Secretary reports the most important business before the T.U.C. General Council to the Executive or General Council of the union, and the feeling of the meeting may be taken to guide him and his two colleagues.

The Union's Work in Trades Councils

It would not be possible to give an adequate account of the work of the union on hundreds of Trades Councils throughout England, Wales, Scotland and Northern Ireland. Suffice it to say that the main function of these Councils is to direct and co-ordinate action on many issues of local importance which are unlikely to arouse much interest outside their own areas. In this work the union's branches and districts play their part along with the others, and probably as competently and loyally as the others. From time to time personal interests and local feuds or rivalries may disturb the harmony of the Councils. The N.U.G.M.W. may be concerned in such difficulties, but so may any other union.

The Trades Councils have little authority in general or

national matters, or on matters within the scope of industrial collective agreements. They may pass resolutions, but these resolutions bind no one, and the most that can be done with them is to refer them to the attention of those who have authority. These resolutions may seem to be of more importance than they really are, for they are likely to get greater attention from the press than other sides of Trades Council activity, particularly if they are Left-Wing resolutions. In this regard the N.U.G.M.W. may come in for criticism from the Left, for its branches are more likely than most other union branches to oppose Left-Wing resolutions. If they do not, district committees may enforce discipline against members who publicly oppose union policy.

The N.U.G.M.W. has consistently opposed extension of Trades Council powers and functions into any field which it regards as within the territory of the unions, including collective bargaining and recruitment. It had doubts about the part proposed by the T.U.C. General Council for Trades Councils during the General Strike, and felt afterwards that those doubts had been confirmed. But so long as the Councils do not stray outside what the union regards as the limits of their authority, it takes its fair share in their work.

CHAPTER III

THE N.U.G.M.W. AND THE LABOUR PARTY

SINCE 1918 Local or Constituency Labour Parties have taken the place of Trades Councils and I.L.P. branches as the main local organs of the Labour Party. In some centres Trades and Labour Councils remain, with separate funds for industrial and political work, but most Trades Councils are now confined to industrial work. Union branches may be affiliated to these local Parties, fees being paid from the district political fund, and union members may also join as individual members.

During the second world war the Labour Party decided to set up regional organizations. Districts may affiliate direct to Regional Labour Parties, fees again being paid from the district political fund.

Unions affiliate directly to the Labour Party itself. The number of delegates which a union may send to the Annual Conference is in proportion to the fees paid. The N.U.G.M.W. chooses its delegates to the Conference in the same way as it chooses its delegates to the T.U.C.

The Annual Conference chooses the Party's National Executive. Since the Party is a semi-federal organization, means have to be found of ensuring that the various sections secure representation on the Executive. In 1918 it was decided that the affiliated organizations (predominantly the unions) should have thirteen representatives, Constituency Labour Parties five, and that four places should be reserved for women, to make, with the Treasurer, an Executive of twenty-three members. Nominations were restricted to the groups represented, but the whole Conference was to vote for each place; and the block votes of the unions have always been sufficient to carry Conference with ease.

As they grew in strength the Constituency Parties came to think that they were under-represented, especially in view of the fact that they included the bulk of the active membership;

in their view the union strength was paper strength. During the 'thirties they agitated for increased representation, and the Executive proposed to increase their numbers by two to allow two additional representatives to the Constituency Parties, and to allow those Parties to elect their own representatives separately, without intervention of the union vote. Both proposals were carried, the former by a narrow majority. The N.U.G.M.W. had opposed them strongly. Charles Dukes said that it was not arithmetically justified, and that:

'I can say this, speaking for my own Union, that in the thirty years of my association with it, never once has my Executive given an instruction to those who happen to be on the Party Executive. We have sent on men, and they have pooled their ideas with other representatives, totally regardless of whether they represented Unions or Constituency Parties, and we deplore the idea, which unfortunately too many people appear to enjoy, that there is a distinct point of view between those who represent the Unions, and those who are elected by Conference to represent the Constituency Parties.'[1]

The union has always had a representative on the National Executive as one of the representatives of affiliated organizations. For many years J. R. Clynes headed the poll for affiliated organizations. He was replaced on retirement by Mark Hewitson, a National Industrial Officer. During the war, Mark Hewitson volunteered for military service, and his place was taken by Tom Williamson. After the latter became General Secretary, Mark Hewitson, now an M.P., served once more until 1953, when Jack Cooper took his place. The union may also have members or 'associate' members (for all Labour Party members are encouraged to join Unions, and for Party leaders membership is almost obligatory) in the Executive places reserved for the Local Parties and for women. George Lansbury, for instance, was a member of the union. In 1930 five Executive members — Clynes, Lansbury, Miss Lawrence, Lady Mabel Smith and Mrs. Ayrton Gould — were members of the union.

There is also the National Council of Labour, on which sit

[1] *37th Report of the Labour Party*, Bournemouth, 1937, p. 144.

representatives of the Party Executive, the T.U.C. and the Co-operative Union. It is used mainly to ensure co-ordination of policies and major activities. The union may be represented on it both from the T.U.C. and the Party. In 1937, for instance, both Clynes and Dukes held places.

The Party was founded to secure Labour representation in Parliament, and, as it grew, its main object became to secure a Labour majority and a Labour Government. The Labour M.P.s and peers form their own Parliamentary Labour Party, which chooses its own leader, and determines its course of action in Parliament. When the Party leader is asked to form a government, however, he chooses his own cabinet, restrained only by the knowledge that his choice must not arouse violent antipathies amongst large sections of the Party, and his government becomes, in effect, the leadership of the Party. For, although the Parliamentary Party might vote against a Labour Government, and the Annual Conference might repudiate the Parliamentary Party, only in the gravest of emergencies is it conceivable that such measures would be taken. Within these extreme limits, the Government may be influenced, but it cannot be controlled, and whatever policy it announces, or whatever action it takes, is almost certain to be accepted by the Party.

Within the Parliamentary Party and a Labour Government unions have no formal representation. Their strength depends on the number of M.P.s and ministers who are members of unions, and the influence over them that each union is able to exert. The proportion of candidates and of M.P.s officially sponsored by the unions has declined heavily. In 1918 the unions sponsored 49 out of 57 successful Labour candidates. Owing to the stigma of pacifism attached to I.L.P. candidates in a 'coupon' election, this result may be regarded as exceptional, but in 1922, 85 out of 142 successful candidates were sponsored by the unions. In 1945 the proportion was 121 out of 393. The loss of seats in 1950 brought the figure up to 110 out of 315, due to the relative safeness of union-sponsored seats. In 1951 the proportion remained almost the same at 103 out of 295. In all Labour Governments ministers officially sponsored by unions have been in a minority, and the influence of leaders closely linked with the unions has clearly declined since the days when J. R. Clynes, Arthur Henderson and J. H. Thomas were in the front rank of party leaders. Since 1945 only Ernest Bevin has been in this category.

Despite, then, the statement of Charles Dukes quoted above there have been grounds for conflict between the unions and the rest of the Party, and there has in fact been conflict. The unions have feared the domination of the Party by the 'intellectuals', and yet the 'intellectuals' have come to play an ever larger part in the making of the Party's policy, and, when a Labour Government is in office, they fill most of the posts. The N.U.G.M.W. has shared these fears, and its relations with the Party can only be understood if they are kept in mind.

Labour Party Finance

The unions may not call the tune, but they must pay the piper. In 1949 the contributions paid by unions affiliated to the Party amounted to nearly 87 per cent of the total contributions. At the same time the unions subscribed £148,000 to the General Election Fund, or nearly 96 per cent of the total of £156,000. The N.U.G.M.W. subscribed £20,000 — certainly its fair share and more. Besides this the unions sponsored, and, therefore, paid a considerable proportion of the expenses of, 140 candidates at the general election of February, 1950. In 1951 the unions again provided nearly 87 per cent of the Party's income from contributions. The number of union-sponsored candidates was 137. The General Election Fund, at £117,000, was considerably smaller than in 1949, and on this occasion the N.U.G.M.W. gave only £10,000.[1]

Direct contributions, subscriptions to special funds, and sponsoring of candidates are the three important means by which the unions give financial assistance to the Party. It is clear that there is almost no limit to the ability of a political party to spend money, and the Labour Party has frequently pressed the unions for more. Neither side has been entirely happy about constant 'special appeals' for elections or for cam-

---

[1] It must be remembered that individual subscriptions account for a larger proportion of Constituency Labour Party income than of national affiliation fees.

paigns built up around the Party's programmes — 'Labour's Bid for Power', 'Labour's Immediate Programme'. But increases in contributions would be unlikely to provide a remedy. The Party would spend the money and still come back for more. The more the unions pay to the Party in direct contributions, the less they have left to meet special appeals or to support their own candidates, and it may have occurred to the unions that this would be likely to reduce any control they may have over the Party.

Since 1939 the Party's income has much more than doubled. One reason for this is the increase in affiliation fees, which went up from 4½d. per year per member to 5d. in 1942, and to 6d. in 1948 (on both occasions the N.U.G.M.W. supported the increases); more important than this was the increase in the membership of trade unions and the effect of the change of the law from 'contracting-in' to 'contracting-out' in 1946. Since the fee has not increased with prices (on any calculation) the Party's real income per member has fallen, and like the unions themselves it has not extended its services *at the same rate* as its membership has grown. Despite appeals from the Party, most unions have not changed the amount of their political contributions (which vary considerably between unions — the N.U.G.M.W.'s 1s. 4d. compares with the T.&G.W.U.'s 1s., the Mineworkers' 2s. and the Railway Clerks' 4s. 4d.), so that increased Party contributions per head leaves less per head for special subscriptions and the support of candidates. The unions' only remedy for this is to affiliate to the Party on a number less than the total of their political contributions. For many years the N.U.G.M.W.'s affiliation figure was frozen at 242,000. As we have seen,[1] the number of political contributors in the union hardly increased with the rapid rise in numbers during the later 'thirties and the war, so that there was no ground for changing the figure. In 1948, however, the union affiliated on a figure of 400,000, or about 50 per cent of its total membership. This was a smaller proportion of the total than the 242,000 had been in 1933. And by that time the change in the law had raised the proportion

[1] See p. 99.

of political contributions to over 90 per cent of the union's 800,000-odd members. In 1933 the number of union members affiliated to the T.U.C. was 3,367,911 and in 1949 the number had increased to 7,937,091 — this may be taken as a fair indication of union growth. Over the same period union affiliations to the Party have increased from 1,899,007 to 4,946,207, roughly at the same pace. Since a number of small unions are affiliated to the T.U.C. and not to the Party, it is clear that, on average, unions are affiliated to the Party on considerably more than 50 per cent of their membership. Since the affiliation fee is a standard rate per thousand members, it is easy for a union with a larger *per capita* political contribution to affiliate on a greater proportion of its total membership. At the Amalgamation Conference of 1924 it was stated that 'we all know that the craft unions do not give the support they should' to the Party, and an unfair burden, therefore, rested on the general unions. That is not true today of direct contributions, although the N.U.G.M.W. usually contributes more generously than most to election funds.

Special appeals have come thick and fast in recent years. The appeal for the 1945 election was followed by a decision in 1947 that each affiliated organization should pay 1s. per member on their 1946 (pre-repeal) affiliation figures, payment to be spread over two years. In 1949 came a new election appeal, followed by still another in 1951. The N.U.G.M.W. can hardly be blamed for trying to keep as much as possible in hand to meet these appeals and to look after its own candidates.

Affiliation fees to Constituency Parties are a matter for the union's districts, so long as the rule limiting affiliation fees to 'Trades Councils and Similar Bodies' to a maximum of £8 for any one branch is observed. Districts work out their own schemes for ensuring some fair gradation between the total affiliation fees paid for large, middle-sized and small branches. Constituency Parties themselves settle the *per capita* fee for affiliated organizations, so that the proportion of members on which affiliation is based varies between branches of the same size according to the amount of that fee. Most large branches are affiliated to Constituency Parties. At the beginning of 1951,

161 of the 292 branches of the London district were so affiliated. The financial membership of these branches was 76,800 out of a district total of 90,000.

Parliamentary Representation

The following table shows the number of candidates the union has sponsored and the number which have succeeded in elections since the amalgamation, and the relation of these figures to the total.

Year	Numbers on N.U.G.M.W. 'official Panel'	N.U.G.M.W. 'official' candidates adopted by Constituencies	N.U.G.M.W. 'official' candidates returned	Total of union* 'sponsored' candidates returned
1924†	7	7	4	86
1929	8	8	6	114
1931	12	11	2	32
1935	11	11	6	79
1945	10	10	10	121
1950	14	9	6	110
1951	12‡	7‡	6	103

*The totals of union-sponsored candidates are taken from the Annual Reports of the Labour Party. Unfortunately union 'sponsorship' and official union support do not necessarily mean the same thing. In 1950, for instance, an unsuccessful candidate who, as a union member, had received a small donation towards his expenses, was returned by the Labour Party as sponsored by the N.U.G.M.W.; and in 1951 two members of the official panel who were elected were returned as sponsored by other bodies. Discrepancies affecting other unions cannot be checked.

†In 1918 and 1922 four candidates officially supported by the N.U.G.W. were elected to Parliament. In 1923 the number was five.

‡ In addition two officers of the Scottish district stood for Scottish constituencies, with the permission of the Executive, but not with full financial support. Both were defeated.

It was natural that the leaders of a union with the strong political interests of the old Gasworkers should find themselves constituencies in which to stand as Labour candidates, and it was equally natural that the union should help to meet the cost of the election campaigns and of maintaining a constituency organization between elections. So Will Thorne and J. R. Clynes entered Parliament and stayed there, to be joined later by Jack Jones, Miss Bondfield and Arthur Hayday. Meantime a political fund had been set up under the terms of the Act of 1913 and aid for these 'official' candidates of the union had to come from it.

During the 'twenties, however, the union's Executive and Congress began to notice that although this development was most natural and desirable, it had brought forth a number of problems which the union must sooner or later face. Should all union candidates be officers, or should some be lay members? If so, how many? On what terms should officers be allowed to sit in Parliament? Could a member of Parliament carry on full union duties? How many official candidates should there be? Who should choose them? Could the union ensure that those whom it chose would be accepted by constituencies? How could the union get the most value from its members of Parliament? The attempt to find satisfactory answers to these questions during subsequent years has taken up considerably more of the time of Congress, the General Council and the Executive, than any other aspect of the union's political work.

It was agreed at the Amalgamation Conference to leave aside two resolutions, one of which demanded that officers of the union should terminate their services if returned to Parliament, and the other that such officers should receive only a retaining fee of £200 a year. Had the resolutions been pressed and strongly supported amalgamation would surely have become much less attractive for the union of Will Thorne and J. R. Clynes. At the 1926 Congress a resolution on the same subject was, in the end, not moved. At the 1930 Congress, however, the platform showed a lively interest in Parliamentary representation, although not on this particular point. Meanwhile the Executive had ruled that no officer could become a candidate for Parliament without its permission, and in fact since that time officers have gone forward only when chosen as official union candidates.[1]

[1] There were two exceptions to this in 1951. See footnote to Table on p. 304.

Constituency Parties choose their own candidates, from names submitted either by local affiliates or by Party Headquarters. The union's first task is to ensure that its branches put forward its official candidates in any constituency which it feels is suitable. Thereafter a union-sponsored candidate may have an advantage over candidates not so sponsored if the leaders of the Constituency Party are impressed by the financial support which his adoption will bring them. Prior to 1935 one union-sponsored candidate might have an advantage over another since the support which different unions were prepared to give to an official candidate varied. By 1935, however, some constituencies were showing a preference for candidates not closely bound to the 'Trade Union steamroller' despite the funds which these candidates might bring. In 1929 the union had sponsored more candidates than ever before, and the Executive wanted to increase the number further. Not all the candidates had been of the calibre of the union's leading M.P.s and one or two of them had had difficulty in finding constituencies. The Executive was doubtful how far the union was committed to continued support of defeated candidates whom it had sponsored. To meet these points the Executive proposed to Congress that it should sanction an increase in the number of official candidates to twelve, and should give the General Council authority 'to deal with circumstances as they arise during the period between one Congress and the next', so that union members who seemed promising and likely to be selected for a good constituency could be put on the list and unsuccessful candidates could, in case of need, be dropped. Congress agreed to these proposals.

The decision of Congress was interpreted to mean that the vacant places could be filled by the General Council, but need not be filled at once. In fact, after consulting the districts, two lay members were included along with the six sitting members — Fred Marshall (later a district officer), who had been returned for Brightside, Sheffield, in 1929, and Walter Windsor, who had been one of the two unsuccessful official candidates in 1929. When Parliament was dissolved in 1931 four more were added to the 'panel' after a 'semi-exhaustive ballot' of the districts, but too late to secure constituencies. In the heavy electoral defeat, only two of the union's official candidates were returned — Will Thorne and Jack Jones — and the Executive ruled that none of the rest could assume that the union's support would continue automatically, although after consideration all but two were endorsed.

Meanwhile the Executive had felt the need to set up a Political Sub-Committee. This was originally intended to make sure that constituency organizations supported by the union were maintained at a reasonable level of efficiency, and to check election expenses. It took on the task of advising on appointments to the official panel.

After the defeat of 1931 a search for constituencies began. Candidates on the official panel had to have the approval of the General Council before they could allow themselves to be accepted by a new constituency. Since the Council normally met only once in three months this procedure was impossibly slow, and by the end of 1931 the Council had granted the Executive and the Political Sub-Committee power to act in an emergency. Even under this procedure, approval might come too late and candidates might have grounds for blaming the union for failure to be selected for a good seat. Ultimately it was agreed that the General Secretary should be granted power to deal with an emergency at once.

In 1933 the Labour Party Conference at Hastings decided to limit the contributions which affiliated organizations could make towards the election expenses and the maintenance of organization between elections in constituencies whose candidates were sponsored by them, in order to avoid 'financial competition' for constituencies.[1] The N.U.G.M.W.'s Executive decided to oppose the resolution, but agreed to put it into effect when the majority supported it.

Some of the difficulties were thus settled, but others arose. During the 'thirties there was at least some check to the political current which had before flowed so strongly in the union. In the early 'thirties Congress twice reduced the proportion of the

[1] The Hastings 'formula' was revised in 1948 in view of the Representation of the People Act of that year, which altered the legal maximum of election expenses.

political fund at the disposal of head office.[1] The failure of the union after 1934 to match increased membership by an increase in contributions to the Political Fund must be attributed at least in part to apathy. In most other unions the number of 'contractors-in' rose, although not so rapidly as total membership.

There was a growth of feeling in the union that no officer could do his work for the union and sit in Parliament at the same time. The General Secretary had given a pledge not to stand for Parliament, and it became understood that district secretaries and National Officers would not be likely to find a place on the official panel in future.

In 1934 Congress heard a proposal to reduce by two-thirds the salaries of officers returned to Parliament in order to pay for the assistance necessary to do the work of the union during their absences on Parliamentary business. J. R. Clynes countered this by saying he would have been better off in 1929-31 if this had then been the rule. But this hardly met the point, for he was then a member of the government, and as such debarred from accepting a union salary. The motion, however, was lost. The next question to be decided was whether officers who retired under the new compulsory rule were entitled to remain on the official panel. It was ruled that they were,[2] and Will Thorne and J. R. Clynes continued to receive official support up to their retirement from Parliament in 1945. Miss Bondfield stayed on the panel for some time, but she had been defeated in the 1935 election, and eventually gave up the search for a constituency.

In 1940 the Executive itself took the initiative in securing a decision that, in future, officers returned to Parliament should receive only a retaining fee of £200, but this decision did not stand for long. During 1942 the Party issued a circular appeal to the unions asking if it was not possible for 'the practice which prevents the Industrial Officers of Trade Unions becoming members of Parliament unless they resign their posts' which

[1] See p. 99.
[2] In 1948 Congress ruled that candidates for the official panel should be under sixty-five years of age, and that the position of those on the panel should be reviewed at that age.

'has become almost universal' to be gradually modified, since it 'excludes from Parliamentary discussions Trade Unionism's most authoritative representatives, and reduces the status of Trade Union M.P.s to a secondary position in industry'. After some months the Executive decided, and the General Council approved, that the union should revert to its former practice, although opinions on the matter were closely divided.

The decisions of some of the older of the union's M.P.s not to stand at the next election brought forward a new problem. The union had some bitter views concerning constituencies into which they had poured funds for many years and which apparently felt no loyalty to the union in choosing a new candidate. In one constituency this was attributed to the machinations of the agent whose salary was subsidized by the union, and feeling ran very high. The general practice was now, however, that younger officers should be allowed to submit their names in approved constituencies, on the understanding that if they received the nomination they would be placed on the official panel. This practice was approved by the 1942 Congress, which removed the limit on the number of those on the official panel, to reflect the growth in membership, and to allow greater flexibility. In 1945 the union had ten official candidates in the field, and all ten were successful.

The post-war Parliament was a more business-like institution than any of its predecessors. It was more than ever impossible for the unions to get value for the salary which they paid to an officer who was an M.P.; and salaries paid to M.P.s were considerably increased. The experience of the war had shown the trade unions that the new devices for the consultation of both sides of industry by the various departments gave them at least as much influence over the government as did the union-sponsored M.P.s. In 1946 Congress rejected a proposal to pay officers who became M.P.s only a retaining fee, but at the next Congress a proposal that Tom Williamson, the new General Secretary, should not be required before the next election to honour the pledge to resign from Parliament, which he had given on becoming a candidate for that post, was heavily defeated. In fact his retirement was delayed for some time to meet the wishes of the Party, who did not want to fight a by-election in his constituency (Brigg) at that time. In 1948 the Executive itself proposed to Congress that after the next general election the salaries paid to officers in Parliament should be reduced by 50 per cent on account of the very limited amount of work which might be expected of them, and the increase in M.P.s' salaries. Congress agreed.

There matters might have remained. The Executive's report on political matters included, however, a recommendation that the practice of selecting members for the official panel be altered. Flexibility had been found to have disadvantages. If a candidate was put forward for a constituency in a hurry, he had little chance 'of establishing his status in the Division concerned with the result that frequently we met with no success'. The Executive suggested a return to selecting members for the panel before they had found constituencies, in order to give them an opportunity to establish themselves in a constituency. It suggested that the panel might consist of twenty and that it would be satisfactory if twelve of these could be 'placed' in any election. Both these numbers might be exceeded if the Executive thought it desirable. Congress approved, and subsequently the Executive sought to fill the vacancies thus created with young officers or promising lay members who might be able to secure constituencies for the coming general election. Jack Cooper, the Southern district secretary who was at that time, as we have seen,[1] Acting-Secretary of the London district, and had just been elected to the London County Council, sought and obtained a place on the panel, and was later accepted for the Deptford constituency which he carried with a handsome majority in the general election of 1950. In 1945 the union's opinion had so far veered round that two National Industrial Officers — Mark Hewitson and Tom Williamson — had been allowed to go forward as candidates, but no district secretary had stood for Parliament since Arthur Hayday retired. The Executive were faced with the problem of whether or not to allow a man who had taken up two heavy political burdens

[1] See p. 129.

(and to them was added a Parliamentary private secretaryship) to retain high offices in the union which carried very heavy responsibilities. Not unnaturally the Executive took the view which Tom Williamson reported to the 1950 Congress that:

'. . . When these proposals were drawn up in 1948 we never envisaged that a District Secretary would be going to Parliament. He is quite entitled, as a member of the Union, to come along and say: "I would like to go on the official list", if he has the capabilities and the qualifications. If he is put on the list and goes to Parliament, he cannot do his District Secretary's job and his Parliamentary duties. The responsibilities of a Trade Union officer are arduous in these days. If he goes to Parliament, we have to appoint somebody else in his position, because the work of the Union must go on. Obviously, if a District Secretary went to Parliament, we could not have a temporary District Secretary for five, ten, fifteen or twenty years. There is a limit to it. So we have had to say that everybody must make up his mind. If he wants to stay with the Union, he can stay. If he wants to go to Parliament, he can go, but we must appoint an officer in his position if he does go.'

The proposals thus prefaced were that any officer of the union on the official panel who should be elected to Parliament at or after the next election should 'relinquish his industrial duties and be paid an honorarium of £250 per annum while he retains his seat'; that arrangement should be made for officers with more than ten years' service, and, therefore, entitled to a pension, to continue to contribute to the superannuation fund if they wished; and if an officer was defeated or retired from Parliament, the Executive should appoint him 'to the most suitable post available at that time and subject to there being no guarantee that he will be offered the same or a similar position to that previously held by him'. The proposals were warmly praised by a number of speakers, and carried unanimously.

Officers of the union are not likely to enter Parliament on these terms unless they have a strong ambition for a political career which outweighs their regard for the safety of their future. District secretaries and National Industrial Officers are most unlikely to go, for they have most to lose. Lay members of the union are taking their place. In 1950 four of the fourteen places on the official list were held by lay members. All four were among the nine who were chosen by constituencies to be candidates, and three were among the six who were returned. After the election, F. Tomney, a lay member who defeated D. N. Pritt, K.C. in Hammersmith North, was placed on the official panel. By June 1951 several officers had withdrawn their names, and on an official list of fifteen there were nine lay members. But most of the union members who have the abilities to cut an important figure in the trade union world, or in the Parliamentary Party, become union officers. Several of those who have come on to the panel as lay members, like Fred Marshall, have later become officers of the union. It is not likely that the union will produce any more J. R. Clyneses or Miss Bondfields under this rule, and, indeed, perhaps one of the reasons for its passage, was that this seemed no longer possible or desirable. The job of the trade union leader is recognized as full-time, and trade union influence on governments must come in the main from extra-Parliamentary devices.

The union has long maintained an Unofficial Parliamentary Panel, on which may be placed the names of members who have not served their apprenticeship in the union's industrial work, but whose work in Parliament is valued by the union. They now receive a contribution of £100 from the union towards their election expenses, and £52 a year towards the upkeep of their constituency organization. In addition a number of Labour candidates join the union in order to comply with Party rules. In 1950 there were seven candidates on the unofficial panel; five of them were successful. These five candidates remained on the list, and were all again returned in 1951. Twenty-six other candidates were union members in 1950, and thirteen of them were successful. These two groups include some well-known members of the Party, but they are all, or almost all, 'intellectuals', their connection with the union is not of great importance, and the contribution towards the expenses of those on the unofficial panel is not more than a gesture.

Under the second Labour Government there was widespread

criticism of some union members who voted against some proposals which were thought to be 'union policy'. The N.U.G.M.W., therefore, formed a House of Commons Committee which was to consult and try to agree a common line of action on any matter in which the union had an interest. At the Congress of 1930, Arthur Hayday, supporting a proposal to increase the number of official candidates, remarked:

'Six of our eight official candidates were in the House, but we had a total of nineteen M.P.s, some of whom, however, could not safely be called into consultation with the House of Commons Committee, because they were not cognisant of the Union's policy on industrial matters.'

The Union and Labour Party Policy

The trade unions have not normally been the policy-makers of the Labour Party. They have followed behind the 'intellectuals', grumbling at times, now and again requiring a great deal of persuasion, and once or twice trying to lay down an absolute veto. The N.U.G.M.W. has not acted differently from other unions in that respect. As a union led by men who had long called themselves socialists, the union accepted the adoption of socialist programmes by the Party after the end of the first world war, and equally accepted the gradual toning down of those programmes during the 'twenties. It showed as strong support as any union of the two minority Labour Governments, proud of its officers in them, but by 1930 even Clynes was moved to tell Congress that 'the Trade Union Group within the Labour Party in the House of Commons have found that they must now become more emphatic in pressing the industrial point of view than hitherto'. By this time all unions were beginning to grumble at the Party leadership, and no wonder, for MacDonald often refused to consult the T.U.C. — a mistake rarely repeated by Mr. Attlee's Labour Government — and in the end, trade union opposition merged with the revulsion of the whole Party against the treachery of its leaders — treachery by which those leaders did more for the unity of the Party than they could have in any other way.

The one important controversy of that period, besides

unemployment insurance, concerned the whole range of social services. The unions feared that extension of social services would cause employers to reduce wages in compensation, and were particularly hostile to family allowances. They felt these would lead to general wage reductions for which only married men would be compensated by the allowances. The N.U.G.M.W. had been a supporter of extension of social services. Arthur Hayday had made strong appeals to include widows' pensions in the T.U.C.'s Industrial Charter, but when the Party and the T.U.C. publicly disagreed on family allowances in 1929, the union unhesitatingly took the side of the T.U.C. In a debate at the union's Congress next year a resolution in favour of family allowances received only six votes against sixty-three after several references had been made to occasions on which employers, particularly the engineering employers, had called attention to the value of social services when making proposals for wage reductions.

After the disaster of 1931 the Party pulled itself together as best it could, and the unions supported the various detailed plans which were made by various research groups within the movement for the guidance of the next Labour Government. The only major point of difference was 'workers' control' over which the Labour Party Conferences were as divided as the T.U.C. Foreign affairs grew in importance and here the union was entirely with the majority in rejecting pacifism, in opposing fascism and in its attitude to the Spanish Civil War. The union was opposed to any association with Communists, and, therefore, rejected the device of the Popular Front, which Cripps and other leaders were at this time striving to get the Party to accept. The N.U.G.M.W., like most other unions, was thoroughly in favour of Cripps's expulsion, and again like some other unions, saw the conflict in terms of 'intellectuals' against trade unionists. In the *Journal* of March 1939 Charles Dukes compared Cripps with Mosley, and wrote:

'I venture to assert that if any trade union leader had announced during a Congress that he proposed calling a special conference of Constituency Parties in an attempt to influence the vote against the Executive, the Congress would have demanded immediate disciplinary action. Yet Sir Stafford did that and not even a murmur was heard. So long as in our movement the convert of yesterday can be made the leader of tomorrow, so long will these unstable and disruptive elements be attracted to our Party. Let anyone who has been in the Party twenty-odd years think over the long list of opportunists who have wrought havoc in our movement. . . .'

Perhaps Cripps's expulsion did almost as much for the unity of the Party as MacDonald's treachery.

During the war the union and other unions were entirely in support of the Party's policy on all major issues, both outside Chamberlain's Government and inside Churchill's. The union, and other unions, were gratified by the extent of consultation with government departments. It joined in the attack against Morrison when he failed to consult the unions before issuing his first fire-watching order which he was ultimately compelled to modify to please the unions. The adoption in principle of the 'Beveridge plan' by the Party entailed the acceptance of family allowances. At the 1941 Party Conference Charles Dukes had withdrawn a motion to 'refer back' the Party's proposals for post-war reconstruction which included family allowances, on Dalton's plea that it was a document intended for discussion only. Thereafter it became clear that both the T.U.C. and the Party would accept the Beveridge scheme and the union decided to withdraw further opposition. When the Party's proposals for the post-war reform of local authority areas and powers were made known the union declared its opposition most strongly. Regionalism, declared Charles Dukes, 'would destroy what had been the most democratic form of government in the world', and at the Party Conference of 1943 the union moved that the matter be the subject of further inquiry.

The most important aspects of post-war policy have already been discussed.[1] In its policies of wage restraint and of increasing productivity the Labour Government of 1945-51 received the union's support. Nationalization and the extension of the social services were approved, and in 1950 the union

[1] See pp. 260-268.

also agreed with the Party's decision to 'go slow' in its electoral programme of that year. The growing coldness of the government towards the Soviet Union, and its outspoken hostility to Communism were readily accepted by the union.

Throughout most of its term of office the Labour Government avoided disputes between the unions and the Constituency Parties. In 1951, however, Bevan resigned from the government, and the 'Bevanite' controversy thus begun continued after the defeat of the government in the 1951 election. Along with most other unions the N.U.G.M.W. remained stolidly loyal to the leaders of the Party. The union's spokesmen have not taken nearly so large a part in the dispute as have Arthur Deakin of the T.&G.W.U. or Lincoln Evans of the Iron and Steel Trades Confederation, but its voting strength has invariably been cast against the 'Bevanites'.

The Union and Local Authority Representation

The constituent unions of the N.U.G.M.W., particularly the M.E.A., were strongly in favour of securing the return of as many Labour candidates as possible to local authorities. The M.E.A. had gone so far as to give financial support to candidates who were not members of the union. This practice was stopped on amalgamation, but during its early years the N.U.G.M.W. gave every encouragement and assistance to members and officers to stand for local authority seats. The attitude of the districts has, however, changed since that time in the same way as the attitude of the union as a whole. We need here only call attention to the two main factors — the change to national wage-rates in the local authority services, and the growing calls upon the time of the union officer. In 1937 the Executive was already pointing out that L.C.C. membership involved almost full-time work, and in the same year the districts were informed that although representation on local authorities was encouraged, it must not take precedence over obligations to the union. In 1945 Charles Dukes advocated stronger action in local elections. 'There were' he said 'within the Districts officers with political aptitudes who could effectively combine political and industrial activity to the Union's advantage'. When questioned on this statement, however, he explained that the encouragement was not intended for officers alone, that union duties must come first, and that there were to be no interferences with district autonomy.

In some districts a number of officers still sit on local councils, but in others there are only one or two, and, in general, the practice seems to be declining. We may expect that this will continue. The union has now less to gain than formerly from such representation, and officers have less time to give to such work. On the other hand the lay members have won more leisure since 1939, and may now be paid for time lost on Council work. Most of the union's many local authority representatives have always been lay members, and under these conditions, more of them are able to take the place of officers who give up this type of work.

CHAPTER IV

INTERNATIONAL AFFILIATIONS

T HE union, like all other unions affiliated to the T.U.C. has owed allegiance to a series of international trade union organizations, first the International Federation of Trade Unions, then, after 1945, the World Federation of Trade Unions, and now the International Confederation of Free Trade Unions. The union's part in those bodies is only through its membership of the T.U.C., and insofar as their affairs are of importance for a full description of the union's work, they have already been discussed in the chapter on the union's part in the T.U.C. The union is, however, also affiliated directly to several international trade secretariats, to which we must now turn our attention.

International organization of trade unions by trade goes back to the nineteenth century. The first secretariat, of leather-workers, was founded in 1889, and several more followed during the 'nineties. Interest came first of all from the Scandinavian countries, from Germany and from Holland. The Latin countries and insular Britain usually came in later. By 1914 many trade secretariats were established and showed considerable stability, re-establishing themselves rapidly after the war, and again in 1945.

The more logical organization of trade unions in countries on the Continent — by the early years of the present century division on industrial lines was normal in many of them — lent itself more easily to international affiliations by trade than did the more complex British trade union structure. This difficulty has been greatest with the general unions. The N.U.G.M.W. is now affiliated to five secretariats, to each of them on a fraction of its total membership — the International Federation of Industrial Organizations and General Workers' Unions (at one time the General Factory Workers' International), the International Federation of Metalworkers, the International Union of Food and Drink Workers, the International Federation of Public and Civil Service Employees, and, through its membership of the National Federation of Building Trade Operatives, to the International Federation of Building and Woodworkers.

The union's interest in the affairs of the secretariats is mainly confined to those who actually attend their conferences, or go as fraternal delegates to the national conferences of other affiliated unions, and particularly to those who are elected to the governing bodies of the secretariats. The work of the internationals is from time to time given a page in the *Journal*, but its affairs are never debated at Congress, and only very rarely discussed by the General Council and the National Executive. Decisions are normally left to the delegates themselves. Since these are naturally chosen in the main from amongst the Executive itself and from the National Industrial Officers, even the active members of the union and the district organizers have little reason to concern themselves with the secretariats. For all that, the union probably plays a greater part in their work, and is more ready to exchange conference delegates with unions abroad than are most British unions.

The best method of describing the work of the union in the secretariats is to take as an example the International Federation of Public and Civil Service Employees, with which its ties have been as close and as firm as with any other. This organization was founded at Stuttgart in 1907, and its first members were unions from Denmark, Holland, Germany, Sweden and Switzerland. The original intention had been to set up a body — its name was then the Public Service Workers' International — to include all municipal and state employees, but applications for membership came only from unions of municipal employees (including workers in the gas and electricity industries). Congresses were held every three years, and at the third Congress, at Zurich in 1913, the M.E.A. was accepted into membership. At this Congress the International appointed its first full-time officer, a general secretary. The presidency remained a part-time office, filled by a leading officer of one of the affiliated unions.

The work of the International was in abeyance during the

war, but the Fourth Congress was held in 1919. In 1924 the newly formed N.U.G.M.W. took over the M.E.A.'s affiliation, but Peter Tevenan remained the union's main representative at Congresses and Executive Committee meetings. He was elected President in 1929, and since that date the presidency has been continually held by an officer of the N.U.G.M.W. Dukes succeeded Tevenan, and when he resigned owing to pressure of work in 1935, he was succeeded by Mark Hewitson. In 1938 Tom Williamson took over and has held the office since. After the withdrawal and subsequent suppression of the German union in 1933 the N.U.G.M.W. had the largest affiliated membership.

During its early years the International did not attract unions of state employees into membership (some of these suffered from legal disabilities before 1918) and in 1925 a separate International was established for Civil Servants. From the first the Public Service Workers sought unity by various means. The 1925 Congress proposed that it should be pursued by individual amalgamations within each country. When this proved Utopian, direct negotiations were started with the new International and at Copenhagen, in 1935, the two organizations amalgamated. The British Civil Service Clerical Association joined as soon as the repeal of the 1927 Trade Disputes and Trade Unions Act in 1946 permitted them to do so. N.U.P.E. was affiliated for a short period after the reconstitution of the International in 1945.

The governing body of the International is its Congress, which meets at least every three years, and at which the number of delegates and votes is determined by the numbers affiliated. This elects a General Council of from one to three members from each country, according to the numbers affiliated. The General Council meets at least once a year, and elects from its number eight members who form, with the General Secretary, an Executive Committee. The Secretary and the President are elected by Congress. The affiliation fees are enough to pay the salaries of a small staff, the expenses of General Council and Executive meetings, and to cover the cost of administrative work and a bulletin, but little more. The expenses of Congress delegations are met by the affiliated unions. In 1910 the second Congress rejected a proposal for compulsory financial aid to members engaged in disputes.

The International is, therefore, mainly a consultative body. Its only sanction is expulsion, and this would not be sufficient to secure the consent of any of its members if it wished to force them to adapt their domestic policy to its wishes. Its chief function is to secure contact between union leaders from different countries, and exchange of information, for instance on the different problems of other countries, and on different methods of tackling common problems.

Exchange of information is provided partly through replies to direct inquiries from members — for instance, on wages and prices in other countries — partly through articles in the bulletin (since 1945 a 'News-Letter'), partly through debates at Congresses — the 1949 Congress discussed the administration of nationalized industries — and partly through special trade conferences. Two of these were held by the International, for hospital workers, and for gas and electricity workers, during the 'thirties, but since 1945 they have become one of its major activities. Five such conferences have been held since then.

The International represents the views of its members to international economic organizations. Since 1919 it has maintained contact with the I.L.O., although its work there has not been as important as that of some other International Trade Secretariats, since the conditions of public employees were generally better than in many private industries, and the I.L.O. was chary of embarking on discussion of their civil rights. [This latter question is one of the staple topics of the International.] Since the war the proliferation of public bodies has added considerably to the work of the International. It is one of the two Trade Secretariats recognized as a consultative organization by the Economic and Social Council of U.N.O., and maintains contact with the World Health Organization and O.E.E.C. One of the main debates at the 1949 Congress was on the European Aid Programme.

The International tries to influence the course of events in individual countries by drawing up common programmes on various subjects, for instance on the rights of civil servants. It has occasionally made representations on matters of trade union organization, for instance in 1929 when the Danish T.U.C. decided to transfer certain groups of municipal workers to a general workers' union, but it has never tried to interfere in the complex problem of British union organization. One field of activity which may open out in the future is work to supplement in its own industries the general efforts of the I.C.F.T.U. to encourage trade union organization in backward countries.

During the 'thirties the International concerned itself with the problems of refugees and of illegal trade union work in Germany and other European countries. Its funds were strictly limited but it gave what direct aid it could, and helped with the collection of general trade union funds for refugees, and for aid to Austria and to Spain.

The relative stability of the Trade Secretariats is largely attributable to their concentration on industrial topics compared to the mainly 'political' interests of the general trade union international organizations. But the Secretariats have not been able to avoid politics entirely. Relations with Russian unions were debated both in the 'twenties and 'thirties. The International eschewed any relations with the Communist International, and was most chary of considering even exchange of delegates or exploratory meetings with Russian unions. After 1945 the Trade Secretariats attracted attention for their stand against inclusion in the W.F.T.U. They accepted the principle of affiliation to the W.F.T.U. but argued that the proposals for reconstituting them as trade departments of the W.F.T.U. did not allow them sufficient autonomy. They feared that the W.F.T.U. was becoming an over-centralized machine easily amenable to Communist designs. Negotiations on the terms of affiliation dragged on until the 'western' trade unions withdrew from the W.F.T.U. and set up the I.C.F.T.U. The Secretariats, which had come together into a loose federation with a Co-ordinating Committee in order to negotiate better with the W.F.T.U., have willingly recognized the new body. Contact is maintained by exchange of delegates between the Co-ordinating Committee and the governing bodies of the I.C.F.T.U.

The N.U.G.M.W. has taken its part in all this work. During the 'thirties its role was rather that of an 'elder brother' relatively remote from the difficulties of illegal work, exile, civil war and mass sit-down strikes which beset many of its continental fellows. During the war it held in trust such of the International's funds as had been sent over from the headquarters in Paris. Since the war it has played an important part in the provision of information and in industrial conferences, in response to the great demand from continental unions to learn of the experience of Labour Britain, and especially of the experience of workers in the nationalized industries and in the Health Service. Since the war the International has established its headquarters in London.

During the 'thirties the N.U.G.M.W., as might have been expected, argued strongly against any direct contact with Russian unions, which was then advocated by unions in one or two countries in which 'Popular Front' alliances were in force, and by some Scandinavian unions. After the war, during the troublesome negotiations between the W.F.T.U. and the Secretariats, its position was not easy, but it maintained throughout support for the official T.U.C. policy that the International *should* affiliate, while agreeing that this could only be done on terms which would be acceptable to the majority of the members of the International.

Relations with the other Secretariats to which the union is affiliated have not always been as good as with the I.F.P.C.S.E. In 1937 it withdrew from the old Factory Workers' International, which it had joined in 1929, on the grounds that fascist expansion had left the Dutch union in a dominant position, and the N.U.G.M.W. was in disagreement with that union on several points. But it reaffiliated to the International when it was reconstituted after the war. Mark Hewitson has taken a prominent part in its work and has been its representative on the Co-ordinating Committee of the Secretariats and one of the five delegates of that Committee to the I.C.F.T.U.

The N.U.G.M.W. has had other international contacts besides those through the Secretariats. One of its National Industrial Officers is a trade union representative on the Tin Commodity Study Group. It has given donations direct to many international funds, and taken part in the T.U.C.-sponsored loan to the Belgian unions in 1934. During and since the war it has taken under its wing organizations of trade unionist refugees or displaced persons working in British industry. But for all that it remains true that international work means little to most of its members, and influences the union's domestic policies hardly at all.

PART V

AN APPRAISAL OF THE GENERAL UNION

AN APPRAISAL OF THE GENERAL
UNION

THE purpose of the preceding chapters has been to describe one of the two great British general unions. Such a description cannot provide the material for a full and satisfactory appraisal of the N.U.G.M.W., or of general unionism. For appraisal must rest on comparison, and this study has not been comparative. It may not be amiss, however, to suggest some conclusions in the light of the evidence here presented, even though the limitations of that evidence prevent a final judgment.

That the general unions have been of value in the past is undeniable. The labourers' unions were founded because men who were unprotected by the type of trade union which had existed hitherto determined to protect their industrial interests by bringing together in 'new unions' those excluded from the old unions. When the conditions of 1910-20 swept millions of unorganized workers into the unions the 'new unions' grew into vast general unions because no other unions were willing or fitted to look after great numbers of these new recruits. During the difficult years from 1921 to 1935 the two amalgamated general unions maintained secure bases in a few industries, particularly the public utility services — road transport, gas, electricity, the Non-Trading services — and from these strongholds managed to keep remnants of trade unionism alive over a vast area of poorly organized industry. If they had not done this, many more Joint Industrial Councils would have collapsed, there would have been no trade union representatives to serve on many Trade Boards, and the integration of the vast numbers of new recruits of subsequent years would have been more difficult.

During the present century there has been a marked reduction in differences in wages and earnings between the highest-paid and the lowest-paid groups of workers. Important changes in social attitudes and social organization provide the explanation, but these changes would not have been so rapid and so

327

great if low-paid workers had not been organized for industrial
and for political pressure by the two general unions.

We are not here concerned, however, with the past so much
as the present. Is the general union an effective form of organization in Britain today? To judge the effectiveness of an organization requires an understanding of the aims which it pursues.
The aim of a trade union, or, at least, its primary aim, is to
protect the interests of its members *as those members see them*.
To judge the N.U.G.M.W., then, we must estimate how far it is
fitted to give adequate protection to its members, and how
democratic it is, for if it is not democratic it may pursue its ends
effectively, but there is no guarantee that those ends will be its
members' interests, as seen by them.

How Efficient is the Union?

No accurate test can be devised to measure the efficiency of
the union. It would be impossible, and ridiculous, to produce
figures to show that the average increase in earnings of members
of the N.U.G.M.W. over a period of years had exceeded or
fallen short of the average of all trade union members over the
same period, and to give a verdict accordingly. Such a test would
almost certainly favour the N.U.G.M.W., but it would leave
out of account so many factors, upon which no exact value
could be placed, that not even the most fervent partisan of the
union could regard the matter as settled thereby.

We have shown grounds on which the union may be criticized. During the depression of 1929-33 its leaders were growing old, and were perhaps too unadventurous. Some of them
may have given too much attention to politics and too little
service in industrial matters. N.U.P.E. has been able to build
up a large membership in a field which the union had regarded
almost as its own preserve. These shortcomings are, however,
matters of the past, and all unions have some failures and errors
to balance against their successes. We cannot answer our
question only by concentrating on the union's faults.

In fact, the task is beyond us, and we can do no more than
point out some relevant considerations.

The efficiency of a union depends in part on the quality of its officers. This quality cannot be judged without remembering that it is all but essential in a trade union that an officer should have years of direct industrial experience behind him. Only thus will he inspire confidence, and this is part of the union's democracy. The N.U.G.M.W. has so altered its original elective procedure that officers are, in fact, selected by the appropriate committees, and have to serve a two years' apprenticeship, during which some are found or find themselves to be unfitted for the work. The N.U.G.M.W. has opened a second channel of recruitment by encouraging those who have shown promise in administrative work in its offices to compete for jobs as organizers. It is beginning to provide training for its officers or potential officers, by sending some to courses arranged by the T.U.C. and other bodies, and particularly by its own scheme for one month courses at technical colleges. It now provides more opportunities for training to its officers than do most unions. It is clearly impossible to say that the officers of the N.U.G.M.W. are more or less capable than the average. It is possible to say that the union does more than most unions to ensure that the right men are selected, and are equipped for their task. Through the work of its Research Department it does more than most unions to service them in carrying out their task.

On two important questions concerning efficiency, opinion within the union is divided. Should there be greater specialization? An officer who deals with only one or two industries has greater opportunity to master his work, but a wide experience of collective bargaining in many industries may also assist him. Secondly, is the small branch better than the large branch? The small branch permits more local specialization and greater contact between members, but the large branch can provide the service of a whole-time branch secretary. Under the influence of the Lancashire district, opinion in favour of specialization amongst officers and in favour of the large branch has grown. The appointment of more National Industrial Officers and reorganization of some districts has allowed more specialization, and it may well be that this trend will continue. Since the majority of members are concerned mainly with their interests within their own industry, a strong case can be made out in its favour. Whether the N.U.G.M.W. would be well-advised to go as far in this direction as does the T.&G.W.U. is a matter to which we must return.

The leaders of the N.U.G.M.W. would claim that their 'business union' methods[1] enable them to give better service to their members than can a union which regards its task as one of open class warfare. But this again is a matter of controversy, if not so much within the union itself, within the movement as a whole. The general unions have been accused of holding 're-actionary' views, and therefore of playing into the hands of the employers. It is true that both of them, the N.U.G.M.W. perhaps more than the T.&G.W.U., have been on the right rather than on the left of the Labour movement over the last twenty or thirty years. This is in part due to their strong opposition to Communism and to the identification, or at least the confusion, of Left-Wing views with Communism and 'fellow-travelling'. But that is not the whole story. The readiness of the general unions to 'do business', to concern themselves with the immediate task, has been accompanied by less interest in general theories and particularly revolutionary theories than some other unions have shown. This may be seen in the excision by the N.U.G.M.W. of its Marxist address from its rulebook. Speakers at N.U.G.M.W. Congresses who use phrases such as 'the only war we should be concerned with is the war against the boss class',[2] sound oddly out of place. The general unions would claim that their rejection of revolution was in line with the tradition of the British Labour movement, and that they have striven to do their best for their members in the world as they have found it. To those who would accuse them of opportunism, they might reply that trade unionists who hold a revolutionary theory rejecting compromise with the society in which they live are not likely to provide the best protection for the interests of their members who must earn their bread in that society.

A frequent criticism of the general unions is that their size

[1] See pp. 254ff.
[2] A Scottish delegate on the 'Peace' Resolution at the 1950 Congress.

renders them unwieldy, and removes their leaders too far from their members. No one would deny that large-scale organization has its peculiar difficulties. Size in organization has few intrinsic virtues. The general unions are necessarily large, because they organize in many industries. They are today the largest unions because they have been able over the last fifteen years to increase greatly the degree of organization in the industries in which they maintained a precarious hold in the difficult years of the 'twenties and early 'thirties. It is, therefore, sensible to criticize their size only if an alternative form of organization can be suggested. Since craft unionism entails labourers' or general unions, that alternative must be industrial unionism. And there are not lacking supporters of industrial unionism who argue that the general unions should be split up. To argue that once the general unions had firmly established trade unionism in an industry they should hand over to an industrial union, in order to concentrate on further extension of trade unionism's frontiers, would show a misunderstanding of the nature of general unionism. It was only because the general unions were able to establish those secure bases that they could maintain and extend trade unionism elsewhere. The industrial unionist may, however, argue that the services of the general unions have been valuable in the past, but that today, when trade unionism is more firmly established in Great Britain than ever before, those services are no longer necessary, and the general unions should be split up. Such an argument is unrealistic, since there is no likelihood that the general unions will disband and no one has the authority to break them up, or seems likely to gain that authority. Many trade union movements abroad are organized on more industrial lines than our own, but this has been due in part to the development of such a structure early in the history of the movement, as for instance in France, to the greater powers of the central authority of the movement, as in Norway, or to the political influence of state or party as in some Communist countries. In Britain the structure of our trade union movement seems firmly established, the T.U.C. and its General Council have neither the power nor the desire to change it, and, revolution excepted, there seems no likelihood of state or party intervention. Large sections of the trade union movement, however, still have strong leanings towards the doctrine of industrial unionism, and there is sense in asking not only whether change is likely, but also whether change is desirable.

We cannot be sure that the general unions will not be called upon to do once more what they did between the wars. There are many industries in which trade unionism is not yet so firmly established that it might not collapse before the gales of economic crisis and depression if it had not the external support which the general unions give. Judgment on this point rests on speculation about the economic future. There are also industries, such as the laundry industry, in which trade unionism is still not established. If it is to be established there, who other than the general unions can do the job?

The argument for industrial unionism would be stronger if it could be shown that the economic interests of particular groups of workers within the general unions were neglected by those unions. In certain instances there is some evidence. It is at least arguable that London busmen might have done better for themselves had they remained outside the T.&G.W.U., although credit is due to them for remaining within that union, for destroying a break-away when one was formed, and for throwing in their lot with other less well-organized and less militant road passenger transport workers.[1] Most of the Aircraft Inspectors who amalgamated with the N.U.G.M.W. in 1944 appear to have drifted away since then, many to other unions. But these instances are exceptions. Certainly the shipbuilding and engineering labourers have reason to be thankful that they have been organized by the general unions. There is no reason to suppose that any grade of gasworker would have done better outside the N.U.G.M.W. N.U.P.E. may have pursued individual grievances and organized the more backward areas of local government Non-Trading services with more energy than the general unions, but its great expansion was due in the main to getting rapidly off the mark during the 'thirties, and to recruiting groups of workers whom the N.U.G.M.W. had

[1] See my *Labour Relations in London Transport*, Blackwell, 1950, chap. III.

failed to organize rather than groups of the latter's members who had been neglected. There is little to show that general increases, or grade differentials, in those services would have been different but for N.U.P.E. Finally, we must ask whether other types of union look after small groups better than the general unions. Craft unions may protect craftsmen, but that form of organization requires labourers' or general unionism if other grades of workers are to be organized at all. Industrial unions have given as good grounds for accusations of neglect as have the general unions. The winding enginemen and the National Union of Mineworkers, the London postal sorters and the Union of Post Office Workers testify to this.

It is now frequently said that the functions of trade unions have radically altered under full employment and in the social service state. Their task, it is claimed, is to take a far greater interest in increasing productivity, and to cast aside many of the methods of protection which were appropriate to a period of unemployment, but which hinder increases in output, since only by these means can the standard of living of their members be radically improved. Furthermore, in order to fulfil these functions union officers and executives should offer courageous leadership in advocating new policies, and should educate themselves and their members in the need for those policies and in the new methods by which those policies must be carried out.

Are not the general unions at least as well fitted for these tasks as most other unions? The N.U.G.M.W. has encouraged its members to welcome systems of payment by results and is trying to give both its officers and selected shop stewards the means of understanding and, therefore, of controlling the systems of work-study and time-and-motion study which are now widely used to increase productivity and earnings, and to lighten work-loads.[1] Constitutionally its officers and governing committees are in a better position to give outspoken leadership than their counterparts in many other unions and the N.U.G.M.W. has consciously adapted its methods and propaganda to conditions of full employment. It is perhaps easier for a general union to do this, for, by and large, its members

[1] See p. 267.

have in the past placed less reliance on 'restrictive practices' than have the members of the craft unions. In fact, it has been in their interest to oppose craft restrictions. Insofar as full employment makes desirable more centralized leadership for the trade union movement as a whole, in order to avoid leap-frog wage-claims and the danger of a wage-price spiral, little fault can be found with the general unions. The T.U.C. and the General Council have little more than moral authority, and there is no great likelihood that they will gain more. The general unions have shown more willingness than some other large unions to support the views of the General Council, and since they provide centralized leadership for the considerable proportion of the whole movement which they themselves organize, they have been able to back that support with their powerful voting strength and to see that the General Council's policies are followed by a quarter of the country's trade union-ists. It is true that the policies adopted over the last ten years have been more easily acceptable to general unions than to some other unions, but this does not entirely explain away the facts that the success with which the moral authority of the T.U.C. and the General Council has been upheld over that period has been largely due to the support of the two general unions, and that the rejection of the policy of continued wage-restraint in 1950 was due least of all to these two unions.

One strong argument in favour of industrial unionism is that in a welfare state and a more socialistic society, trade unions should play a growing part in the formation and execution of industrial policy, and their organization should be suited to that purpose. Clearly a general union is structurally less well fitted for this task than a union confined to a single industry. It is, however, important to remark that there are other obstacles in our trade union movement to development on these lines. For unions to take a larger part in industrial policy-making there is need for the training of union officers for this new task. There is even more need for encouragement and training for lay members (who know much less of collective bargaining, but who may know more of the general problems of their own industry than the full-time officer) to become

334

members of the consultative bodies which are set up in nationalized and in private industry, and to take an active part in their
work. Since much of this work must go on in each individual
company and each unit of industry there is also great need for
the encouragement and training of shop stewards and workshop representatives to play their part. The general unions are
doing more in some of these ways than many other unions.
They are more willing to provide training for officers and for
other members, and they are expanding their training schemes
rapidly. The N.U.G.M.W. has recently adopted more sensible
policies concerning its shop stewards and is showing a greater
understanding of their problems than it has done in the past.[1]
In many of the firms which are experimenting with the
development of co-operative techniques of industrial management the general unions and their local representatives are
showing more readiness to work for the success of the experiments than many craft or even industrial unions and their
members.[2]

Participation by workers and by unions in the direction and
management of industry is only in its infancy. It may well be
that in a future society in which the infant had grown to man-
hood, general unionism would be an anachronism. There are,
however, no grounds for thinking that the dismemberment of
the general unions would aid the growth of the infant now;
growth might even be retarded thereby.

A practical problem which must be faced in any discussion of
the comparative merits of general and industrial unionism,
is the way that the change from the one to the other, if desirable,
could be made. To endow each industry with unions like those
of the Boot and Shoe Operatives, or the Pottery Workers, or the
Iron and Steel Workers, might seem attractive. If, however, the
proposal was to hand over the engineering and allied workers
in the general unions to the A.E.U., all electricity workers to
the E.T.U. and so on, the general unions and their members
would fight harder than ever against it, and with reason. Their
argument that such a step would place the interests of the
workers whom they represent at the mercy of the craftsman

[1] See pp. 115ff.   [2] See pp. 226ff.

could not be easily answered, particularly in the light of the recent history of the Confederation of Shipbuilding and Engineering Unions.

In a radically different society general unionism might be out of place. In a society in which participation in industrial management became trade unionism's central function, in a society as free as that which William Morris envisaged in *News from Nowhere*, or in a society in which the closed shop was the rule and trade unions became administrative agencies of the state, general unionism would perhaps be unsuitable. It is also true that to suit societies of this sort the other sections of the British trade union movement would require radical reorganization. But in our present society, which combines a considerable degree of freedom for individuals and for organizations with great concentrations of economic power, in which trade unionism's strength varies greatly between different industries and different groups of workers, and in which no satisfactory solution has been found to the conflict between the need for centralization and the strong human desire for decentralization and local autonomy, the evidence seems to show that the general unions have served their members, trade unionism, and society as well as have most other unions. So far as we can see into the future, there is no reason to suppose that they will not continue to do equally well.

How Democratic is the Union?

Our second question is no easier to answer than our first. There is no definition of democracy adequate to cover all the ways in which we commonly use the word, and there is no perfectly democratic institution which can serve as a standard for comparison. Institutions are more or less democratic, and about the more and the less there is opportunity for endless argument.

The rulebook need not detain us long. Written constitutions may help or hinder democracy, but they cannot make democracy. Our inquiry must be directed towards the actual working of the union. Members of other unions criticize the rules of the N.U.G.M.W., saying that officers are placed in too strong a position, that it is wrong for officers to be members of the Executive, and that the powers of the Executive are too great. But it is clear that within the rules there remain sufficient constitutional channels by which the members can, if they are determined to do so, control its policy and activities. And we must ask whether in practice they do so.

A sturdy local independence is an important element in any democracy. This study has not provided the material for a judgment of the virility of branch and factory democracy in the N.U.G.M.W. Only a thorough study of a large number of branches spread over several districts could provide the material for such a judgment. The most that can be said as a result of more casual and haphazard acquaintance is that although there are no doubt many instances which may be justifiably brought up against the union, there are instances of local interest and activity which can be cited in its favour. Low attendance at branch meetings is a problem which faces all unions. There may be N.U.G.M.W. branches which have failed to find an attendance for a succession of meetings. There are, however, branches which are as well and democratically run as any union branches. District officers and whole-time branch secretaries undoubtedly sometimes disregard the wishes of the members, and the constitution of the union may make this relatively easy, but there are groups of members, and particularly shop stewards (by no means always politically Left-Wing) who question officers closely and intelligently, and who, if they disagree, show it in no uncertain manner. Unofficial strikers have been threatened with expulsion and even expelled.[1] Whether or not this is desirable, most of the union's unofficial strikers are not punished in that way, and an observer of a strike meeting at which an officer pleads with angry members to refrain from passing a strike resolution in order to allow more time for negotiations, could never say that the union was entirely controlled by its officers. Unofficial strikes are rare, and perhaps not a happy example of democracy at work, but observation of a briefing meeting at which an officer and a group of stewards decide how to pursue a number of grievances

[1] See p. 132.

or complaints in a factory, would teach the same lesson, perhaps less dramatically but no less certainly.

Small attendances at branch meetings open the way to electoral abuses, and this cannot be remedied by activity within the factory. Branch officers and holders of higher posts in the union must be chosen at the branch meeting. There can be no doubt that abuses do arise. Small groups — not always Communists — have 'packed' ill-attended meetings to ensure that the whole weight of the branch vote may be swung behind their own candidates for particular offices, whatever the general attitude to those candidates. Here again we can only offer an opinion based on inadequate and unsystematic inquiry that abuse is exceptional, and that, on the whole, delegates at Congress, and District Council or Committee members, are representative of the members, and removable by the members. Certainly some of the elections for these positions are keenly contested and sometimes won by only a narrow majority. A whole-time branch secretary has been elected by a chairman's casting vote. If that did not augur well for the successful candidate's tenure of office, it indicated an open contest.

The previous chapters have provided more evidence on which to base judgment of the formation of union policy and the working of its national and district organs. The control of policy is primarily the function of Congress. And for convenience its decisions may be placed into three groups — those determining the way in which the union's vote shall be cast at the major conferences of the Labour Movement; those concerned with the constitution of the union; and those concerned with industrial action.

Each year a number of resolutions come forward, from the branches and from the National Executive, dealing with the policy of the movement. Unless the views of the platform arouse the opposition of the Left-Wing delegates, and a small storm blows up, Congress is apathetic towards them. They are normally treated as occasions for a few rousing, non-controversial speeches; Congress cheers and passes on to the next business, content to accept the views of its leaders on the matter. Only in 1951, when Congress took a strong dislike to the wording of the Executive's motion on the control of prices and profits, has there been an important exception. It is from amongst resolutions passed in this way that the union chooses the motions it wishes to offer to the T.U.C. and the Labour Party Conference. How to vote at those meetings on matters on which Congress has not determined policy must be decided by the delegates sent to them, unless the matter seems so important that the Executive feels the need to take a formal decision for the guidance of the union's delegates.

This relatively low level of interest is probably representative of the attitude of most union members. Such matters are certainly not their primary concern in the union, and in its discussions of them Congress probably reflects accurately the general sentiment of the union because Communists and their sympathizers are not encouraged to come forward as delegates from most districts. Left-Wing spokesmen there are at Congress, and their opinions are given a fair hearing, but they are in a small minority. Unions whose conferences are under Communist influence could not pretend that the *political* resolutions which are passed by them accurately reflect the attitude of their members.

When we turn to the government and administration of the union itself there is a far keener tang in the air. Even in the pages of the reports one can feel the increased attention of Congress delegates, who are certainly concerned about the amounts of contributions and of benefits, the amount of the branch secretary's commission, compulsory retirement for officers, and the terms on which officers may sit in Parliament. There have been differences amongst the union's leaders on some of these issues, and in some of them the union's nearest equivalent to party organization at Congress — the district divisions — have been brought into play. Once or twice, when contributions, branch officers' commissions and the frequency of Congresses have been debated, a division between the platform and the members has been visible, and Congress has not hesitated to disagree with the union's leaders over the amendment of rules. The considerable extensions of the powers of district committees and the General Council which have been approved by Congress over the years cannot be explained by apathy. They were granted by Congresses accustomed to give keen attention to constitutional matters, and ready to disagree if they felt disagreement. We must, therefore, conclude that they were passed by delegates who had listened to the arguments and been convinced by them. It may be that the delegates have been too ready to be convinced when the argument for a change of rule has been that it is necessary in order to deal with 'subversive elements', but there can be no doubt that opposition to Communism has been a genuine conviction amongst the great majority of delegates each year, and not only the view of the platform.

To the members, interest in the constitution itself must take second place to their concern with the union's attempts to maintain and improve wages and conditions of work in each industry and each place of work. The continual increase over the last twenty years in the time given by Congress to questions on the General Secretary's report, the bulk of which outlines the results of negotiations in each industry over the previous year, has made it more representative of general opinion. The National Industrial Officers must explain and defend actions of the union to those who are affected by them. But Congress cannot determine what is to be done in industrial matters. Resolutions relating to matters which can only be settled by the negotiating bodies of each industry are ruled out of order. Rightly so, for how could Congress lay down in a few days the steps to be taken during the coming year in two hundred industries? Even if time was unlimited, decisions concerning each industry would be taken by a body in which those directly concerned are necessarily only a small fraction of the whole. In industrial matters Congress must be, and is, supplemented by other means of control.

The methods by which this control is exercised differ according to the pattern of collective bargaining in each industry. Where many matters of importance are settled at the place of work or with the individual firm — particularly where some system of payment by results is in force — control is direct. Shop stewards take part in the discussions, and the responsible officer must make sure, through consultation with them, and, if necessary, by addressing mass meetings of the members, that he has support before he comes to an agreement. If an offer seems acceptable to his stewards and members, he will have to show them solid reasons for objection to it if he wishes to carry on negotiating for different terms. If they reject an offer which seems to him favourable, he must try to win them round, for he will only store up trouble for himself if he accepts without their support.

In industries such as gas and electricity, and in the Non-Trading services, the trend towards centralization has left relatively little to local negotiation, and even in engineering and shipbuilding many issues are settled nationally. Decisions in such matters are normally left to the workers' side of the regional or national bargaining body concerned. Doubtful points are referred to the district secretary or General Secretary, and by them to the district committee or National Executive. Apart from questions at Congress, the members are brought into the process in two ways. Branches are informed of the progress of negotiations, and of agreements in each industry in which they have members. They may send their opinions on these reports to the district office, and thence, if need be, to Head Office. When the district committee or National Executive feels the need to consult representative opinion, they may call delegate meetings of the branches or districts concerned to hear reports and to offer them advice. As we have seen, in some industries, particularly in the London district, such meetings are held regularly.

The main burden of decision thus falls on the negotiating committees, and therefore on the union officers within them. They must make the decisions, knowing that they are accountable to the members in these ways, and that they may be called upon to justify their actions before the union's governing committees. Behind these lies another sanction. The closed shop is the exception still in British industry. In many places of work the member suffers little by leaving the union; in many others he may transfer his allegiance. General unions are probably more vulnerable in this way than most other unions.

District officers in the N.U.G.M.W. are largely judged by changes in membership in the branches or industries entrusted to them, and the district secretary has an equal interest in the figures for the district. Control over industrial decisions in the A.E.U. is more direct than in the N.U.G.M.W., for the A.E.U. officers must be re-elected at intervals, and the National Committee exercises the right to decide on the submission of claims to employers; but the officers of the N.U.G.M.W. are certainly not free to disregard their members' wishes.

Union leaders must have freedom to act. Union business would become impossible if every decision had to be made by ballot, and conferences can meet only for a few days each year. At the same time the leaders must be made responsible for their actions. There is clearly room for argument over whether the N.U.G.M.W. or any other union has established the right balance between these two needs. In a general union the officers are bound to exercise greater power than in most other unions, both because general representative conferences are unsuitable for the settlement of industrial matters, and because there is less common interest between the various groups of members than in a craft or industrial union. The union is therefore cemented together by its relatively small body of officers, and the power of these officers is accordingly increased. Furthermore, the proportion of actively interested members is almost certainly smaller in a general union than in most craft unions, although only a small minority in each. All that can be concluded with confidence is that though the constitution of the N.U.G.M.W. would certainly not suit a craft union, the rule-book of the A.E.U. would make it impossible for the N.U.G.M.W. to carry out its work.

We have argued that the strength of democracy in any institution depends only in part on the written constitution, and in part on the practices which grow up within and around the formal rules. These practices are influenced by the tasks which must be done and the situations in which they must be carried out; they are also influenced by the character of the men and women who carry them out. The division between policy and administration is not sharp and distinct. It is possible to argue that democracy or autocracy are descriptions of the way that policy is made, and that all that remains in execution is better or worse administration. In fact, methods of administration can do much to strengthen or weaken democracy. Union members may be bullied and bludgeoned into obedience to democratically-determined policy decisions, or they may be helped and persuaded. Decisions may be applied without regard to the men and women to whom they are applied, or they may be tempered to suit individuals without destroying their purpose. Which method is chosen depends far more on the character of the administrators than on the rules. All great men have their faults. Charles Dukes was a great man, and gave of his best to the union, but he was a strong-willed man, accustomed to having his way, sometimes too impatient of criticism, and of different views. J. R. Clynes was a very different type of man, but also perhaps too intolerant of views opposed to his own. Some of the early district secretaries, who built up the union out of nothing in the face of opposition from both employers and craft unions, retained as administrators the forcefulness with which they built up the union. Some district officers have carried out their duties in the same way. The position and power of the officer in the N.U.G.M.W. perhaps makes it easy for him to adopt methods of this kind. Some of the criticisms of the union's democracy, and there certainly are criticisms, may have been due to dissatisfaction with administrative shortcomings rather than with policy-making methods.

Whatever weight should be given to these shortcomings, there is certainly no evidence that the union is less democratically administered under Tom Williamson and the present district secretaries than under their predecessors. The evidence is rather that the union's administrative methods are more human and sympathetic.

There are dangers for democracy in the N.U.G.M.W. The general understanding that Communists are not acceptable for high office is a limitation of freedom of choice. The leaders of the union would say it is a limitation necessary for the preservation of union democracy, but there remains the danger that the label 'Communist' might be extended to cover any opponent on the Left. The small numbers attending branch meetings and voting in union elections, the authority granted to the union's officers and the great powers entrusted to the governing committees, might all serve to provide opportunities for the limitation or perversion of democracy should the leaders of the union wish to use them for that purpose and should the members fail to offer active opposition.

All these dangers, and others, exist, but they must not be over-emphasized. The leaders of the union do show regard for the spirit of democracy. The General Council and National Executive have withdrawn the restriction on the London district and bans on individual members which they felt it their duty to impose after the Savoy dispute.[1] They have revised penalties imposed by a district committee which they felt to be too harsh.[2] They have submitted to Congress their actions in some matters of major importance in which they might have claimed to have acted within the limits of their constitutional powers.[3] Organs of popular control exist and are used. Congress has defeated the platform; and a district secretary has been dismissed by his district council.[4] Instances of this kind are to be found mainly in recent years, which seems to reveal — and this is a conclusion which personal acquaintance with the union has strengthened — that the machinery of democracy within the union — admittedly imperfect, as in any other democratic institution — is not rusting for lack of use, but used more than ever before. Despite the vast increase in numbers, which has probably materially reduced the proportion of active members to the total, the dangers to democracy within the union are, for this reason, more remote than in the past.

Comparison with the Transport & General Workers' Union

Since this study has been confined to the N.U.G.M.W., we are in no position to make a general comparison of the methods and achievements of the two kindred unions, but in the matter of democracy we must give some attention to the very different provisions for union government in the T.&G.W.U., the more

[1] See p. 130.   [2] See p. 63.   [3] See p. 139.   [4] See p. 51f.

so because we have attributed some of the practices of the N.U.G.M.W. to the inability of a general union to act otherwise.

The outstanding constitutional differences between the two unions are that the T.&G.W.U. has an entirely 'lay' executive, and that it is divided into 'trade groups' as well as into regional divisions. The trade groups overshadow the regional divisions, and it is fair to say that in the T.&G.W.U. decentralization is by industry as compared to the territorial decentralization of the N.U.G.M.W. Because of this the national secretary of each trade group is in a more important position than the regional secretary. The trade groups have national and regional committees, consisting entirely of elected lay members, who are the final authorities within the group. The T.&G.W.U. is not, however, a federation, as officers of the N.U.G.M.W. often say, for by rule trade groups have only such specific powers as the Executive chooses to delegate to them, and these powers may be, and on occasion have been, withdrawn.

It might seem that the officers of the T.&G.W.U. are kept in a more subordinate position than those of the N.U.G.M.W. and that the members of the T.&G.W.U. have a far greater control over industrial decisions than have the members of the N.U.G.M.W. This conclusion must, however, be accepted with caution, for several reasons.

At the level of a union executive the distinction between officers and 'lay' members is not always as sharp as might appear. Leading lay members of such important unions as these two often spend considerably more time on union business or sitting on negotiating bodies than at their industrial jobs, and this must affect their attitudes. For all this a senior officer is a much more powerful figure than any lay member. His experience is normally greater; he is often an important figure in the trade union movement as a whole, and a member of various government committees. For this reason the effect of the rule which excludes officers from the Executive of the T.&G.W.U. is not only to place its senior officers, the trade group national secretaries, in a less powerful position than that of the district secretaries of the N.U.G.M.W., but to elevate the one officer with a voice on the Executive — the General Secretary — to a position of eminence and authority which the General Secretary of the N.U.G.M.W. cannot hope to attain. The National Executive of the N.U.G.M.W. is clearly in a better position to control its General Secretary than is the General Executive of the T.&G.W.U., and it may be that its greater expertise makes it a more effective working body.

The more subordinate position of the trade group national secretaries compared with the district secretaries of the N.U.G.M.W. entails greater centralization in the T.&.G.W.U. and this centralization is increased by the latter's method of selecting officers. They are appointed and supervised by the General Executive (although it delegates selection to examining committees, and supervision naturally falls on the General Secretary and his chief subordinates) so that they constitute a more unified corps than do the officers of the N.U.G.M.W. in which much of the work of selection and supervision falls on the districts. For this reason practices are far more standardized in the T.&G.W.U. There is more room for local variation and experiment in the N.U.G.M.W., with also the inevitable result of local authority, a greater gap between the most efficient or most democratic and the least efficient or least democratic sections.

Finally, the difference in power between officers of the two unions must not be exaggerated. Because the T.&G.W.U. is a general union, even larger than the N.U.G.M.W., it must be held together largely by its body of officers. And because it is more centralized, decision on many matters is further removed from the members in any locality than in the N.U.G.M.W., so that in practice their control may be no greater, or even, in some instances, less. Certainly in recent years the T.&G.W.U. has shown more obvious signs of the strain which large-scale organization involves.

Any judgment on the merits of these different constitutions must be personal. In the view of the author the greater decentralization of the N.U.G.M.W. is commendable, even though in certain instances it may involve less efficiency. Since it depends in part on the presence of district secretaries on the

National Executive, that provision of the rules may be justified. There is, however, much to be said for the trade group structure of the T.&.G.W.U., the more so since their industrial interests are of first concern to most trade unionists. That structure is incompatible with the organization of the N.U.G.M.W., but, in the author's opinion, some districts of the union would do well to make greater use of the practice of calling representative meetings of working members for consultation on important matters affecting their own industries; and those districts which fill all or almost all of the seats on the workers' sides of negotiating bodies with full-time officers (a state of affairs which also exists in some sections of the T.&G.W.U.) unduly limit the participation of the members in the work of the union.

The cautions offered at the beginning of this chapter must be remembered. The conclusions here set forth can be no more than tentative, and subject to qualification or revision when further evidence is available. On the basis of the evidence we have, however, it seems that general unionism has not only justified itself in the past, but is now, and will remain in the foreseeable future, a useful form of trade union organization. The N.U.G.M.W. can fairly be said to be a democratic organization. The two great general unions differ, and advantages can be claimed for each. During the years following the amalgamations the T.&G.W.U. forged ahead more rapidly in numbers and in reputation. Today only a rash man would be willing to attribute clear superiority, except in numbers alone, to the one or to the other.

LIST OF NATIONAL INDUSTRIES IN WHICH
THE N.U.G.M.W. ORGANIZES

THIS list includes the industries which were allocated to the National Industrial Officers in June 1953, grouped according to Officer responsible. It does not include localized industries which are dealt with entirely by the districts concerned.

1. Asbestos
   British Broadcasting Corporation
   Cable
   Cement
   Chalk
   Fire Service
   Gloves
   Hide and Skin
   Hospital Services
   Leather Tanning
   Nursing
   Papermaking
   Rubber

2. Agricultural Machinery
   Bacon Curing
   British Oxygen
   Canteens — Industrial and Staff
   Coal Distribution
   Electricity Supply
   Forestry Commission
   Iron and Steel Scrap
   Keg and Drum
   Milk Distributive
   Motor Vehicle Retail and Repairing
   Oil and Petroleum
   Timber:
      Fencing
      Home Grown
      Packing Case and Wood Container

Plywood
Saw Milling
Tin Box
Thermal Insulation

3. Agriculture and Fisheries
Catering
Flax Processing
Government Workers:
  Admiralty
  Air Ministry
  Ministry of Supply
  Ministry of War
  Ministry of Works
  H.M. Stationery Office
  Crown Land
  Board of Trade
  Ministry of Pensions
  Ministry of Food
  Home Office
  Foreign Office
  Civil Aviation
  Miscellaneous Trades Joint Council
Gypsum
National Service Hostels Corporation

4. Aerated Waters
Blast Furnaces
Breweries
Carlisle State Management Scheme
Coal Mining
Coke Ovens
Copper Mining
Film Processing
Furniture
Gas (including Staffs and intermediates)
Iron Ore
Linoleum
Patent Fuel and Briquette
Rediffusion
Remploy

Sugar Beet
Sugar Refining
Tobacco

5. Cocoa and Chocolate
Corn
Electricity (Staffs)
Flour Milling
Ophthalmic and Optical
Paint, Colour and Varnish
Road Haulage Wages Council and J.I.C.
Road Passenger Transport:
   Municipal
   Private Company
Seed Crushing
Sugar Confectionery

6. Ball Clay
Brick and Allied Industries
Building Trade
Building and Civil Engineering in Electricity Supply
Cast Stone and Concrete
Civil Engineering
Clay Industries
Demolition
Glass Container
Glass Processing
Glass, Sheet and Plate
Horticultural Pottery
Iron and Steel
Monumental Masonry
Mastic Asphalt
Quarrying:
   Roadstone
   Limestone
   Freestone
Refractories
Road Roller Hire
Roofing Felt
Salt Glazed Ware
Sand and Ballast

Sand, Lime, Brick
Silica and Moulding Sands
Stoneware
Slag

7. Civil Air Transport
   Coal Trimming
   Cellophane Paper
   Drug and Fine Chemical
   Engineering
   Fat and Bone Degreasing
   Fertilizers
   Foundries
   Fountain Pen
   Glue and Gelatine
   Heavy Chemicals
   I.C.I.
   Ironmongery
   Lead Mining
   Light Castings
   Metals (all sections)
   Metal Finishing
   Metal Mining
   Needle, Fish Hook, Fishing Tackle and Allied Trades
   Plastics (Chemical)
   Plastics (Engineering)
   Railway Shopmen
   Shipbuilding and Ship Repairing
   Soap and Candle
   Tin Mining
   Wire Rope and Wire Netting

8. Civil Air Transport Canteens
   Cold Stores
   County Council Roadmen
   Docks and Fish Docks
   Local Authorities Services (Non-Trading) Manual, Administrative, Professional, etc.
   Match
   River Authorities (land drainage)
   Waterworks Undertakings

9. Aluminium
Biscuits
Buffer food
Button
C.W.S.
Engineering (Women)
Food Manufacturing
Fustian Cutting
Laundries and Dyeing and Cleaning
Narrow Fabrics
Ostrich and Fancy Feather
Rayon
Rope, Twine and Net
Sack and Bag
Silk
Stamped and Pressed Metalwares
Surgical Dressings
Toys
Unlicensed Places of Refreshment (Cafés)
Waste-Cotton and General
Wholesale Grocery and Provisions

Boot and Floor Polish
Brush and Broom
Carpet
Corset
Cotton
Cutlery
Dressmaking
Drift Net
Domestic Workers
Flax and Hemp
Hat, Cap and Millinery
Hair, Bass and Fibre
Hollowware
Hosiery and Knitwear
Jute
Light Clothing
Linen and Cotton Handkerchiefs
Made-up Textiles
Paper Bag
Paper Box
Perambulator
Wool Textiles

INDEX

353

INDEX

INDEX

INDEX

357